NOUS·SOMMES·PRETS
SIMON FRASER UNIVERSITY
W.A.C. BENNETT LIBRARY

Designing with Blends

Designing with Blends

Conceptual Foundations of Human-Computer Interaction and Software Engineering

Manuel Imaz and David Benyon

The MIT Press
Cambridge, Massachusetts
London, England

MIT Press books may be purchased at special quantity discounts for business or sales promotional use. For information, please e-mail <special_sales@mitpress.mit.edu> or write to Special Sales Department, The MIT Press, 55 Hayward Street, Cambridge, MA 02142.

This book was set in Stone Sans and Stone Serif by Graphic Composition, Inc. Printed and bound in the United States of America.

Library of Congress Cataloging-in-Publication Data

Imaz, Manuel.
Designing with blends : conceptual foundations of human-computer interaction and software engineering / Manuel Imaz, David Benyon.
  p. cm.
Includes bibliographical references and index.
ISBN 978-0-262-09042-1 (hc : alk. paper)
1. Human-computer interaction. 2. Software engineering. I. Benyon, David. II. Title.
QA76.9.H85.I53 2006
004'.019—dc22

2006044045

10 9 8 7 6 5 4 3 2 1

Contents

Preface

For the last twenty-five years, we have witnessed some important changes in the way we think about knowledge, the mind, and the relationship between literal and figurative meaning. We are moving away from a framework where the mind was seen as separated from a body built to contain it, and the mind alone governed all the rules of searching for an objective and comprehensible world. Mark Johnson's *The Body in the Mind: The Bodily Basis of Reason and Imagination* (1987) was one of a number of texts that showed how the meaning of a discourse has to be found out, ultimately, in our bodily interaction with the world—a world that is physical, social, and cultural. In this new framework, abstract things such as ideas, thoughts, and cognitive processes are seen to be embodied—that is, determined by the way our bodies interact with the environment. George Lakoff and Mark Johnson's *Philosophy in the Flesh* (1999) is another powerful evocation of this.

Another component of this new framework is the discovery of how significant the use of metaphors is in both our everyday language and more specialized discourses. Metaphors are a fundamental part of our comprehension of the world, as Lakoff and Johnson showed in *Metaphors We Live By* (1980). People usually consider metaphors to be rhetorical figures (and they certainly are often poetic); accordingly, it is hard to think that metaphor might be considered as a fundamental cognitive process underlying most of our thinking.

A third crucial strand of this new approach is the concept of *conceptual integration* or *blend.* In 2002, Gilles Fauconnier and Mark Turner completed *The Way We Think,* a book that aims to explain how new concepts originate as a blending of older concepts, giving rise in the process to new, emergent properties.

The story we are telling in this book is how the evolution of the concept of mind means that the use of stories, metaphors, blends, and figurative language is becoming increasingly important in software engineering (SE) and human-computer interaction (HCI). This is quite contrary to traditional ideas of basing computing principles in algorithms, mathematical theories, and formal notations to avoid "sloppy intuitive thinking." We want to encourage well-informed, sensitive design by providing software engineers and HCI professionals with a new framework of concepts.

Francisco Varela describes how the mind works: "The mind is not in the head." The immediate question this raises is, Where is it then? But this question itself is a consequence of using underlying metaphors whereby *concepts are things*. If we believe that concepts are things, it is evident that if the mind is not in the head, it must be somewhere else. Yet, if we adopt a different stance by saying that the mind is in the interactions with other people and things, we no longer look for a simple container that holds these things called concepts that make up this thing called "mind." This simple exercise of questioning the classical ideas about the mind shows how the use of different metaphors and concepts may help us to uncover new aspects of something. This is what we want to do to SE and HCI.

Turner called one of his books *The Literary Mind* (1996). In it, he explains that the same cognitive processes that are used in everyday language and literary writings are used in scientific discourse as well. It has been assumed for a long time that something opposed the literary mind—characterized as vague, obscure, and figurative—with the rigorous, precise language of the sciences and technology. It is a big surprise to discover that tales and novels are able to describe and predict exactly many of the complex human, social, and cultural phenomena. In *Designing with Blends* we are trying to develop a digital literacy, a fluency in the concepts of software and the interaction of people and software.

This book has evolved and developed over an extensive ten-year collaboration between the two authors. Manuel Imaz has a background in SE and has taught software design methods to professional software engineers. David Benyon has a background in systems analysis, and has taught database systems and HCI to university students. Benyon supervised Imaz's MSc and PhD, and they have published several papers together. Along the way, a number of people have contributed to and influenced the ideas here, and the authors would like to acknowledge their debt to them.

At the same time, the concepts that make up the framework here have themselves been evolving as the group of linguists, philosophers, psychologists, and others involved in this loose-knit community have argued about as well as collaborated on theories of metaphor, meaning, and thinking. This evolving framework is ongoing, and is broadening to include people from a phenomenological background interested in embodied cognition.

We hope, then, that this book is the start of another process. We are at the beginning of a fascinating period when digital "new media" will dominate people's lives in a way hitherto unimagined. We believe that this change demands a shift in our approach to SE and HCI. With this book, we hope to provide a foundation for that change. We also hope to offer some provocations and inspirations for a new generation of software designers and new media creators.

Finally, one of the authors (Imaz) is grateful to Mauricio Milchberg for his revision of the manuscript and valuable comments.

Acknowledgments

Grateful acknowledgment is made to the publishers, authors, and designers listed below for permission to reproduce material copyrighted, designed, or controlled by them.

Figures 2.1, 2.3, and 2.4 are from Mark Johnson, *The Body in the Mind: The Bodily Basis of Reason and Imagination* (Chicago: University of Chicago Press, 1987). Reprinted by permission of the University of Chicago Press.

Figure 2.2 is from George Lakoff and Mark Johnson, *Philosophy in the Flesh: The Embodied Mind and Its Challenge to Western Thought* (New York: HarperCollins, 1999). Copyright © 1999 by George Lakoff and Mark Johnson. Reprinted by permission of Basic Books, a member of Perseus Books, LLC.

Figures 3.2, 3.3, 3.4, and 3.5 are from Gilles Fauconnier *Mappings in Thought and Language* (Cambridge: Cambridge University Press, 1997). Reprinted by permission of Cambridge University Press.

Figures 6.1, 6.8, 7.14, and 8.6 are from David Benyon, Phil Turner, and Susan Turner, *Designing Interactive Systems: People, Activities, Contexts, Technologies* (Boston: Addison-Wesley, 2005). Reprinted by permission of Pearson Education EMA.

Figure 6.3 is from Don Gentner and Jakob Nielsen, "The Anti-Mac Interface," *Communications of the ACM* 39, no. 8 (1996): 70–82. Reprinted by permission of ACM.

Figure 7.13 is from John Carroll, *Making Use: Scenario-Based Design of Human-Computer Interactions* (Cambridge: MIT Press, 2000). Reprinted by permission of The MIT Press.

Figures 6.2, 6.4, 6.10, and 8.1 have been reproduced from the Mac OS X user interface. Mac is a trademark of Apple Computer, Inc.

Figure 5.15 has been kindly designed for this book by Luis Pérez.

Designing with Blends

1 Growing Up in the Digital Age

There is a fundamental problem for people living in the digital age. People and digital artifacts are different. People struggle to understand and use their computers, cameras, and phones. Certainly, many of these devices are quite complex, but many features of them are also poorly designed. This is not to blame designers; they are people living in the digital age too. They have grown up with the same understanding of people and the same background of computers as the rest of us. We do feel, however, that if designers were more sensitized to the problems people have using digital technologies, they might come up with better designs. If they were more literate in things digital, they could better express their intentions through their designs.

The digital is about to come of age. For sixty years, we have seen a steady development of digital technologies. Now everything is going digital. Once-separate things like cameras and phones are now converging, creating new artifacts. Indeed, it is right to say that the very fabric of the world is increasingly becoming digitally enhanced. The designers of these new environments, artifacts, and forms of interaction need to understand the things they create and the impact that they may have on people's lives.

Unfortunately, there is good reason to believe that our understanding of people, and particularly how people think, has been dominated by a serious misconception for the last sixty years. This misconception is that there is an objective world that people understand by holding and manipulating symbols in their heads that, in turn, stand for the things in the world. In place of this view is a conception that thinking is inherently embodied, rather than disembodied, literal, and based on the logical manipulations of abstract symbols. It is creative, figurative, and derived from our experiences as humans living in a physical, cultural, and social environment.

With this alternative view of cognition we can revisit the design of digital technologies. We can understand where the constructs used in the design of digital artifacts have come from and better explain how they may be used. We can help software designers and engineers understand their technology. Most important, we can develop literacy in digital technology design that will enable people to interact with and through those technologies in a satisfying and fruitful way.

Things Digital

Digital technologies, of the sort that we are familiar with today, first arrived in the form of electronic computers at the end of the Second World War. The concept of an electronic calculating machine had arisen during the 1930s, and found a real need in the work of the code-breaking group working at Bletchley Park in Buckinghamshire, England, and the war effort in the United States. Soon, general-purpose computers with names such as ENIAC and EDVAC were being developed. At much the same time, psychologists were doubting the prevalent theories of psychology. These theories focused on the observed behaviors of people, and a fierce debate raged between the behaviorists and the "cognitivists" about how best to describe and understand the psychology of people. Whereas behaviorists had looked at the observed behaviors of people, cognitivists believed that people had mental representations of things in the world that they stored, manipulated, and transformed in their minds.

Since the 1950s, there have been many developments in both computing and cognition. They have drawn from each other and have contributed to the understanding of each other. The fundamental design of a computer's memory and the way in which it processes data are much the same now as they were in the 1950s. Data—whether text, video, audio, or graphics—is represented as bits (binary digits), manipulated in the computer's main memory, and stored on some more permanent secondary storage device. Data can be transmitted over communications links to other devices. In a similar way, people could be described as having a long term memory for more permanent storage, a short-term memory for transitory data, and some processing capability, and of course they can transmit as well as receive data through hearing, seeing, smelling, touching, or tasting.

Digital technology has been very successful. The speed and capacity of computers have increased at a phenomenal rate—far beyond anything the early pioneers dreamed of. Thus we now have digital technologies (that is, computers) that are ubiquitous and pervasive, embedded in the fabric of the world. People increasingly wear computers in their clothes or jewelry, or carry computers in their phones or audio players. Ambient technology describes computers that are embedded in the fabric of buildings. These new media are characterized by their interactivity. They are interactive media—people alter the behaviors, presentation, and content of the media through their interactions with them. Interactive media continue to evolve and converge so, for example, a phone might include a camera, display live video transmissions, and connect automatically to receive e-mail when in range of a communications network. In interactive media, data is digital so it is transferable between devices, transmittable across wireless networks, and transmutable from one representation to another. The stuff of digital media that allows all this to happen is known as software.

Alongside the successes of digital media, however, there have been some notable failures. In the 1960s, the new field of artificial intelligence (AI) was established, and courses were set up at the University of Edinburgh in Scotland and Stanford University in the United States. Expectations were high. An AI computer would understand people when they talked to it. Computers would be able to wander around a house, recognize faces, and think in much the same way that people do. From the 1970s onward, huge amounts of investment have been put into "natural-language" processing to try to get computers to understand and use language as we do. In the 1990s, the Japanese "fifth-generation" project predicted highly "intelligent" machines within five years with automatic translation between languages. In the United States, President Ronald Reagan envisaged an umbrella of intelligent missiles in the "Star Wars" project. None of these has been realized.

Cognition, or cognitive psychology, has also come a long way since the 1950s. In particular there have been great advances in neurology, which is concerned with how the brain functions, where the functions are located, and how these functions can be identified and repaired, if necessary. But we are still no closer to understanding how people understand what each other say, how they recognize objects, nor how they play games like chess. If we could only understand the representations that people have (so the argument goes), we could program computers to do the same. Yet, some commentators have asserted that computers could never be intelligent in any way approximating what we understand by human intelligence because of the way that computers represent the outside world. They might do some clever things (which indeed they have done), but this has to do with size and speed, with brute force rather than understanding.

This difference between the representations of things that computers have and people's ways of understanding and acting has also made interacting with the computer difficult. The human-computer interaction (HCI) discipline grew out of the computing and cognition discussions of the 1970s, and became a central arena in which the psychologists could explore their theories. Software systems became to the cognitivists what the rat-in-a-maze had been to the behaviorists. People could be studied and questioned about the thinking that they were engaged in. The first theories of HCI were based on the idea that people are "human information processors" (see, for example, Card, Moran, and Newell 1983). Theories of human information processing had developed during the 1960s and 1970s. They examined how people could encode, transform, create, and output information. Applying this to people interacting with computers seemed an ideal laboratory in which to explore the cognitivists' ideas.

Many metaphors were used during this time to try to characterize HCI. HCI was often called the human-computer dialogue in the early days, suggesting that the person was communicating and discussing things with the computer. The notion that people interacting with computers could be considered a dialogue had its origin in the early design of computers too. In the early 1950s, "instructions" were given to computers by setting switches. Each switch could be set; either it was on or off (hence binary). Six or eight such switches (binary digits or bits) taken as a group would represent a character. With eight switches there were 256 different combinations (2^8), which was enough to represent all the letters of the alphabet, the numbers 0 to 9, special characters such as commas and periods, and spaces, with some to spare. Eight bits were known as a byte. As the process of using computers became more automated, paper tape was used to provide a sequence of instructions. Holes were punched in the tape to represent the bytes, and the sequence became known as a program, instruction set, or procedure. The process worked much the same as the original automated knitting machines, the Jacquard loom. By the late 1950s, general sets of instructions were stored in the computer to enable it to undertake frequently used procedures (such as storing and retrieving data). These were known as supervisor programs, monitor programs, or the operating system.

And so the scene was set for the first period of the digital age. Metaphors were used to describe the actions of computers and the representations that they used. Data was stored in "files." Programs were written in a programming "language." Programs were "executed" on the computer. People engaged in a "dialogue" with the computer. Since then, of course, we have a very different form of HCI and such metaphors have proliferated. We have "menus" of "commands." We "cut" and "paste." We "open" and "close" files. We "quit" programs and "import" data.

The Felt Sense of Thinking

In 1980, George Lakoff and Mark Johnson published their book *Metaphors We Live By*. This groundbreaking work argued that language and thought were based on a limited number of fundamental, conceptual metaphors. Metaphor was much more than a literary trope; it was central to how humans thought. Many metaphors were not recognized as such because they had been so ingrained into our ways of thinking and talking that we no longer saw them at all. The coauthors gave examples such as "knowing is seeing" (for instance, I see what you mean) and "up is good" (one is climbing the ladder of success). The computing examples above would not be recognized as metaphors by many; they are what we do with computers. This discovery of the systematic embedding of metaphors was accompanied by another key insight. These metaphors were based on embodied experience. These fundamental, conceptual metaphors derive from the fact that we are people living in the world: "three natural kinds of experience—experience of the body, of the physical environment, and of the culture—are what constitute the basic source domains upon which metaphors draw" (Rohrer 2005, 14).

Lakoff and Johnson's work and that of some other commentators represented a major shift in cognitive theory that may, in turn, have significant impact on how we view cognition (the debate on this continues). Given the intertwined history of computing and cognition, we suspect that the various theories that Lakoff and Johnson's ideas spawned will have a significant impact on software engineering (SE) and HCI too. In this book we explore exactly these issues.

Consider the following story based on reports of an air accident (Imaz and Benyon 1996, 106–107):

On 27th November 1983 there was a Boeing 747 accident near the Barajas airport. It was an Avianca (Colombian Airlines) regular flight from Paris to Bogota with a stop at Madrid. Even if the total scenario is quite complex, it could be said that the main cause of the accident was the misuse of the Ground Proximity Warning System (GPWS). According to the official report on the accident, the GPWS was insistently warning about the fact that the plane was below a minimum altitude.

The captain reacted saying: "OK, OK" meaning "I know it is a GPWS malfunction, so I will continue the approach procedure." The official reports says:

Captain answers "Bueno, bueno" (OK, OK).

However some people very close to this Official Commission (and some magazines of that time) say that the real captain answer—registered in the CVR (Cockpit Voice Recorder)—was:

"Calla gringo" (Shut up gringo).

"Gringo" is an expression used by some Latin-American people referring to (north) American people. In this context the captain was Colombian (south American), the aircraft north American and a warning system (GPWS) that speaks English. There is also a known fault in the artifact that in certain circumstances it gives a false warning. This determines a mistrust reaction by the captain. The captain has used a way of anthropomorphizing the GPWS by using the metaphor: THE DEVICE IS A STUPID PERSON.

This story illustrates that the relationship the captain establishes with the GPWS is not neutral. It shows some type of mistrust or a pejorative attitude. It appears that the GPWS has caused some unconscious reaction as if it were a real person. As this GPWS was a device that in certain circumstances gave erroneous information, this malfunction determined that in a critical moment, the captain did not accept the warning as a real one, but just another malfunction.

This analysis draws on a concept that we might call "sociocultural embodiment." The interaction of the captain and the device is not a simple, disembodied exchange. An HCI specialist could look at the design of the device as well as that of the human-computer interface and conclude that all HCI guidelines (derived from a traditional view of cognition) had been met. Such an analysis, we argue, would miss some key aspects of the human-computer relationship that derive from the embodied nature of cognition.

Tim Rohrer (1995) discusses "zooming windows" as an example of the power of physiologically embodied metaphors. When a person double clicks on a file icon on a computer, the image zooms out toward the person much in the same way as a page gets larger if you move a book toward your face. Similar animations have been adopted on personal data assistants and in the "genie" effect on the Macintosh operating system OS X when an item is moved on or off the temporary holding location, the Dock. Rohrer (1995, 8) says that:

> zooming is more than just a nice touch however; it is one of the best examples of how user interface design can draw on common patterns of feelings. Zooming is a pattern of feelings that takes place in and through time; the realization that all feeling takes place in and through time is the most important step in thinking about users' bodies. . . . Zooming windows are an extension of the PHYSICAL WORLD metaphor, which draws on the common pattern of feeling we experience when an object approaches us. Though computer events usually happen fairly instantaneously by our standards, zooming windows are a deliberate attempt to make the PHYSICAL WORLD metaphor of the user interface to include both three-dimensional space and time.

Rohrer (2005) emphasizes the felt sense of embodied interactions. It is not just a case of knowing some interaction is good or bad; it is sense of feeling it. In this book, we explore the design of computing systems—including the process of SE and HCI—from the perspective of "embodied cognition." This term covers a number of theoretical positions that oppose the traditional "objectivist" view of cognition that has dominated the discipline since its beginning. Our interests are with computers, how people use computers, what they try to do with computers, and designing for new interactive media. In the remainder of this chapter we introduce some of the key concepts in both people and computers.

A Short History of Cognition

Throughout the 1940s and 1950s, disciplines such as psychology, linguistics, computer science, and philosophy found that they were thinking and talking about similar concepts. This gave rise to a new discipline, called cognitive science. Indeed, one history of the subject (Gardner 1985) points to September 11, 1956, as the real starting point—the middle day of a symposium on information theory at MIT when papers were presented by Noam Chomsky (on linguistics), George Miller (on human memory), and Allen Newell and H. A. Simon on computing. Each person was to become a central figure in their own field.

Cognitive Psychology was the title of Ulrich Neisser's (1967) book that applied these concepts specifically to understanding human thought from an individual perspective. The computer-processing metaphor was used just as it is, taking *meaning* as almost synonymous with information, and describing people in terms of an input, a process, and an output: "Cognitive psychologists investigate human information processing—how people encode, transform, create, and output information" (Haberlandt 1994, 25).

The computer metaphor THE HUMAN IS AN INFORMATION PROCESSOR was used to understand cognition. The two main assumptions of cognitive psychology are representation and process. Within cognitive psychology, there are many debates about what these representations might be like, such as whether the representations are analogous to the physical entities or whether they are abstract. But the question of representation is not controversial. Moreover, for the adherents of a strong cognitivism, knowledge has uniformly the same structure and format, whether it is a transient image, a memory, the meaning of a word, or a problem to be solved.

Once the question of representation has been established, the next issue concerns how to store such representations in memory. Cognitive psychologists ask, for example, whether there is a specific storage location (as in a computer), which is always the reference of a representation. Others argue that information is distributed over many locations as a neural network. Cognitivism is a term usually reserved for an individual, isolated approach to cognitive psychology. It has a whole repertoire of processes, strategies, moves, operations, procedures, algorithms, plans, goals, and so on that manipulate the representations. For example, if a person is to remember a phone number the processes would involve listening, writing the number down, trying to remember it, and recalling it when needed. In terms of cognitive psychology this would be encoding, recoding, storing, and retrieval. Encoding means that the number is recognized, next it is recoded for writing it down, and assuming that the number has been stored in memory, then it may be retrieved for later use.

This notion of cognition dominated psychology throughout the 1960s and 1970s. In the 1980s, a new computing paradigm emerged: parallel distributed processing (PDP). People such as David Rumelhart and James McClelland (1986) used this different computing metaphor to discuss cognition. The classical paradigm of centralized processes and an executive program in control was replaced by a new one: THE BRAIN IS A NEURAL NETWORK. In this model, thousands of relatively independent processing nodes are linked into a network. The strength of the different connections is altered during processing until the network settles down (or "relaxes") to provide a solution.

Another development in cognition is the notion of "distributed cognition." Starting his work in the 1980s, Ed Hutchins published *Cognition in the Wild* in 1995. Since then, he has been working with colleagues at the University of California, San Diego, to develop these ideas. One of them, Jim Hollan (et al. 2000, 175) states that unlike traditional theories, distributed cognition "extends the reach of what is considered cognitive beyond the individual to encompass interactions between people and with resources and materials in the environment."

In traditional views of cognition the boundaries of the unit of analysis are those of individuals, while in distributed cognition the unit is the cognitive process, wherever it may occur and taking into consideration the functional relationships of elements participating in the process. Distributed cognition is also concerned with the range of mechanisms that are assumed to participate in cognitive processes. This is a broader spectrum of cognitive elements than those assumed to exist in the limits of an individual brain. As an example of distributed cognition, researchers point to flying an aircraft. The successful completion of a flight is shared across the instruments in the cockpit, a pilot and copilot, the air traffic control staff on the ground surrounded by all their computers and notebooks, and so on.

Hollan and colleagues (2000) identify three different kinds of distribution of cognitive processes: across people, across representations, and across cultures. Socially distributed cognition focuses on the role that a group of people have in thinking and knowing and on the phenomena that emerge as a result of these social interactions. Second, cognitive processes make use of external as well as internal representations. These external representations are things such as notes, entries in logbooks, specialist measuring instruments, and other cognitive or information artifacts. An important ramification of this view is that designers cannot simply automate something. By changing the information artifacts that are involved in an activity, the distribution of the cognition required to undertake the activity changes.

People are social agents who live in cultural environments. Hence, there is an intertwined relationship between agents and culture. On the one hand, culture emerges as a result of the activity of human beings, and on the other hand, in its various forms of artifacts and social practices, culture shapes cognitive processes. Hollan and colleagues claim that this influence is particularly important in processes that are distributed over social agents, artefacts, and environments. This has a crucial knock-on effect for our analysis. If concepts are culturally shaped, then so is cognition. How we think about things is affected by history.

A conceptually related view of cognition is activity theory. Activity theory has its origins in the works of the Russian psychologist Lev Vygotsky beginning in the 1920s, but has only recently been recognized in the Western scientific community (see, for example, Leont'ev 1978; Bødker 1991; Bannon 1991; Nardi 1995). The concept of *activity* consists of a subject (one or more individuals), an object (held by the subject and motivating the activity), actions (goal-directed and conscious processes that must be undertaken to fulfill the object), and operations (former actions that have become routine and unconscious with practice). An activity is "a system that has structure, its own internal transitions and transformations, its own development" (Leont'ev 1978, 50).

An activity is directed toward a certain object (that is, a purpose or goal), and is mediated by one or more artifacts (which may include pieces of software, "thinking" artifacts such as language, and so on). Activities can only be understood given some knowledge of the object and the motive behind the activity. Significantly, activities need to be seen within a cultural and historical context; the term "cultural historical activity theory" (CHAT) is often used to emphasize this.

Since its beginnings in the 1950s, then, cognition has gone through many transformations as researchers have grappled with better ways of understanding and describing how people think. This quick tour through some of the main influences inevitably leaves out much detail and many other competing theories. The purpose of the tour is to illustrate that cognition is not a simple well-understood concept or theory. Yet these folk views of cognition have been profoundly influential on the design of computer systems and digital media.

Concepts of Software

There are many levels at which a computer (or any digital medium) can be described. There is the overall "architecture" of secondary storage, primary storage, processing unit, input and output mechanisms, and power source. Each of these has an impact on what can be done with the device, and each is becoming smaller and faster all the time. People are now predicting "speckled computing"—fully functional computers that are one millimeter cubed that can be sprayed from a spray can or spread around like "smart dust." We have seen the amazing increases in secondary storage that allow people, for example, to put their whole music, photo, or video collection on a device no bigger than a pack of playing cards. We have mobile phones that contain more computing power than the standard computer of five years ago. Such features of digital media are incredible, but our interest here is in what we can make these devices do, using software. We take the basic digital architecture as given. We are interested in some conceptual description of what the computer does, the constructs of computer programming languages, and the different ways in which programming the computer has been conceptualized over the years. Even at this level, there is a huge amount that can be said, and there are specialist groups that research the psychology of programming and related areas.

A computer works by manipulating the contents of the locations in its memory. In the early days, computers were programmed in a machine *language.* This specified the location in the computer's memory where data or instructions were stored, and where the result of any calculation should be placed. Soon after this, symbolic programming languages were developed that used more abstract terms to specify the actions of the program. Words such as move, add, store, and so on, included the specification of a storage location using names such as rate, pay, and so forth. These more abstract descriptions were then "assembled" into the machine code. This assembly language was still quite obscure, so more abstract means were used to program the computer, and more and more of the processing was moved from software into hardware. The main hardware revolution happened in the 1970s, when general-purpose microchips were developed. These have subsequently become incredibly small, and can be tailored and manufactured for specific purposes such as controlling the fuel input to a car engine or telling the time. The trade-off between hardware and software is one of flexibility. A more general-purpose hardware can be programmed to do many different things. Hardware with a more specific function is less flexible.

The more abstract programming languages began appearing in the 1950s and 1960s, and included FORTRAN (standing for "formula translation"), the common business-oriented language (COBOL), and the beginner's all-purpose symbolic instruction code, BASIC. These languages adopted a procedural paradigm and are known as procedural languages. Sequences of instructions are written in the order in which they are to be executed. Other competing programming paradigms included the functional language LISP (for "list processing language") and the logic programming language, Prolog. These latter two were particularly popular for programming AI applications. Another important change that took place during this period was that the preferred term for describing instructing the computer changed from *computer programming* to *software engineering*. Software development was depicted using an industrial plant metaphor: SOFTWARE IS CONSTRUCTION.

The "object-oriented" (OO) paradigm of computer programming began at the Xerox Corporation's Palo Alto Research Center (PARC) with the development of the programming language Smalltalk in the early 1970s. In OO methods, the domain of interest (some "sphere of activity") is represented in terms of the objects that exist, the relationships between objects, and the messages that are passed between objects. This was an important change. The metaphor for thinking about software development changed from SOFTWARE IS A SEQUENCE OF STEPS to SOFTWARE IS A COLLECTION OF OBJECTS.

There were many competing methods during the 1990s for OO design and programming. Toward the end of the century, three of the main competing OO methods became united in the Unified Modeling Language (UML).

Objects are defined as: "an encapsulation of attributes and exclusive services [behaviors]; an abstraction of something in the problem space" (Coad and Yourdon 1992, 31). They correspond to "real-world" entities. The benefits of OO techniques include abstraction and encapsulation (otherwise known as "information hiding"). All computing is concerned with abstractions: with finding generic methods of representing things so that people can attend to the significant aspects and not get confused by the details. Objects are "viewed" from the outside, and people need not be concerned about how they are implemented. Objects can send and receive "messages"; they encapsulate the structure and processing that enables them to deal with those messages. Other features of the OO paradigm include polymorphism (that different object classes will treat the same message in different ways) and inheritance; objects can inherit characteristics from more abstract objects. The most popular OO programming languages are Java and C++.

The OO paradigm is still the dominant approach for software development. Recently, however, software objects have been programmed to be more independent. Rather than sitting and waiting to be instructed to do something, objects can be given higher-level "intentions" that they actively seek to achieve. Such systems are known as software agents. Agents operate in a variety of domains. For example, agents can move around a computer network, optimizing the flow of network traffic or checking for breaches of security. Agents in mobile phones actively seek out the strongest signal and automatically switch connections. Software in car engines optimizes fuel flow in order to maximize efficiency.

Increasingly, software agents are taking on these mundane tasks, leaving us, as people, to concentrate on the more interesting aspects of life. There are dangers and concerns of course. Computer viruses are software agents. Computers and other digital technologies connect autonomously with one another and can exchange data without us being aware of it. The advantages of the agent approach, though, is that they can be given relatively abstract, high-level instructions and be left to satisfy those as best they can. And so we see another change in how we think about software: SOFTWARE IS A SOCIETY OF AGENTS.

Human-Computer Interaction

People and software come together in the discipline of HCI. The concerns of HCI were expressed intermittently during the early part of the digital age. J. C. R. Licklider's "Man-Computer Symbiosis" in 1960 and Brian Shackel's 1959 paper are counted among the first writings to address the issues of people making use of devices along with the difficulties they might face. But the subject really started to attract interest with the publication of Ben Shneiderman's *Software Psychology* in 1980 and Don Norman's "The Trouble with UNIX: The User Interface Is Horrid" in 1981.

As with the development of both psychology and software, HCI was originally concerned with a person using a computer. Stuart Card, Thomas Moran, and Allen Newell published *The Psychology of Human-Computer Interaction* (1983) and introduced the discipline to the information-processing view of people that was so dominant in psychology. Applied to HCI, this perspective resulted in a number of detailed methods for analyzing and designing human tasks. Task analysis was to dominate HCI for the next twenty years. The basic conceptualization of HCI was that a person had a goal that they wanted to achieve. This goal could be accomplished by undertaking a number of tasks in a given order. Tasks consisted of subtasks and actions. Thus people formed a plan of action and followed it through: HCI IS FOLLOWING INSTRUCTIONS.

During this period, the emphasis was firmly on the human-computer interface: all those parts of the system that the user comes into contact with, whether physically, perceptually, or conceptually. HCI was practically synonymous with interface design.

Later in the 1980s, a new field emerged that focused on people working together through computers. This became known as computer-supported cooperative work. The stress here is on multiperson, distributed systems and issues of awareness of others, supporting collaboration and peripheral information. The centrality of tasks to HCI was also challenged by Lucy Suchman, who published *Plans and Situated Actions* in 1987. In this work, she argues that people do not simply follow plans; they react to changing situations.

When considering HCI, we recognize an initial constitutive metaphor: THE INTERACTION IS A DIALOGUE, CONVERSATION, OR COMMUNICATION. This had its origin with the introduction of operating systems in the mid- to late 1950s. These new "supervisor programs" were the intermediary software needed to represent the computer in all the interactions with the operator, programmer, or user. The consequence of using a linguistic metaphor applied to the code is that the interaction between humans and computers could be considered as a DIALOGUE. The user interface at this time (up until the late 1970s) was known as a command line interface. The interaction between person and computer consisted of the person typing in instructions, or commands, and the computer undertaking some processing and displaying the output.

A new metaphor, INTERACTING WITH THE COMPUTER IS DIRECT MANIPULATION, was formally characterized in 1983 by Ben Shneiderman. Yet it had begun to take form many years previously when Ivan Sutherland was defending his PhD thesis, *Sketchpad: A Man-Machine Graphical Communications System* (1963). It is interesting to note that Sutherland conceptualized this interaction in terms of communication—the dominant paradigm at that time—although it was a true interactive computer graphics. Shneiderman (1983, 57) described the new computing of the late 1970s that were using interactive computer graphics as follows:

> In trying to understand the commonalities across these diverse interfaces, I began to notice a certain pattern. The first was a visual representation of the world of action. The objects of interest and the actions of interest were shown on the screen. . . . These new systems showed the objects of interest, and when actions were taken the results were also shown immediately and continuously on the screen. A second set of principles that also seemed important were that the actions were rapidly executed, incrementally

described and reversible. Furthermore, in direct manipulation systems, pointing, selecting and dragging replace the need to type commands. For example, you could drag an icon towards a folder or you could bring it back.

While Shneiderman is credited with coining the term "direct manipulation," it is fair to say that the designers at Xerox PARC were responsible for creating the interfaces that he was observing. Shneiderman detected some patterns or principles of interaction—visibility of the objects of interest; rapid, reversible, incremental actions—to introduce a new paradigm and a new metaphor. It was the Xerox Star computer, the Apple Lisa, and finally the Apple Macintosh in 1984 that demonstrated the principles.

Finally, another approach called ubiquitous computing (Weiser 1991, 1993) appears as enhancing or generalizing direct manipulation. Weiser (1991, 94) says that:

> the idea of a "personal" computer itself is misplaced, and that the vision of laptop machines, dynabooks and "knowledge navigators" is only a transitional step toward achieving the real potential of information technology. Such machines cannot truly make computing an integral, invisible part of the way people live their lives. . . . Such a disappearance is a fundamental consequence not of technology, but of human psychology. Whenever people learn something sufficiently well, they cease to be aware of it. . . . Only when things disappear in this way are we freed to use them without thinking and so to focus beyond them on new goals.

Here a new slogan is emerging: THE COMPUTER IS DISAPPEARING or THE COMPUTER IS BECOMING INVISIBLE, according to Norman (1998). In order for computers to disappear from our awareness, they would have some features that everyday objects have: a natural, intuitive form that indicates functions and content that resides in the background, or periphery, coming to the fore when needed. At this point it is interesting to listen to some skeptical voices about ubiquitous computing, who observe that "we will still be frustrated, but at a higher level of functionality, and there will be more of us willing to be frustrated" (Odlyzko 1999, 1).

Framing the Problem

And so we arrive at the present, and the digital age continues apace. The problem we have is how to design digital artifacts, how to design for new spaces that are full of computing devices, and how to design for people who are wearing these devices. Information, data, and multimedia content are easily passed from one person or place to another, transformed from one medium to another, and displayed on one device or another. What new forms of interaction will there be, what are the potential pitfalls, and what are the potential benefits?

Unfortunately, we cannot answer these questions yet. What we can do is to develop literacy in designers, and provide designers with an understanding of the underlying concepts of the digital medium and its interaction with people. We may even influence some changes in design—moving it away from the idea that we are trying to make something literally happen toward an understanding that interaction with and through digital media is fundamentally figurative.

We have seen that SE methods have changed over the years according to the metaphors that people have used to conceptualize what they are doing: THE SYSTEM IS AN INDUSTRIAL PLANT; THE SYSTEM IS A COLLECTION OF OBJECTS; and THE SYSTEM IS A SOCIETY OF AGENTS. HCI is still grounded in both metaphors: HCI IS COMMUNICATION and HCI IS DIRECT MANIPULATION. There are new proposals, such as informal interaction or sketching interfaces (Landay and Myers 2001), that try to assist people with new, informal activities, such as writing, drawing, or designing. Pattie Maes (1994) has conceptualized HCI as A SOCIETY OF INSECTS, and Alan Kay (1993) has a vision of HCI as the INDIRECT MANAGEMENT OF AGENTS. Indeed, there have been debates between protagonists of these different metaphors for HCI (Shneiderman and Maes 1997).

We are moving into yet another new era: THE COMPUTER IS DISAPPEARING. We expect interaction with digital media to become much more physical and less screen based. People will interact with digital technologies through touch, manipulation, and gesture; interaction will increasingly be embodied. People will move through environments embedded with digital artifacts, and will interact with and through technologies in new ways. These new environments promise to be highly complex in terms of their accessibility, functionality, and usability. Conceptually, it will be difficult to determine what can be done, how it can be done, and where it can be done.

We also suspect that our traditional understanding of cognition is flawed. Hence, the principles of HCI are based on an inappropriate view of how people think and act, and on the relationships between action and cognition. SE methods are predicated on an objectivist view of the world that is inappropriate.

Finally, we point to a fundamental difficulty for the design of digital media: people and digital media are different. This is the problem of HCI-SE. In order to design digital artifacts, we have to specify instructions in some way that the computer can process, but this is inevitably fundamentally different from how people want to work. There is a mismatch between the rich, complex, nuanced activities of people and the inflexible demands of digital artifacts.

In the next few chapters we explore these three intertwined issues. We introduce a view of cognition that is grounded in ideas of embodiment: we think and act the way we do because we have bodies and live in human societies. We use this to provide an alternative perspective on HCI and SE, the conceptual foundations of these subjects, and methodologies for the analysis and design of human-computer systems. The aim here is to offer insight and develop literacy in the analytic approach that we adopt. We also look at design and how embodied cognition can change the way we approach design by foregrounding the figurative (as opposed to the literal) nature of interaction, and then move toward a critical approach to the design of digital media.

2 Cognition and the Body

When René Descartes wrote the famous words "Cogito ergo sum" (I think, therefore I am), he established a period of thinking about cognition that separated mind and body. Apart from one or two key thinkers, it is only relatively recently that philosophers and psychologists have recognized this and have tried to bring the body back into thinking. The critical concept underlying embodied or "experiential" cognition is that humans only think how they do because they are human; people have human bodies and live in human societies. This is quite a fundamental shift in thinking about thinking. It has resonances with Ludwig Wittgenstein's (1953; excerpts in Margolis and Laurence 1999, 190) famous pronouncement that "if a lion could talk we could not understand him." The experience of a lion is so different from that of a human that the lion would have vastly different concepts.

In this chapter, we examine the main cognitive structures that people have. Our principle sources for the discussion come primarily from the field of linguistics where the relationships between cognition and language have been explored. What we seek to do in this chapter is to establish a view of cognition suitable for looking at SE and HCI.

The threads of embodied cognition can be traced back to the writing of authors throughout the latter parts of the twentieth century such as Hilary Putnam (1975, 1981), Hubert Dreyfus (1972; Dreyfus and Dreyfus 1988), Martin Heidegger writing in the 1930s (Heidegger, Macquarrie, and Robinson 1978), Maurice Merleau-Ponty (1962), and Wittgenstein (1953; excerpts in Margolis and Laurence 1999). These philosophers argued that human understanding was a skill akin to knowing how to find one's way in the world, rather than knowing a lot of facts and rules for relating them. For these thinkers, the philosophy that attempted to treat intelligence as rational or at least analytic had never worked (Dreyfus and Dreyfus 1988). The role of the body in conceptualization and thought was critical.

Lakoff's philosophy has also been known as *experientialism,* which stresses the embodied, experiential nature of the approach. Elsewhere it is also known as *cognitive semantics,* which reflects its historical links with linguistics. Our analysis draws mostly from this group of linguists, particularly on George Lakoff and Mark Johnson (1980, 1999), Gilles Fauconnier (1994, 1985), Lakoff (1987), and Fauconnier and Mark Turner (2002). Most of these authors have criticized the objectivist theory of mind—also known as *cognitivism*—and focus their theory on a different approach that gives a central role to the body in characterizing meaningful concepts and cognition in general.

In the design of new media, ideas of embodied cognition have recently been championed by authors such as Paul Dourish (2001) and Malcolm McCullough (2004). Dourish, in particular, emphasizes the two sides of embodied cognition. It is both the fact that we have a body and that we live in human societies that provide the basis for our thought processes. Concepts are socially constructed.

Experientialism or cognitive semantics offers a sound basis for the notion that cognition is embodied (as opposed to disembodied) because it argues that the basic building blocks of cognition are derived from bodily and social experiences. There is a "human scale" to this description of cognition. Cognition and action are intrinsically linked and grounded in human experience.

We consider the principle components of this view of cognition in terms of cognitive models, basic-level categories, and image schemata. Cognitive or mental models refer to the thoughts and ideas that we have. Basic categories refer to the ways in which we organize and structure these, and image schemata refer to the spatial relationships between them that we experience. These establish a foundation for looking at other conceptual processes, primarily metaphors and blends, which we consider in chapter 3.

Lakoff and Johnson (1999) contend that experientialism is grounded in neurophysiology and that there is sound empirical evidence for supposing that a description of thought in these terms is a sensible one. They also argue, however, that there is no single conceptual metaphor that can consistently describe all our ways of thinking and experiencing. For us, cognitive semantics provides a set of conceptual tools for reasoning about people and their interactions with digital media.

Cognitive Models

One of the main contributions of cognitive psychology to HCI is the concept of mental models. A mental model, also called a conceptual or cognitive model, aims to provide a description of how people's thoughts and ideas about things are structured. The mental model construct covers a wide spectrum of ideas, ranging from classical functionalist views to others closer to cognitive semantics.

Mental models are popular in cognitive psychology and HCI where they are often synonymous with trying to understand how people think some device or system works. Psychologists try to understand people's mental models of electricity, a central heating system, or an automated teller machine. People might use mental models to solve problems when there is a breakdown (for example, your car does not start), work out the mapping between actions and events, or fill in the details of some description. Norman's (1983, 8) point of view is that:

1. Mental models are incomplete.
2. People's abilities to "run" their models are severely limited.
3. Mental models are unstable: People forget the details of the system they are using, especially when those details (or the whole system) have not been used for some period.
4. Mental models do not have firm boundaries: similar devices and operations get confused with one another.
5. Mental models are "unscientific": People maintain "superstitious" behaviour patterns even when they know they are unneeded because they cost little in physical effort and save mental effort.
6. Mental models are parsimonious. Often people do extra physical operations rather than the mental planning that would allow them to avoid those actions.

Mental models are not simply recipes or procedures written in the mind. In point 5 above, Norman indicates that mental models may include some external conceptual artifacts. When he says that "people maintain 'superstitious' behavior patterns even when they know they are unneeded," it is clear that people have consciously adopted such behavior as something external and convenient as it saves mental effort. In this case, it is suggested that mental models are not the result of the interaction between the user and a system but of a given external representation of the system.

There are many interpretations of the concept of a mental model in Dedre Gentner and Albert L. Stevens (1983) that explore the different uses that they can be put to, and the different structures and functions that they may have. Ed Hutchins (1983) provides one of the early descriptions of distributed cognition in his work on the mental models used by navigators in Micronesia. He argues that navigators reason with the environment rather than translating features of the environment into some type of representations or, in Hutchins's terms, "material anchors" (such as charts and navigational instruments), and then reasoning with these and translating them back into real-world analogues. James Greeno (1983) points to the importance of choosing the appropriate ontology for the mental model so that relations between domains can be recognized and hence reasoning can be simplified. Richard Young (1983) observes that mental models can be used for either helping the performance of some activity, learning, reasoning, and solving problems in some domain, or design. Different representations (mental models) will be more or less useful for different activities.

Dedre Gentner and Donald Gentner (1983) explore the conceptual role of analogy in reasoning. They point out that people sometimes use implicit analogies in their reasoning. The title of their piece, "Flowing Waters or Teeming Crowds: Mental Models of Electricity," captures the issue concisely. The concept of a mental model is not homogeneous but embraces a set of multiple theories. Each theory is based on different assumptions varying from a classical approach (Williams, Hollan, and Stevens 1983) premised on metaphors such as THOUGHT IS OBJECT MANIPULATION or THOUGHT IS LANGUAGE, to an approach such as that proposed by Gentner and Gentner that recognizes the important role of metaphor in mental models.

For Lakoff (1987), the concept of a cognitive model is close to the ideas of mental models explored here, along with other structuring concepts such as frames (discussed below). He distinguishes between cognitive models and idealized cognitive models (ICMs). A cognitive model provides the structure for a "mental space," which is seen as "a medium for conceptualization and thought" (Lakoff 1987, 281). His concept of mental space is based on Fauconnier's (1994) ideas. Mental spaces are purely mental constructs (that is, cognitive structures) that may be related to one another (connected) in a person's mind.

Despite the proliferation of similar terms, the underlying view of all these writers is that people engage in thinking, acting, and reasoning by making use of some abstract, conceptual structures that we can call mental or cognitive models. There are many differences of opinion of where these models come from, what form they might take, and how they relate to things in the world. For Lakoff and Johnson (1999, 266), "The word mental picks out those bodily capacities and performances that constitute our awareness and determine our creative and constructive responses to the situations we encounter. Mind isn't some mysterious abstract entity that we bring to bear on our experience. Rather, mind is part of the very structure and fabric of our interactions with our world."

There is a group of related concepts, which have been used by different authors and would be useful to clarify their differences and similarities, and how we will use them in the book. The first author to use the concept of *cognitive schemata* (or schemas) was Frederic Bartlett (1932). According to his schema theory, when reading a text our background knowledge and the linguistic cues contained in the text are organized into patterns related to one another, which are made use of in reconstructing meaning. There are clear similarities here with mental spaces when Fauconnier (1994, xxii) writes that "as discourse unfolds, much is going on behind the scenes: New domains appear, links are forged, abstract mappings operate, internal structure emerges and spreads, viewpoint and focus keep shifting."

Bartlett studied the process of memory, which had up until his time been considered to be a static phenomenon. He changed the perspective of memory, proposing that remembering is an act of reconstruction, not one of reproduction. After experimenting with storytelling to determine how the same story is successively modified as it passes from one subject to another, Bartlett's findings were that:

- Interpreting plays a large role in what we remember.
- What is remembered has to have some connection with what is already familiar.
- Memory is a constructive process.

He concluded that human memory involves the formation of abstract cognitive structures he called schemata. What we remember is built on what we have experienced in our past. Another way of seeing schemata is to consider them as frameworks for organizing information in memory. Bartlett's point of view is more complex than traditional cognitive psychology that considers just an encoding, storing, and searching process in memory. In the encoding process there is an interpretation determined by previous experience, and what is stored is also determined by connections to what is already familiar. There is not just a search, but it is about a whole constructive process when remembering, implying the activation of other schemata associated to the one we are looking for. A schema is an abstract cognitive structure, which may be considered as a pattern or framework for organizing such cognitive structure.

Another important concept is that of *frame,* which has been employed by Marvin Minsky (1975) and Charles Fillmore (1977), and means according to Minsky a data structure for representing a stereotyped situation. Minsky envisages a frame as a network of nodes and relations. According to Fillmore, frames are rich conceptual structures from which lexical items draw their meaning and function. There is an online lexical resource called FrameNet (2001), based on Fillmore's approach, and where examples and bibliography may be found.

Frames have frame elements. For instance, the *commerce* frame has elements *buyer, seller, goods,* and *payment.* So the following sentences might describe the same interaction:

1. John bought a car from Paula for two thousand dollars.
2. Paula sold a car to John for two thousand dollars.

The sentences are framed by the same frame, commerce or commercial transaction. Minsky's conceptualization includes default values in frames. These standardized, or stereotyped, domains allow people to fill in details from the default values if they are not given explicit information about some element, or facet, in a frame.

Also related is the work of other authors, notably Roger Schank and Robert Abelson (1977), who use the term *script;* a script describes a frequent event sequence. Schank and Abelson (1977, 38) used examples such as a birthday party script or a restaurant script to show how stories are told and understood: "when someone decides to tell a story that references a script, he recognizes that he need not (and because he would otherwise be considered rather boring, should not) mention every detail of his story."

Lakoff introduces a further term: *scenario.* According to Lakoff, a scenario has an initial state, a sequence of events, and a final state. If we are to see any difference between frames (as defined by Fillmore) and scenarios (as defined by Lakoff), frames are elementary scenarios with some roles as well as a few actions and events. In the example of the commerce frame, there is just a buyer, a seller, some goods, and a payment with a transaction (an event) whereby the goods pass from the seller to the buyer and money passes from the buyer to the seller.

A scenario (or script) such as the restaurant scenario implies a series of events: arrival, waiting for a table, sitting at a table, receiving the menu, asking for food, eating, and so on. In this sense, a scenario or script is an enlarged frame, seen from the point of view of one of the roles.

We will use the terms as follows. Usually, the term schema will refer to an image schema (see below). We will prefer to use the term frame in a similar way as discussed above, avoiding script and scenario since they have particular meanings within SE.

Frames are an example of cognitive models of a particular type: they are propositional cognitive models. That is to say, frames have some elements (or an ontology) and some structure that expresses relations between the elements. Nevertheless, it must be stressed that frames are mental constructs; they do not describe the world *as it is*. They are a representation of the world. Recalling Norman's view of mental models above, frames may contain "erroneous" beliefs, "unnecessary" facts, and so on.

Lakoff, however, argues that propositional models are only one type of cognitive model. He has identified four main types of cognitive models, which he calls ICMs. Each ICM is a complex structured whole, a gestalt, which uses any of four kinds of structuring principles:

- Propositional models specify elements, their properties, and the relations holding among them. These are frames.
- Image-schematic models produce representations based on bodily and cultural experiences. They have basic elements organized into a gestalt structure and hence have a logic that is inherently meaningful because of people's bodily experiences.
- Metaphoric models are derived from mappings from a model in one domain to a corresponding structure in another domain.
- Metonymic models are those derived from the relationship between one element of the domain to the domain as a whole. In metonymy, a member of the category stands for the whole category. Concepts such as "Wall Street might crash" or "Downing Street refused to comment" use the place to stand for the institution. In answering a question such as "How did you get there?" with "I hopped on the bus," you are using the embarkation process to stand for the whole journey.

A key observation here is that only the first of these is in any way factual and declarative, or "literal." The other three types of cognitive models are created by projecting imaginatively from one representation to another. Importantly, they are derived from bodily and social experiences. Cognitive models as described here are ecological and holistic.

Concepts and Categories

The classical theory of concepts holds that most concepts have a definitional structure. That is, most concepts embed necessary and sufficient conditions for their own application, if possible in sensory or perceptual terms. In this classical theory, there is also a classical example: the concept bachelor. It is possible to think of this concept as a complex mental representation that specifies the necessary and sufficient conditions for somebody to be a bachelor: "So BACHELOR might be composed of a set of representations such as IS NOT MARRIED, IS MALE, and IS AN ADULT. Each of these components specifies a condition that something must meet in order to be a bachelor, and anything that satisfies them all thereby counts as a bachelor (Margolis and Laurence 1999)."

As clear and simple as this example might seem, the question of defining concepts is not as easy as it looks. Moreover, one of the difficulties of the classical theory of concepts is what Eric Margolis and Stephen Laurence call Plato's problem: for most concepts, there simply aren't any clear definitions.

In the classical view, it is thought that we automatically categorize people, things, and animals. This way of grouping similar things into sets leads to the impression that we just categorize them as they are. Things come in natural kinds, and our mental categories naturally fit the kinds of objects there are in the world. In fact, the use of classical categories worked perfectly for a long time, up to the publication of Wittgenstein's (1953) later work. Lakoff points out, however, that this classical view was not the result of empirical study; it was instead a basic assumption of philosophy.

Wittgenstein questioned the classical theory of categories, pointing out that things were related in many different ways. He used the example of the category game:

Consider for example the proceedings that we call "games." I mean board-games, card-games, ball-games, Olympic games, and so on. What is common to them all?—Don't say: "There *must* be something common, or they would not be called 'games'"—but *look and see* whether there is anything common to all.—For if you look at them you will not see something that is common to *all,* but similarities, relationships, and a whole series of them at that. To repeat: don't think. But look! (Wittgenstein 1953; excerpts in Margolis and Laurence 1999, 171).

The conclusions drawn by Wittgenstein are that we observe a complex network of similarities in categories. Sometimes these are overall similarities and sometimes they are similarities of detail. He called these similarities *family resemblances.*

Basic-Level Categories

In the mid-1970s, Eleanor Rosch took up the Wittgensteinian analysis about the difficulties with classical categories and tried to offer an empirical foundation. Her research is an attempt to explain the idea of family resemblance (such as applied to games) as a new concept of category. When considering a group of objects as equivalent, we call it a category, while a system by which categories are related to one another is a *taxonomy.* The usual way of representing a taxonomy is by a hierarchical diagram, and associated to such diagrams is the idea of the level of abstraction. A higher level of abstraction is associated to a greater inclusiveness of a category within a taxonomy diagram, and lower levels of abstraction distinguish subcategories.

One important result of Rosch's work is the concept of basic-level categories. Basic-level categories are at a middle level of abstraction. They refer to subcategories or category members that have a special cognitive status: that of being a "best example." She conducted a number of experiments in which participants judged certain members of the categories as being more representative of the category than other members. For instance, when considering the category of bird, some exemplars, like robins, were judged to be more representative than chickens, penguins, and ostriches. Rosch proposed a prototype theory of categories, summarized by Lakoff (1987, 56) as follows.

Some categories, like tall man or red, are graded, that is, they have inherent degrees of membership, fuzzy boundaries, and central members whose degree of membership (on a scale from zero to one) is one. Other categories, like bird, have clear boundaries; but within those boundaries there are graded prototype effects—some category members are better examples of the category than others. . . . Human categories are not objectively "in the world," external to human beings. At least some categories are embodied. Color categories, for example, are determined jointly by the external physical world, human biology, the human mind, plus cultural considerations. . . . The properties relevant to the description of categories are interactional properties, properties characterizable only in terms of the interaction of human beings as part of their environment. Prototypical members of categories are sometimes describable in terms of clusters of such interactional properties. These clusters act as gestalts: the cluster as a whole is psychologically simpler that its parts. Prototype effects, that is, asymmetries among category members such as goodness-of-example judgments, are superficial phenomena which may have many sources.

Basic-level categories are *basic* in a number of respects. From a perceptual point of view, basic-level categories map to an overall shape, to single images with fast identification. From a functional point of view, basic-level categories are associated with a general motor program or cultural functions. In order to organize our knowledge, most attributes of categories members are stored at the basic level, and the advantage for communication is that they are the shortest and most commonly used words, which we first learn when we are children, and they are the first to be included in the lexicon.

In terms of mental images, we can form a general mental image of basic-level categories like chairs or dogs. But we cannot form a mental image for superordinate categories like furniture or animals. We have mental images for elements of the furniture category: chairs, tables, armchairs, beds, and so on, but not for a generic piece of furniture. Similarly, we have general motor programs for using chairs and tables, but not for using furniture in general.

Basic-level categories are formed by entities we physically interact with, thus determining basic elements of perception and function. The communication aspect and knowledge organization ground both perception and function. Basic-level categories are defined by how we interact with the world given the bodies we have, our cognitive models, and our culturally defined purposes. A consequence of these considerations is that most of our knowledge is organized at the basic level.

Forming New Categories

Lakoff distinguishes two kinds of cases, depending on whether the nature of categories is an aspect of the mind or is determined by the nature of the human body:

- Cases where the nature of the human body (perception or motor capacities) determines some aspect of the category;
- Cases where some imaginative aspect of the mind—schematic organization, metaphor, metonymy, or mental imagery—plays a role in the nature of the category.

A typical way of defining categories by means of an imaginative aspect of the mind is by using metaphors. The typical expression "time is money" defines a conceptual structure for time. As a consequence of this way of categorizing, it is possible to say somebody is *stealing* time to mean that the person uses their job's time for a personal concern.

Other categories are sometimes the result of using a metonymy in the projection, such as the case of the housewife mother stereotype. This subcategory is used to stand for the entire category of mothers in defining social expectations (Lakoff 1987, 84). Most of social stereotypes are a special way of categorizing selecting a subcategory and projecting on the entire category the attributes of the source subcategory; these are metonymic models of categorization. Most of the metonymic models are, in fact, not models of categories but of individuals, such as when using the White House expression to indicate the U.S. government. But there are also more general metonymic models like when referring to a delicious plate in place of a delicious salmon.

Much has been discussed about metaphorical concepts or concepts defined by metaphors—like LOVE IS A JOURNEY—regarding its very nature. There are at least two possible views about metaphor-structuring conceptual representations. One of them is the strong view, which states that there is no a literal definition of such concepts, but they are only defined by metaphorical projections to knowledge in different domains (Gibbs 1998). Is it possible to have an independent, nonmetaphoric concept for love? Some authors answer that it is not possible to have a literal definition for love, something that is essentially metaphorical.

It may be argued that concepts like love may be essentially metaphorical, but most concepts, including scientific ones, are not metaphorical. Let us listen to Lakoff and Johnson (1999, 166) when they point out that

> we conceptualize time using . . . metaphors and . . . such a metaphorical conceptualization of time is constitutive, at least in significant part, of our concept of time. What, after all, would time be without flow, without time going by, without the future approaching? What would time be if there were no *lengths* of time? Would we still be experiencing time if time could not *creep* or *fly* by us? Would time still be time for us if we could not *waste* it or *budget* it? We think not.

This is the strong view as it is stated that a metaphorical conceptualization is constitutive of thought (at least in significant part). The weak view considers that people have well-established, independent concepts, but these are often metaphorically linked to other concepts with similar structure. The problem with the weak view is that it essentially takes into account the metaphorical links from one concept to others when trying to define a given concept. And the question we might ask is, If such independent concepts exist, why not use them directly in place of using a metaphorical detour? Anyway, the important fact recognized by cognitive linguists is that both views consider that metaphors are conceptual. Metaphor plays a major role in people's mental representations of many, particularly abstract, concepts.

The consequence for our purposes is that metaphorical conceptualization plays a crucial part in defining software concepts. The role performed by the metaphor is not only an economic or synthetic one but is at the same time constitutive as the metaphor brings most of its structure to the new concept.

Image Schemata

Cognitive semantics states that the research in many domains indicates that mental processes involved when using language and establishing inferences "make use of image-schemas, which are nonfinitary meaningful symbols" (Lakoff 1988, 120). Johnson (1987, 19) explains that his concept of image schemata is derived from a term first elaborated by Immanuel Kant, meaning nonpropositional structures of imagination, focusing "on embodied patterns of meaningfully organized experience, such as structures of bodily movements and perceptual interactions." This idea of embodied patterns is essential to cognitive semantics as it considers that meaning is based mainly on bodily experiences.

As defined by Johnson (1987, 29), "A schema is a recurrent pattern, shape, and regularity in, or of, these ongoing ordering activities. These patterns emerge as meaningful structures for us chiefly at the level of our bodily movements through space, our manipulation of objects, and our perceptual interactions."

In other words, experience is structured in a significant way prior to, and independently of, any concepts. That's why the term *nonpropositional* or *nonfinitary* is employed in relation to schemata. Image schemata are preconceptual.

The meaning proposed by Johnson for the term schema differs in important respects from what was a standard meaning in the cognitive sciences of the late 1980s. The main difference is that while schemata, frames, or scripts refer to a propositional structure, Johnson's image schemata are essentially imaginary and nonpropositional. In fact, Johnson uses the terms schema, embodied schema, and image schema interchangeably, but we need to be careful about the term image. Image schemata are not concrete images or mental pictures; they are structures that organize our mental representations. The level at which this organization occurs is more general and abstract than that at which we form particular mental images. The important fact is that image does not have to be taken as meaning mental pictures but refers to a more general cognitive process of imaginary.

But even *imagination* is not employed to connote artistic creativity, fantasy, invention, or novelty, as they are only one aspect of imagination, which has other facets that are equally significant. Another crucial aspect of imagination is its capacity to organize mental representations (especially percepts, images, and image schemata) into meaningful, coherent units.

Image schemata operate at a level of mental organization that falls between abstract propositional structures, on the one side, and particular concrete images, on the other (Johnson 1987, 29). They are grounded in physical and social experiences, and these give the basic logic and concepts to the schema. Gibbs (1998) gives the example of the conceptual metaphor that we use to consider anger as containment: “he was boiling over with rage,” “steam was coming out of her ears,” and so on. These ways of thinking about anger arise from our experience of containment and what happens to liquids in containers when they are heated up.

There is a whole collection of image schemata that have been studied and that reflect these (mainly) physical, bodily experiences. They include part-whole (things are made up of components), center-periphery (central to something or on the edge), link, cycle, iteration, contact, adjacency, pushing, pulling, propelling, support, balance, straight-curved, near-far, front-back, and above-below (see Johnson 1987). Here, we will present those that we will use most in our analysis of SE and HCI.

The Source-Path-Goal Schema

A simple and general example of image schema is the from-to or source-path-goal schema (figure 2.1).

The schema consists of three elements: a source point A, an endpoint B, and a vector tracing a path between them. There is also a relation specified as a force vector moving from A to B. This path schema is a recurring structure shown in a number of apparently different events, such as:

- Throwing a baseball to your friend;
- Punching your brother;
- Giving your mother a gift.

Figure 2.1
Source-path-goal schema

There are even some examples that have to be considered metaphorically, such as "the melting of ice into water," with points A and B representing state (for instance, solid or liquid) of a substance (water). In fact, this is a particularly interesting example, as it is different from our three other examples that can be considered as physical movements schema. In the "melting" example, even if there is a physical change, it has to be projected metaphorically from the bodily movements world to a conceptual one. The metaphor used in this case would be THE MELTING IS A PATH (from solid to liquid), so the example is a combination of image schema and a metaphor or a metaphorical projection from an image schema. This melting example is the prototype of many other metaphorical projections, as we will see in the following chapters.

Lakoff (1987) adds to each image schema a basic logic and the metaphors associated with it. In the case of source-path-goal image schema, the basic logic determines that if we go from a source to a destination point along a path, then we will pass through all the intermediate points on the path. Another consequence of such basic logic is that the farther along the path we are, the more time has passed since starting.

The metaphors associated with the source-path-goal image schema are, for example, that purposes are understood in terms of destination. Achieving a purpose is seen as passing along a path from the starting point to an end point. Some of the sentences associated with such a metaphor are that one must go a long way toward achieving one's purposes. Events can also be considered in terms of the source-path-goal schema. Events have an initial state (source), a sequence of intermediate stages (path), and a final state (destination).

The Container Schema

Another important image schema to be considered is the container schema. This is based on the fact that we constantly experience with our bodies both as containers and as things in containers (say, rooms and caves). The structure of the container schema is defined by three elements: interior, boundary, and exterior. This basic structure is arranged so as to yield a basic "logic." Everything is either inside a container or out of it. If container A is in container B and X is in A, then X is in B, and so on. The container schema is illustrated in figure 2.2.

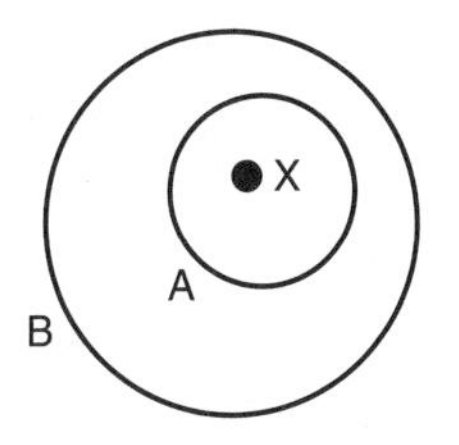

Figure 2.2
Container image schema

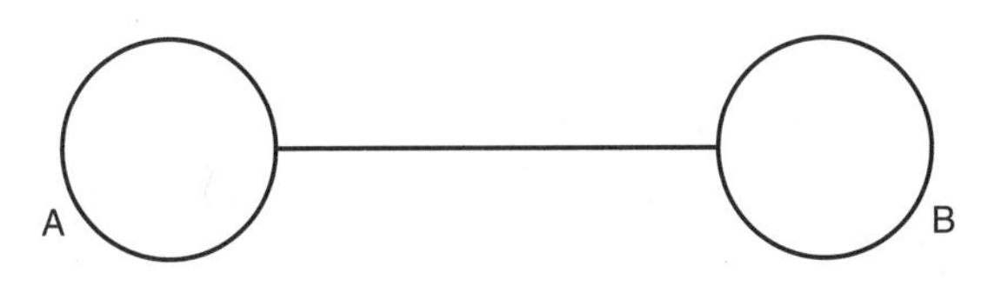

Figure 2.3
Link image schema

A metaphorical projection from this schema is, for example, THE VISUAL FIELD IS A CONTAINER, generating such expressions as "things come in and go out of sight." Memory is also conceived as a container, and "ideas come to our minds."

The Link Schema

A third important schema is link. In relation to our bodily experience, our first link is the umbilical cord. The basic structure corresponds to a couple of entities A and B, and a link connecting them. The basic logic inherent in the schema establishes that if A is linked to B, then A is constrained by, and dependent on, B. There is also symmetry, as if A is linked to B, then B is linked to A (figure 2.3).

Imaginative Processes

In addition to image schemata, we have to consider a set of imaginative processes such as metaphor, schematization, metonymy, and categorization for forming abstract cognitive models from image schemata. In particular, there are metaphors mapping image schemata from their physical, concrete origin into more abstract domains. Typically, such metaphors are not arbitrary but preserve their basic logic and are themselves motivated by structures inherent in everyday bodily experience.

Image schemata also have a main role in producing categories. To recognize several things as structured by the same image schema is to recognize a category.

A surprising result of research in cognitive linguistics is that even though different languages have their own system of spatial relations, all these systems decompose into conceptual primitives, and these primitives are image schemata.

It is interesting to observe that the English word *on,* in the sense used in "the book is on the table," corresponds to a composite of three image schemata:

- The above schema (the book is above the table);
- The contact schema (the book is in contact with the table);
- The support schema (the book is supported by the table).

As George Lakoff and Rafael Núñez (2000, 30) point out:

> The Above schema is orientational, it specifies an orientation in space relative to the gravitational pull one feels in one's body. The Contact schema is one of a number of topological schemas; it indicates the absence of a gap. The Support schema is force-dynamic in nature; it indicates the direction and nature of a force. In general, static image schemas fall into one of these categories: orientational, topological and force-dynamic.

This is a simple example of how we can get the meaning of a given word—in this case, on—in terms of a set of image schemata. It is not establishing a mapping between the word on and some external and objective fact that might assign meaning to words, but associating it with a composite of patterns of embodied experiences (image schemata). Meaning is not in the external world but in the relationship between words as well as the combination of bodily experiences and conceptual projections. Even in German, the word on as in "on the table" *(auf)* is different from the word on as in "on the wall" *(an).*

Image schemata are often used to structure cognitive models. For example, our knowledge about baseball, tennis, or cricket includes a trajectory schema; the ball traveling from one place to another is critical. Our knowledge about projects includes a source-path-goal schema; the project begins, is carried out, and ends. In linguistics, image schemata provide structure and meaning to many phrasal verb constructions, of the type *verb + out* (go out, pull out, take out, and so on).

Consider the following sentence: "Peter went out of the room." This case corresponds to a container and source-path-goal image schemata. Figure 2.4

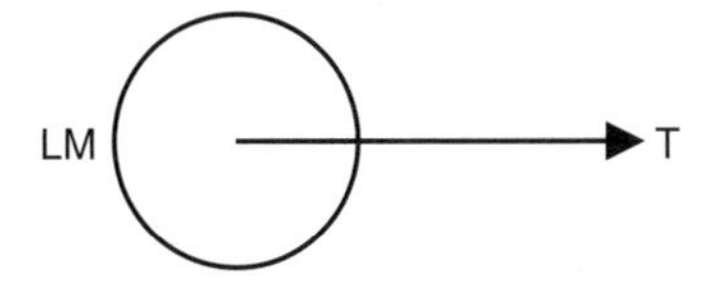

Figure 2.4
Image schema for the particle *out*

shows a composed image schema with a container and a source-path-goal image schema. There is a landmark (LM), which is in relation to a "trajectory" (TR). When applied to the actual sentence (Peter went out of the room), the circle LM represents the room (as container), and Peter moves along the arrow (as TR) out of the room. Lakoff (1987) devotes a long chapter to discussing various instances of the "over" involving various trajectors and landmarks.

Embodied Cognition

In *Where the Action Is,* Dourish (2001) develops his ideas on the foundations of embodied interaction. The embodied perspective considers interaction "with the things themselves." Dourish draws on the phenomenological philosophy of such writers as Heidegger, Edmund Husserl, and Merleau-Ponty as well as recent developments in tangible computing and social computing to develop a theory of embodied interaction. For Dourish, phenomenology is about the tight coupling of action and meaning.

Dourish's main concern is with how we understand the computational world, and with the entities and relationships that we interact with when dealing with digital technologies. A second concern is about how meaning can be shared with others, including both the communication of meaning from designer to user (so that, for example, the system can reveal its purpose and functions) and the communication between users through the system. Another aspect of meaning is intentionality. This has to do with the directedness of meaning and how it relates one thing to another.

Actions take on meaning for people through effective coupling. If objects and relationships are coupled, then the effects of actions can be passed through the system. Dourish uses the familiar example of a hammer (also used by Heidegger) to illustrate coupling. When you use a hammer, it becomes an extension of your arm (it is coupled) and you act through the hammer onto the nail. You are engaged in the activity of hammering. From this theory of embodied interaction—"not just how we act *on* technology, but how we act *through* it" (Dourish 2001, 154)—Dourish develops several high-level design principles.

Philosophy in the Flesh is the evocative title of Lakoff and Johnson's (1999) latest joint work. While acknowledging their debt to previous philosophers, particularly Merleau-Ponty and John Dewey, this book is a major challenge to established philosophical thinking. For us, it gives a foundation for the notion of embodied cognition. The important structures of cognitive models, basic-level categories, and image schemata along with the processes of figurative, experiential understanding and imaginative projections underlie our conceptualization of embodied cognition.

This conceptualization of embodied cognition includes the ideas that thought and action are bound up with each other. There is a felt sense of understanding and thinking that comes from growing up and living in the world as people. We need to design to achieve human scale: to make things understandable to people and enable people to express meaning through the new medium of digital technologies. Others have argued for embodied cognition, or embodied interaction, in HCI. We feel that cognitive semantics provides the philosophical foundation and conceptual tools that will help us understand embodied cognition by developing a literacy of sense making in the digital world.

3 Metaphors and Blends

Metaphors have long been used in the design of digital media, and have come in for both criticism and praise. Metaphors are criticized because they might lead to people developing inappropriate expectations of technologies. They are praised because people can bring their previous experiences to bear on some new interaction. Much of this confusion arises because metaphor is not well understood. In particular, it is not understood in terms of embodied cognition in which the basic categories and processes are derived from our bodily and social experiences.

Our use of the term metaphor is related to the way it is employed in literature, but it lacks the poetics associated with that area. In our analysis, we consider metaphors to be conceptual rather than just poetic. Of course they can be poetic as well, but the focus is on metaphor as a cognitive process. Metaphor is one of the main methods of imaginative projection that enables people to build up rich conceptual structures from the basic categories and image schemata that they start with.

Our treatment of metaphor is somewhat mechanistic rather than artistic. Yet understanding metaphors and how they work together to form blends is an important part of the digital literacy that we are seeking. By providing people with an understanding of how embodied cognition works, we gain insight into how we might design technologies that work better with people.

Metaphor

We begin with the concept of a domain. A domain is a coherent sphere of activity observed and described at some level of abstraction. This might be very abstract, such as talking about the domain of love, traveling, or of games. It might be more concrete, such as talking about the domain of maternal love, sea journeys, or ball games. It might be even more concrete such as the domain of Humphrey Bogart and Lauren Bacall, the Titanic, or Babe Ruth. Abstract domains are more generalized and less detailed than concrete domains. But that does not mean abstract domains provide more insight. The detail of being concrete may offer deeper insight than the looseness of being abstract.

A domain is a coherent sphere of activity observed and described in terms of the elements and relationships that make up the domain. These characteristics may be functional, structural, emotional, psychological, social, and so on. Our understandings of domains are typically quite rich. For example, the domain of Bogart and Bacall includes their on-screen and offscreen romances, their arguments, the ways in which they looked at each other, their relationships with other people, and so on. On the other hand, individuals may know little about domains. Some readers will not have heard of Babe Ruth and so will have few, if any, elements to take from the domain.

Metaphor is a cross-domain mapping. One domain is conceptualized in terms of the elements and relations of another. Metaphor is central to our thought processes. We have already experienced many metaphors. THE HUMAN IS AN INFORMATION PROCESSOR, THE DEVICE IS A STUPID PERSON, HCI IS A CONVERSATION, and so on. As you have probably noticed, we have written the statements in small capitals to indicate when we are using explicit metaphors.

We can refer to this metaphor in terms of names of domains, which gives the following structure: TARGET DOMAIN IS SOURCE DOMAIN. Importantly, the metaphor establishes a true equivalence relationship. Unlike analogy, which asserts that something is like another thing, metaphor says A IS B. This stronger relationship is where the felt sense of embodied cognition comes from. The device really *is* a stupid person.

A commonly used example considers the relationship of love as a journey. This allows us to formulate expressions such as "Our relationship has hit a dead-end street." In this example we have defined two different domains—the source domain (travels) and the target domain (love): LOVE IS A JOURNEY. The mapping between the domains refers to the correspondences between elements and relationships in the two domains. The name of the metaphor is used for this mapping. For the LOVE IS A JOURNEY metaphor we have a set of mappings:

- The lovers correspond to the travelers.
- The love relationship corresponds to the travelers traveling together, possibly in a vehicle.

- The lovers' common goals correspond to their common destinations on the journey.

When dealing with metaphors it is important to realize that while the names of the mappings take a propositional form, the mappings themselves are not propositions. Metaphors are sets of conceptual correspondences. They are cognitive processes that result in a set of propositions. It is critical to differentiate between the metaphor and the resulting propositions. Consider another example of a metaphor and the following statement: "This theory has good foundations."

This sentence uses the metaphor THEORY IS A BUILDING and also shows how, from a concrete domain (construction), we establish a projection to a more abstract domain (that of theories). At the same time, we can see how the meaning of the sentence derives from the original meanings associated with the domains of building and construction. The metaphor reelaborates the original meaning, thereby producing a new one that applies to the domain of theories.

A significant and well-known metaphor is the conduit metaphor, first analyzed by Michael Reddy (1993). He argues that the prevalence of this metaphor has led to some erroneous notions of communication and cognition. The conduit metaphor reflects an objectivist philosophy of cognition; the mind *contains* thoughts, language *transmits* ideas, and human communication achieves the *physical transfer* of thoughts and feelings. The conduit metaphor is embodied in many expressions, such as:

- You have to put each concept into words very carefully.
- Try to pack more thoughts into fewer words.
- Insert those ideas elsewhere in the paragraph.
- Don't force your meanings into the wrong words.

The sentences above show meanings, thoughts, or ideas going into some container (words and paragraphs), but we also find the opposite flow of objects (thoughts) from the container to somewhere else:

- Can you actually extract coherent ideas from the prose?
- Let me know if you find any good ideas in the essay.
- I don't get any feelings of anger out of their words.

Reddy (1993, 171) explains that "in order to investigate the effect of the conduit metaphor on the thought processes of speakers of English, we need some alternate way of conceiving of human communication. We require another story to tell, another model, so that the deeper implications of the conduit metaphor can be drawn out by means of contrast."

Reddy constructs an alternative paradigm (which may be considered as a nonobjectivist one) that he calls subjectivist, and uses it to give another interpretation. From this new point of view, there are no ideas in the words, and therefore none in any books, nor on any tapes or records, or in libraries. He continues arguing that all that is stored in any of these places are "odd little patterns of marks or bumps or magnetised particles (187)." Texts are instructions to create mental spaces ("patterns of thought," in Reddy's terms), which as an active, complex process will re-create or reenact meaning. Indeed, he observes that because the context of reading is different from that in which text has been produced (the expression Reddy employs is a "different world"), the new meaning is likely to be different from the original one.

What Reddy intended to show was how our thoughts, or our ideas about thoughts and ideas, are biased by the underlying conduit metaphor on which all sentences used to speak of communication are based. We can produce a "paradigm shift" by changing the underlying metaphor of a given domain.

The conduit metaphor of language is an example of a more general problem—one that is central to our arguments. Metaphors frame discussions and set the problems that we try to solve. Often, in design situations there is a need to resolve "frame conflicts" (Schön 1993)—different perspectives on (that is, different metaphors for) the problems that are being used by different people in the design situation. By restructuring the frame, we can see the same problem in a new light.

Once a set of correspondences has been established between two domains, there is much opportunity for the creative use of the metaphor. Lakoff (1993) analyzes the LOVE IS A JOURNEY metaphor, giving an example of how we can then use expressions such as "we're stuck" about a relationship. We project from the metaphor—the vehicle is stuck, so we will not reach our destination. We could abandon the vehicle (relationship), reverse, find another way out, and so on. As we will see, choosing suitable, expressive, and relevant metaphors is a key cognitive skill.

Mental Spaces

One way of thinking about metaphors and other expressions is to see them as providing instructions to create mental spaces. The concept of mental space refers to partial cognitive structures that emerge when we think and talk about "allowing a fine-grained partitioning of our discourse and knowledge structures" (Fauconnier 1997, 11). Fauconnier explains that in between language and the real world is a process of mental construction where background experience and cultural history are brought to play in the form of frames or schemata (see chapter 2).

What is intended by this approach is that language expressions do not in themselves have meaning in the classical sense; they do not transmit ideas through a conduit. They are instructions to build certain kinds of mental construction at an intermediate cognitive level. The constructions involved in this process of meaning unfolding are those of interconnected domains. Mental spaces are set up and built on through many sources. There are background frames and domains that may be invoked, cognitive models, behaviors that are observed, and things that people say. Mental spaces may be linked to one another by "connectors." A connector establishes counterpart relations: it establishes a mapping between an element of one space onto one or more elements of another.

This concept of mental spaces and connectors applies to general situations and not only to metaphors. In particular, in the case of a metaphor, there is a source mental space, a target mental space, and connectors that map elements from both spaces. As we talk, mental spaces are established, structured, and linked to other spaces. This results in a network of mental spaces that we move through as an experience unfolds.

Fauconnier (1997) sees the process of understanding meanings in terms of the unfolding of a network or a lattice of mental spaces. A base space sets up the beginning of a discourse and may generate a number of child spaces. At different times the mental space in focus may change. The child space may then establish further mental spaces. The discourse participant moves through the lattice of mental spaces to generate meanings.

A frequently cited example of (at least) two spaces unfolding is that of a movie where a connection is established by a link between actors (real-world individuals) and the characters they portray. Consider this example: "in *Air Force One,* Harrison Ford flies in the presidential Boeing."

The name of the president's counterpart (the actor Harrison Ford) is used to identify a situation of the character. Starting from the base space—that is, the speaker's space—a child space is produced by "in *Air Force One*"—the space of the movie. Initially, this space has no structure as we do not know anything about it (except that Air Force One is the presidential aircraft, inherited from the base space). The second part of the sentence, "Harrison Ford flies . . . ," adds a minimal structure to the base space (the space of the real world, in which the actor Harrison Ford exists), whereby Harrison Ford just flies. This structure can be expressed as "Harrison Ford flies." But there is a connector that links Harrison Ford to the character "the president" of the movie, so the base space gives its structure to the child space, resulting in the clearer structure "the president flies . . . ," which is incorporated then into the child space (figure 3.1).

In the example, the child space, the movie, is in focus, but the viewpoint is from the real-world space because our concern is the film, yet we are actually speaking from the real-world point of view. We name the actor (Harrison Ford) and not the character (the president), and the condition of flying is linked to the character, the president. From an initial structure in which there is only the presidential aircraft, we enrich the mental space of the movie by connecting Harrison Ford to the president and adding to the structure the fact that the president flies.

This is a simple case in which there is no metaphor, but the sentence unfolds in a two-space mental construction. At the same time, it shows us in a practical way the "access" principle: if elements a and b are linked, we can identify element b by referring to element a. In the film example, the application of the access principle clearly shows that the character is described by pointing to its counterpart, the actor. This case results in a different meaning than if the situation had been described directly using the character. The different meaning is the result of the creation of two mental spaces in place of one. In a classical linguistics interpretation it would be only one meaning where the real referent is the same in both cases: the movie.

Sometimes, a mental space is structured by an ICM. The ICM could be a frame—for example, the commerce frame of buying and selling. In such a

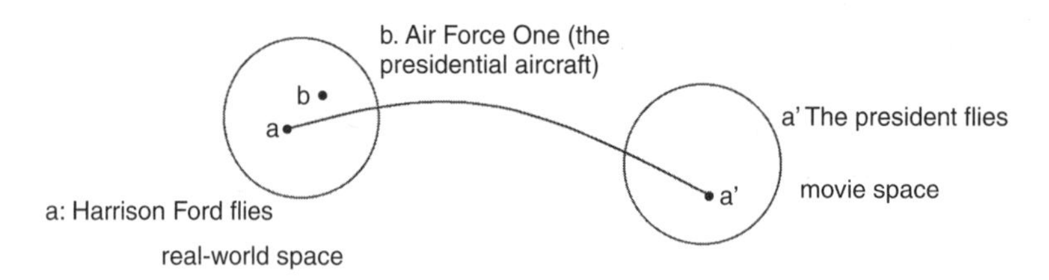

Figure 3.1
Connections between mental spaces

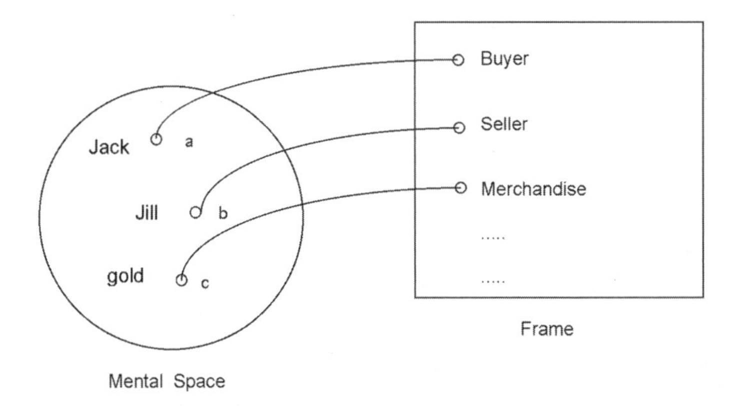

Figure 3.2
Mental space structured by a frame

frame, there is a buyer, a seller, merchandise, currency, and price as well as a rich set of inferences pertaining to ownership, commitments, exchange, and so on. If a sentence like "Jack buys gold from Jill" occurs in the discourse, and if Jack, Jill, and gold identifies elements a, b, and c in a mental space, then those elements will be mapped onto the appropriate slots in the buying and selling frame, as illustrated in figure 3.2.

It is important to realize that the connections between mental spaces are not given: they are creative acts or imaginative projections. We perceive a certain topology of the elements in a mental space—that is, the elements and relations that pertain both within a space and across two or more spaces. For example, the topology of a commercial transaction involves a particular type of relation between a buyer and a seller. It also includes another element: the merchandise. Different types of commercial transactions will invoke different frames: an auction is different from a purchase at a shop.

Blends

The last of the main theoretical constructs is the blend, or "conceptual integration." If the metaphor is a cross-domain mapping, taking elements from one domain and applying them to another, then conceptual integration or blending is an operation that is applied to two input spaces, which results in a new, blended space. The blend receives a partial structure from both input spaces but has an emergent structure of its own. Blending works as follows.

First, there is a cross-space mapping that connects elements and relations between two input spaces (figure 3.3). Second, there is a generic space that maps onto each of the inputs. This generic space reflects some more abstract structure and organization shared by the inputs, and defines the core cross-space mapping between them (figure 3.4). Third, there is another partial projection into a fourth space, the blend (figure 3.5). Importantly, the blend will have a new emergent structure not provided by the inputs. As we explore blends in the forthcoming chapters, we will see a variety of methods and principles at work in the process of blending.

The main principles of blending are:

- **Composition** The projections from the input spaces make new relationships available that did not exist in the original inputs.
- **Completion** Our background knowledge in the form of cognitive and cultural models allow the composite structure projected onto the blend to be

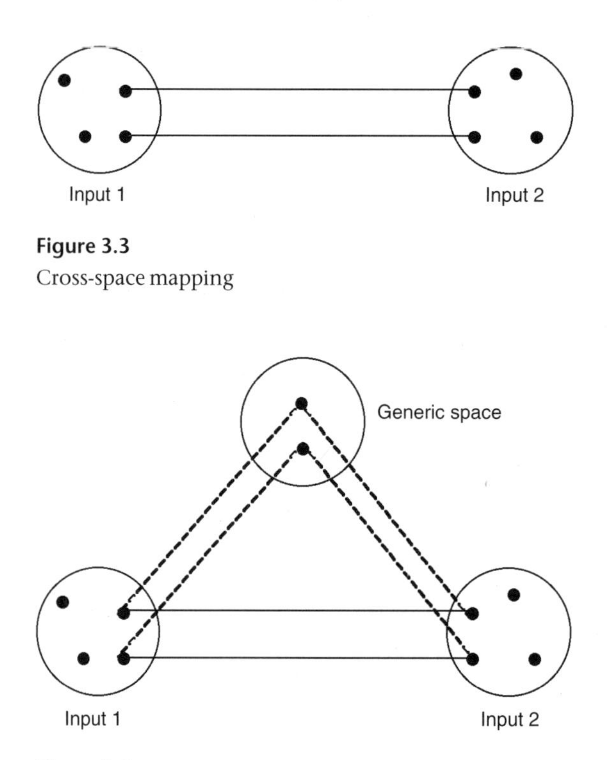

Figure 3.3
Cross-space mapping

Figure 3.4
Generic space

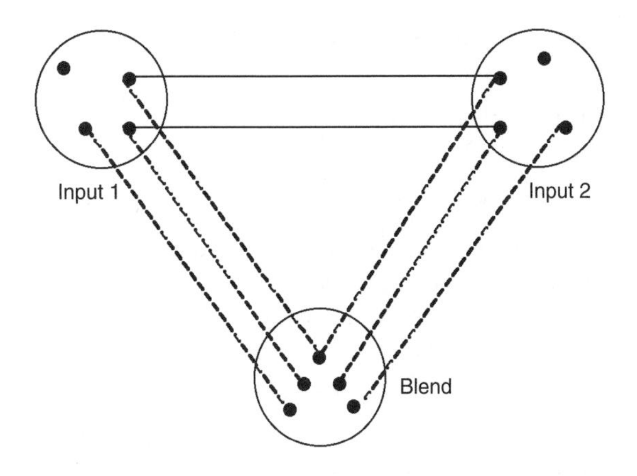

Figure 3.5
Blend (or blended space)

viewed as part of a larger self-contained structure in the blend. The pattern in the blend triggered by the inherited structures is "completed" in the larger, emergent structure.

- **Elaboration** The structure in the blend can then be elaborated. Fauconnier and Turner (2002) call this "running the blend," an elaboration or refinement of the blend. The blend has its own emergent logic, and this can be elaborated to produce new ideas and insights.

When speaking of metaphors as mappings, we consider that there are two input mental spaces and project from one to the other. With blends, we project structure onto a new space and get an emergent structure. Often in everyday expressions we find a blend already exists, and we have to work backward to unpack the blend and hence understand the statement. Consider the following sentence: "This theory has been built on firm evidence."

Here, the metaphor is produced by putting together a noun, *theory,* and a verb, *build,* that originally were not employed this way. One input space is concerned with theories, ideas, and evidence for the validity of theories. Another space is that of material constructions and their own features of robustness, firmness, and so on. Bringing them together as a blend produces a conceptual structure that is qualitatively different. It allows new reasoning such as "undermining" the theory, "knocking down" the evidence, and so on. Arguably, all metaphors are blends because the very power of a metaphor comes from the juxtaposition of ideas from different domains. This is where the “cognitive work” gets done. The converse is not true, however, and most blends are not derived from a metaphor.

A nice story, quoted by Turner (1996) as well as Fauconnier (1997, 151) and originally attributed to Arthur Koestler, shows that the developed structure in a blended space can help us be creative and solve problems and riddles.

A Buddhist monk begins at dawn to walk up a mountain. He stops and starts and varies his pace as he pleases, and reaches the mountaintop at sunset. There he meditates overnight. At dawn, he begins to walk back down, again moving as he pleases. He reaches the foot of the mountain at sunset. Prove that there is a place on the path that he occupies at the same hour of the day on the two separate journeys.

The solution to the problem is to imagine the Buddhist monk walking up as his double walks down on the same day. If there were two monks, they would certainly meet, and clearly this would mean that they were at the same spot at the same time. The input spaces are the outward and return journeys; one space has the monk ascending and the other has the monk descending. The generic space is the space of a journey, a path, and a traveler. We imagine the Buddhist monk walking up and his double walking down in the blended space. We merge the two paths from the input spaces, but we maintain two monks. We do not project things such as which particular day events happened on, or what the weather was like, and so forth. In the blend, we find the solution to the problem because of the emergent structure created from the input spaces and our selective projections into the blend.

There is also an interesting issue in the back projection to both input spaces, so the solution simultaneously provides a new structure for both input spaces, transforming them as a result of the cognitive process of solving a problem. (Note the point above about the creative framing of a problem.) “Blending is a dynamic activity. It connects input spaces; it projects partial structure from input spaces to the blend, creating an imaginative blended space that, however odd or even impossible, is nonetheless connected to its inputs and can illuminate those inputs” (Turner 1996, 83).

Another important characteristic of blended spaces is that they enable inferential work to be performed. A blend produces knowledge. The story of the monk has been solved in a blended space in which some inferences were performed to show how both monks meet each other at a certain time of the day.

In blending, there are a number of key processes at work. These processes may be run in sequence or in parallel, and people work creatively with the elements, their relations, their organizing frames, and entrenched, integrated cognitive models. They will change as features of experience change in a highly dynamic fashion. Mental spaces are established, mappings are created, and blends are produced that themselves may form the generic of input spaces to other blends. In this way, cognition is seen as a dynamic conceptual integration network.

When projecting from the inputs, not all elements and relations are selected but only some of them; there is selective projection. For example, in the Buddhist monk case, there is an important element that is not projected: real time. It is clear that if we need to have both monks traveling along the path simultaneously, the original dates and times when the monks were going and returning have to be eliminated from the projection.

In the blend, there is a composition of elements from the input spaces providing relations that do not exist in the original inputs. Continuing with the Buddhist monk example, the composition produces two travelers making two journeys at the same time on the same path, even though each input has only one traveler making one journey.

The principle of completion concerns our ability to fill in the missing pieces in a blend and infer relationships that are not explicitly stated. The process of blending requires us to bring our wealth of background knowledge to bear to make sense of the blend. In the Buddhist monk story, the composition of the two monks (there is really only one, remember) on the path is completed automatically. We are so familiar with a scenario of two people journeying toward each other that we use this to complete the blend.

Regarding the emergent structure of blends, we run them imaginatively according to the principles that have been established. In the case of the Buddhist monk, we run the blend to get something impossible in the real world: the encounter of the monk with himself, providing the solution to the riddle. The definition of emergence implies that such structure is not projected directly from any input. It arises through a combination of the composition of elements projected from the input spaces, through completion based on recruiting familiar frames and scenarios, and through elaboration. As an interesting aside, Fauconnier and Turner use the term running the blend to describe how we mentally work our way through the logic of the blend. Thus, they have adopted a metaphor from computing (running a computer program) to explain a cognitive process.

Some people have criticized the term blend because it suggests everything in the blend has been mashed up together: THE BLEND IS A SMOOTHIE. Yet this would be a misreading of Fauconnier and Turner's intent, we think. Blends work because they compress and preserve the most significant (or "vital") relations from the input spaces. As we will see later (in chapter 6), there are guiding principles for blends that emphasize how it should be possible to unpack a blend and see the web of relations that it originates from. There are many of these vital relations between elements of mental spaces that Fauconnier and Turner identify, including change, identity, time, space, cause-effect, part-whole, analogy, disanalogy, property, similarity, category, intentionality, and uniqueness. For instance, in the Buddhist monk story, time is clearly an important relation, as is identity and space (or place). In the example of Harrison Ford and *Air Force One,* we see role as particularly critical: Harrison Ford has the role of the president. It is the existence of the vital relations that gives the blend its force.

Metaphor or Blend?

So far, we have been considering the conceptual metaphor theory (MT), based on Lakoff and Johnson (1980), and blending or conceptual integration as two separate frameworks, or at least not showing any relationship between them. The case is that both approaches share important features. First, metaphor is a conceptual phenomenon, not simply a linguistic one. Second, both frameworks involve the idea of projection of structure between domains. Third, they both propose constraints on this projection.

But there are also important differences between the approaches: MT establishes relationships between pairs of domains, while blending considers a network of spaces—usually four. MT considers the metaphor as a directional phenomenon—from the source domain to the target domain—while blending considers projection going from any mental space to any other. Whereas MT typically analyzes entrenched conceptual relationships (metaphors of everyday language), research in conceptual integration is focused on new conceptualizations (see figure 3.6).

Another significant difference between MT and blending is that in the MT framework, the analysis is focused on a stable relationship between two conceptual domains. In blending, on the other hand, the basic unit of cognitive organization is the mental space.

Consider the well-known metaphor, THE SURGEON IS A BUTCHER. The intended meaning is that the surgeon is incompetent. We may try to explain

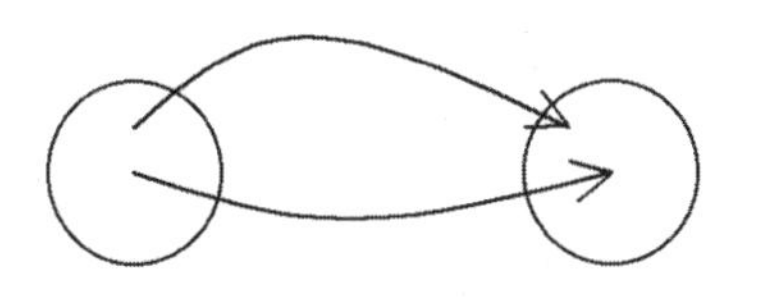

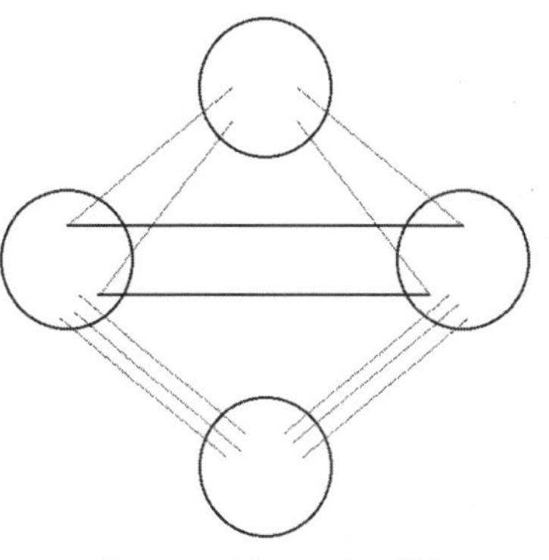

Figure 3.6
Metaphor and blend

the metaphor by projecting some structure from the source domain of butchery to the target domain of surgery. But this analysis based on the cross-domain relationships cannot itself explain a key element of the meaning: the incompetence of the surgeon. As the source domain of butchery includes expert, ordinary, and incompetent butchers, so the target domain of surgery must imply a varied range of competences. The metaphor, by itself, cannot project something not included in the source domain: the incompetence.

This is a typical example where the MT is unable to explain something that blending may easily show as an emergent structure produced by the blend. The incompetence is produced in a third space—the blending space where we project structure from both input spaces (butchery and surgery)—but the new structure is produced as a consequence of blending both spaces. This paradoxical result is explained by pointing to the contrast between butchers and surgeons: in particular, the incongruity of the butcher's means with the surgeon's ends, which leads to the central inference that the surgeon is incompetent.

As conceptual metaphors are well-established metaphoric projections between concepts, they are good candidates to be used in the blending process. As we see in figure 3.7, a metaphor described by its source and target domains will replace both input spaces in the blending process represented on the right hand as $Input_1$ and $Input_2$, respectively.

This is a typical case, as the metaphor offers a ready-made material of mappings between both concepts. It should be noted that it is not always a

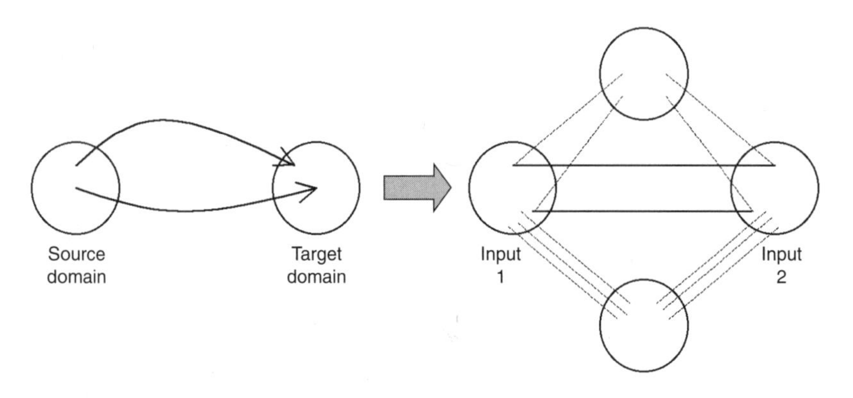

Figure 3.7
A conceptual metaphor brings its concepts to blending

metaphor that is used in the blend (as we have already seen in the example of the Buddhist monk), but what is interesting for our purpose is finding a fair metaphor that might be used as input to a blending process. Many constructs in HCI and SE are derived from well-selected figurative language, or metaphorical projections, that offer the raw material for understanding new ideas.

The Desktop Metaphor

The Macintosh computer user interface and later Microsoft's Windows were designed around something known as the "desktop" metaphor. Originating with the Xerox Star workstation, the designers sought to evoke explicitly people's knowledge of office work to help them understand the operation of the computer. The Xerox Star was the first widely available computer with a bitmapped display that allowed the designers to use complicated graphic images on the display. There were images for documents, folders, files, a printer, and other commonly used things that one might find in an office. Through the Macintosh and Windows, these have evolved into the images that people see on their screens today.

The desktop metaphor is built on the basis of two conceptual inputs: one is that of ordinary work in an office with folders, documents, a desk, a trash can (or wastepaper basket), and so on. The other is the traditional field of computer commands, executed by the computer in the form of an expression in a specialized language (see figure 3.8). This style of human-computer interface soon became known as the desktop metaphor, and computer interfaces

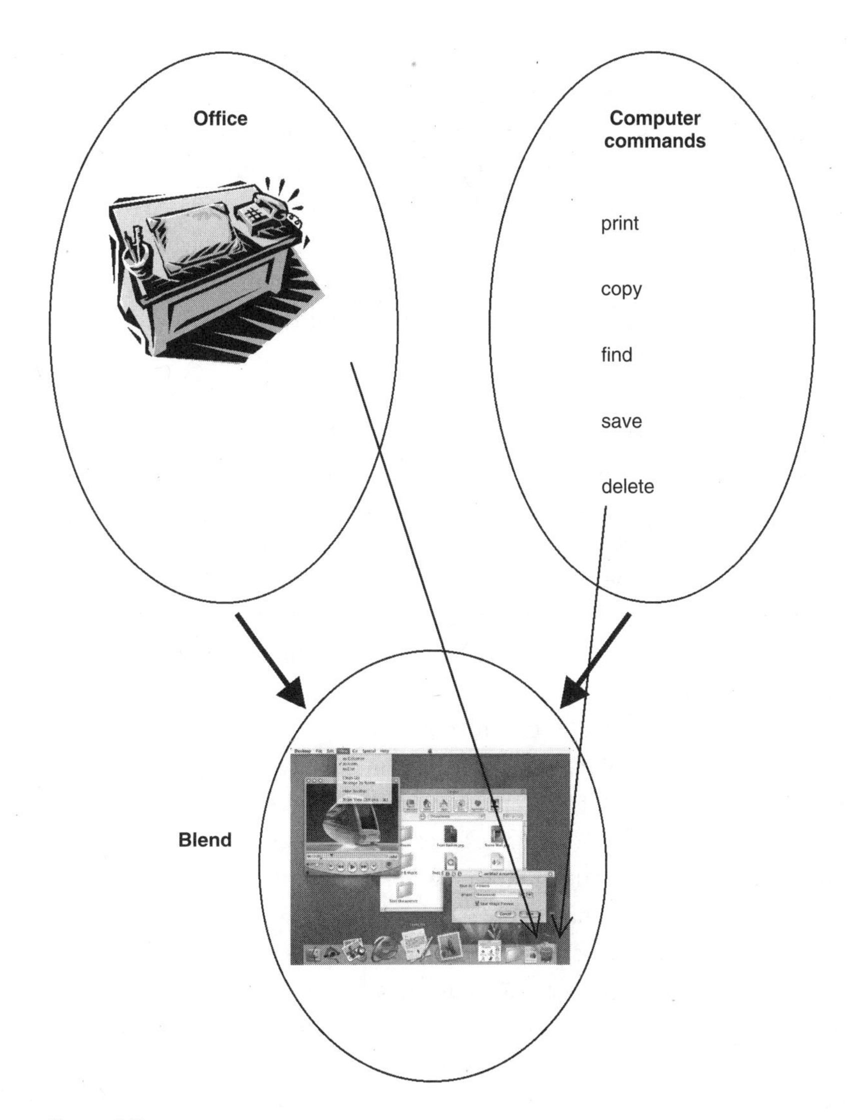

Figure 3.8
The desktop blend

characterized by windows, icons, menus, pointing devices, dragging things, storing things in folders, opening files, and so on were said to be based on the desktop metaphor. Over the next twenty years, more and more interfaces adopted this style, and now it is spreading to other devices such as mobile phones. It is also used on many Web sites. The constraints imposed by different hardware and software affect to what degree other interfaces follow the desktop metaphor. For example, you cannot at present drag icons across the screen of a phone or digital camera, and Web sites offer reduced levels of functionality over the other computer applications.

When we speak of the desktop metaphor now we are really referring to a large blend. We know a computer window is different from a real window and a menu on the computer is different from a menu in a restaurant. The desktop metaphor is the result of a long process of elaboration (in this case, many years) of computer-based signs (icons, windows, menus, and so on). When we say the desktop metaphor, we are employing a metonymy whereby the whole process of blending and producing new spaces that are used in new blends, and so on, is referred to by the original metaphor used as input to the blending process.

It is usually considered to be a metaphor because most of the traditional functionalities of ordinary work have been maintained as expressions in interface tasks. We open folders (or documents), we close them, we throw folders or documents into the trash, we empty the trash, and so on. The tasks we do when dealing with the interface evoke our ordinary office job without thinking of the equivalent computer commands.

So, both input spaces participate in a metaphor, THE OPERATING SYSTEM IS AN OFFICE DESKTOP before they are included in a blend relationship. This is the reason why the desktop interface is called a metaphor. But when observed in detail, it is evident that we are dealing with a blend rather than a metaphor—the blend being based on the metaphor.

One design decision on the Macintosh resulted in the rather odd use of the trash can for ejecting floppy disks when they were no longer needed. People would drag the icon of a floppy disk to the trash can and this would eject the disk from the disk drive. This strange design decision has been used as an argument against metaphors in the creation of interfaces for many years. This trouble was found only in the Mac interface and indeed has now been redesigned in the operating system Mac OS X. The design decision to use the trash can in this way had nothing to do with the metaphor employed to structure the whole interface. It was adopted for expedient reasons to do with the constraints on the memory of the computers at the time.

The desktop interface is actually a blend, and as usually occurs with blends, it has a new emergent structure. In the Mac and Windows interfaces, we can mimic the grasping of an object by dragging an icon and dropping it somewhere else—something without an equivalent in the real world. In the same way, we can close a document by clicking on an associated button or open folders by double clicking on them. These are new functions that exist neither in the real world nor the universe of classical computer commands. They are emergent functions in the blend space, a new conceptual domain that has its own characteristics to be considered when the blend is used to construct new metaphors and blends.

Another criticism of using metaphors at the interface is that people will develop an incorrect understanding of what is happening. For example, Tom Ericksson (1990) argues that people really believe that they are dragging a document from one folder to another when in fact all that is happening is that a "pointer" in the operating system changes to point at a new location. When considering metaphor, then, we need to think about levels of abstraction.

For example, when we employ the sentence "Perform until" in a language such as COBOL, we are using a construct that exists at the COBOL layer, but not necessarily at the layer of the assembler or machine code. The word until has a meaning that does not exist necessarily at lower levels. At lower levels, there are groups of instructions executing and some asking for a termination condition to be satisfied. It is the higher level that adds meaning corresponding to the included intentionality: we repeat the group of instructions *until the condition is satisfied.* That is why the perform until construct seems to us as completely literal, reflecting exactly what the construct does. In fact, we are projecting our intentions in the expression without our being conscious of such projection. We think of *until* as something the computer is really proposing to do and not as a blind process.

In the case of the Mac or Windows interface, there is a metaphor (or blend) on which the computing mechanism is based: the desktop metaphor. This metaphor inspired the mechanism we usually use in order to move one document from one folder to another. As this mechanism, what we might call a computer-based sign, is inspired from some actions from the real world, it is logical that we use the same expressions as those employed in our everyday workplace. But we deal with icons (graphic representations of some other objects) that are blend concepts and not metaphors anymore: they are derived from the real world and the computer domain, giving rise to a new, synthetic concept.

Metaphors and Figurative Language

Metaphor per se is not the source of any pathological symptom. We use many devices without knowing exactly what happens inside the "black box." Metaphors have to be judged according to their convenience and fitness for the current task, even if the user's mental model does not agree with the designer's mental model. The fact that users think they are moving a document from one folder to another is not only irrelevant, it could even be beneficial for their performance in using the graphic interface.

The other arguments against metaphor are that the target domain of a metaphor may have features not in the source domain, the source domain has features not in the target, or some features exist in both domains yet work very differently. But as we have seen, this is exactly the process of blending, and a well-designed and well-chosen metaphor will enable people to understand the blend appropriately. As we will see later (in chapter 6), there are a number of principles that designers can refer to in order to help them select the appropriate metaphors.

There is a general trend in the computer science community to refuse any type of nonformal reasoning. People like Edsgar Dijkstra (1972) have contended that diagrams and other notations lead to sloppy thinking. We argue, on the other hand, that much of the work done by the computer community is not only nonformal and intuitive but commonly uses figurative language. Moreover, figurative language is a way of reasoning that is as valid as one that could be considered as using literal language, and many new concepts arise based on a metaphor or blend.

In the last few years, there have been a collection of works about the relationship between literal and figurative language. One of the most exciting disclosures is that between both types of languages, there is a continuum, a gradient; "distinctions between the types are in fact graded, and judgments of literal versus figurative are accordingly graded" (Turner 1998, 69).

In the traditional view of literal meaning it is usually assumed that the only theory of meaning that could exist is a theory of literal meaning and nothing else (Gibbs 1994). One consequence of this is that there must be literal concepts and literal meaning in order for people to communicate successfully. As Raymond Gibbs (1994, 26) points out, "The idealized, mythical view of literal meaning as being well specified and easily identifiable in thought and language is incorrect. It is, in fact, quite difficult to specify the literal definitions and concepts and the words that refer to these concepts."

In fact, there are many arguments that even in scientific contexts we speak metaphorically, making use of the large number of metaphors we use in everyday language without our noticing it (Lakoff and Johnson 1980). As we will see, the language of software and HCI are littered with examples of figurative language based on metaphors. This provides a number of key benefits. Gibbs (1994) offers three key features of the metaphor. Metaphors are expressive, compact, and vivid.

One of the reasons for using such concepts like "layered architecture" or "broker" in SE is that metaphors provide a way of expressing ideas that would be extremely difficult to convey using literal language. The inexpressibility hypothesis asserts that literal language usually lacks the expressiveness to deal with the complexity of our thoughts. The compactness hypothesis presents the idea that language can only partition the continuity of our conscious experience into discrete units comprising words and phrases that have a relatively narrow referential range. In this case (and using another metaphor), it is a way of freeing language from an oppressive situation. Literal language generally does not enable people to convey a great deal of information succinctly in the same way that metaphor does.

Another interesting issue of metaphor is its capacity to capture the vividness of our phenomenological experience. This vividness hypothesis describes the capability of metaphors to convey complex configurations of information rather than discrete units, thus enabling the communication of more vivid images of our subjective experience. This vividness hypothesis brings us back to the idea of a felt sense of cognition. Embodied cognition is felt when experienced, not just thought.

One classic example of this, again from the design of the Apple Macintosh, was the "bomb" icon. A message, just allowing the user to restart the computer, would be displayed in a dialogue box along with an icon of a bomb taken, presumably, from the computer programmer's expression that a program had "bombed out." A friend of one of the authors (Imaz) phoned saying she was very worried since she had just had a bomb message displayed on her

Mac screen. It was explained to her that in such a case she had to restart the computer and that usually there were no further problems. As they continued talking, it was obvious that she was increasingly worried and was thinking that the bomb might explode. The projection of the frame of the bomb input space, as something more and more dangerous as time goes by, provoked this.

A similar reaction is described by Rohrer, regarding the use of the trash can for ejecting diskettes. People felt nervous that they would lose their work, even though they "knew" it was OK. Even in the latest operating system on the Mac, removing an item from the Dock is followed by an animated puff of smoke and a whoosh sound. MY WORK HAS GONE UP IN A PUFF OF SMOKE.

These reactions to metaphorical interface features once again point to the felt sense of cognition. We do not just have mental ideas, we react to situations in a physical and social way. Metaphors are grounded in human experience from the most basic physical experiences of in and out, up and down, and along and through. They are grounded in categories derived from physical and cultural experiences. From these beginnings, complex networks of concepts are blended to arrive at the forms of communication and action of everyday life.

4 Blends in Human-Computer Interaction and Software Engineering

A blend implies four spaces: two input spaces, a generic space, and the blend space. Conceptual integration is a basic cognitive operation that works on two input mental spaces to yield a third space, the blend. So we can distinguish two different elements: a process or cognitive operation, and the product of such a process, the blend. Another concept used in relation to conceptual integration is that of integration network. This concept is a reference to the set of spaces involved in the conceptual integration, and how projections from the spaces are manifest.

In this chapter, we explore a number of examples of metaphors and blends from HCI and SE, introducing any new features of the blending process as and when necessary. There are countless examples that we could have chosen to illustrate the use of figurative language in HCI and SE. The ones we have selected have been chosen to illustrate the ideas of digital literacy, or software criticism. We want to develop a set of examples that demonstrate how the conceptual tools we have introduced—cognitive models, basic-level categories, image schemata, mental spaces, metaphors, and blends—work together to provide insight into software and interaction design.

Types of Integration Networks

In their analysis of blending, Fauconnier and Turner (2002) identify a number of different types of integration networks. A first type is the frame network, in which the input, generic, and blend spaces share a topology provided by an organizing frame. One of their examples involves two attempts at sailing across the Atlantic performed at different times (the turn of the nineteenth century and late in the twentieth). The aim of this analysis is to see which of the sailing vessels performs better than the other. In the analysis, two input spaces of regattas are created along with a blend space and a generic space. All four spaces have the organizing frame "boat making an ocean voyage," and the blend has an extension of that frame: two boats making ocean voyages and racing as they make them. This type of structure in which all spaces share the same topology of a generic space is called a shared topology network.

Another key feature of integration networks identifies single and double-scope networks. In a single-scope network, there are two input spaces with different organizing frames, only one of which is projected to structure the blend, In figure 4.1, the frame for input space 1 is a square and the frame for input space 2 is a hexagram. The square frame from input space 1 is projected into the blend space. In a double-scope network, the organizing frame for the blend will take parts of the structure from the organizing frames of both the input spaces (figure 4.2).

Turner (1996) gives an example of a single-scope network, "John is the father of James." The input spaces are the specific people involved in the relationships and the abstract space of parenting. Turner comments that these types of blends appear very literal.

In SE, there are many examples of single-scope blends. If we say, for instance, "John Smith is the name of entity Employee," there are also two input spaces. One is an abstract frame, the concept of entity (with an entity name, attributes, and relationships with other entities). The other space is the appli-

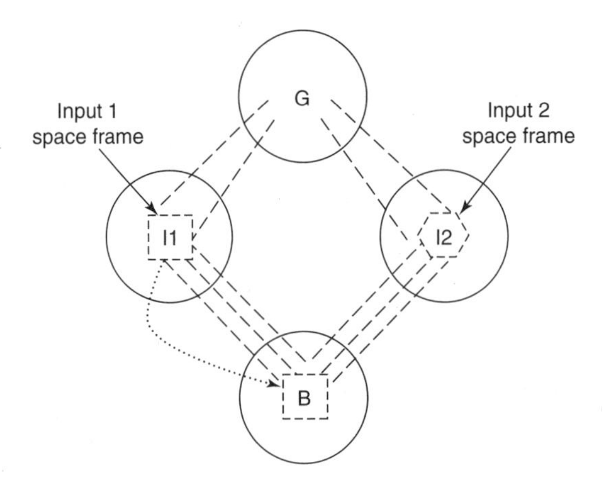

Figure 4.1
Single-scope network: The blend has the same frame as I_1

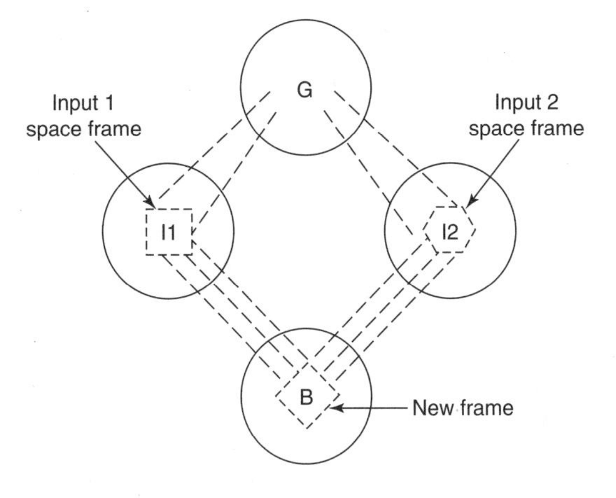

Figure 4.2

Double-scope network: The blend has its own, new frame

cation domain of employees. The domain will have been modeled to arrive at the Employee entity construct, drawing on all the various cognitive processes that we have discussed. The abstract frame of the entity concept is applied to the conceptual domain on which the specific situation is built (figure 4.3).

Once a given blend has been established—for example the Employee entity—it can then be applied to more specific situations dealing with instances of elements belonging to the domain. As the domain is increasingly used, the language constructions used to refer to such situations become increasingly literal, or entrenched. With a word processor, a person literally cuts and pastes now, even though these terms clearly had a figurative history.

In the case when both input spaces come from widely different conceptual domains, the resulting blend space may be a single- or double-scope network. When input spaces are heterogeneous, their shared structure as represented in the generic space is necessarily highly abstract. Since it is abstract, and the input spaces are heterogeneous, the blend is commonly thought to be figurative.

There is no clear-cut distinction between literal and figurative language. Rather, it is a question of grades and degrees of entrenchment. Even double-scope blends like the example of the desktop metaphor that initially are highly figurative, become with time more and more literal. And this results in people believing things that are erroneous. As mentioned earlier, for example, people believe that when dragging a file from one folder to another they are really moving it. As new concepts emerge, they seem figurative at

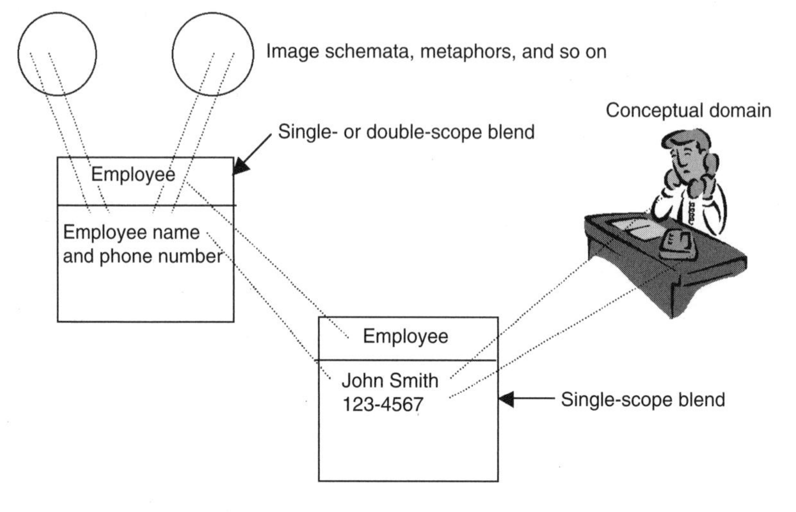

Figure 4.3
Example of single-scope blend: Entity construct

first. After a while, they become more and more literal and entrenched. By entrenched we mean the extent to which the rest of the conceptual system depends on the concept.

The folk theory of categorization leads us to think of entities in the world as composed of features like red, small, or hot. This same folk theory is continuously present in our SE methods such as entity-relationship diagrams or class diagrams of object-oriented technology. In such models, the basic class hierarchy is defined by the features possessed by all the members of the category (or class). These features are inherited as we move down in the hierarchy, so the features of the higher-level categories from which a given category derives will receive all accumulated features in a top-down way. What we argue here is that the objects or entities are not objectively “there” to be discovered; they are created by the systems analyst as a blend of their understanding of the domain and the entity (or object) construct.

Another aspect of categories is that we tend to think of them as fixed and invariable, but they are not. We categorize to operate efficiently in the world. There is no genetic payoff in perceiving differences except where it increases fitness. So we perceive things as being equal at a given level of conceptualization. The question is, How do we decide more or less automatically to equate certain concepts?

Turner answers that how we approach this decision depends on where the two concepts are located within our category structures. There are many degrees of entrenchment between conceptual connections. Some of them are so deeply entrenched in our conceptual systems that we cannot imagine what it would be like to operate without them. Other connections are less deeply entrenched. These levels differ for different people.

Figurative Language in SE

Let us imagine that we are in front of the first electric computer (ENIAC perhaps), which produces a group of electric pulses resulting in a change of state or some other effect. This initial event is crucial, as there are no new meanings yet, only new phenomena that are to be named using the words available at the moment. This will be called an instruction. In order to produce the first blends, we have to select the input spaces from which to project the main structure.

It is likely the meaning from which the word instruction has been selected is that of a detailed direction or procedure. That means a reference to a judicial frame, in which we usually attend to detailed directions on procedures. An alternative meaning points to an authoritative direction to be obeyed—that is, an order. So, from the beginning of the computing era there has been a special agency in charge of the computer. Whether the authoritative direction to be obeyed was given to the computer or the computer gives this instruction to itself, the resulting projection is the same. An alternative name for instruction is command. Analyzing the meanings of this word confirms the idea of an intentional feature transferred to the machine.

In the case of the term "sentence," it is evident that it has been produced using an input domain from linguistics—even if the group of instruction, procedure, sentence, and execution could be wholly referred to the judicial domain. At a given moment in the development of computer science the concept of a symbolic language appears. Logically the unit of any language is the sentence. Trying to trace some concepts to their original meanings might be a highly arduous task, as in the present case where sentence has simultaneously a judicial and linguistic context, and it would be interesting to know whether both meanings have a common root. But such discussions can be left to the linguists. For our purposes, what is interesting is the fact that in our everyday computer language, sentence has an external origin from a linguistic or judicial domain.

One of the meanings of "procedure" points to a series of steps taken to accomplish an end. This sense could be considered as a generic space while a second meaning, that of the methods of conducting the affairs of an organization, is a more specific frame from which the generic space may be projected. In this case, we observe that the generic space—steps taken to accomplish an end—is a concrete form of the source-path-goal image schema, in which some intermediate subgoals have to be reached. So the concept of procedure is guided mainly by pressure from the source-path-goal image schema.

Another common computer term is "abortion." This computing concept receives its sense from terminating an operation or procedure before its completion. But this is also in its origin a figurative meaning derived from a generic space in which the fact of giving birth before the embryo is capable of surviving or ceasing growth before full development contributes to its generic structure. As usual, a series of metaphorical projections deploy a collection of meanings to the same word. Even the dictionary includes the following meaning for abortion: a procedure to terminate the execution of a program when an unrecoverable error or malfunction occurs. The term becomes entrenched in the language and polysemy eventually appears.

It is important to say here that we are considering the role of metaphor in producing new, figurative, meaning in general, independently of the fact that in some examples the name is applied to already-created technological objects like sentences or procedures. We also see how metaphor is chosen for designing new technological objects such as user interfaces. In the first case, metaphors have an explanatory role, while in the second instance they are fundamentally a design tool to help cognition.

In the world of computing the list of metaphors is uncountable. The following is only a sampling organized by their background domain:

- **Construction** Architecture, foundation, platform, frame, framework, hook, and front end;
- **Manufacturing** Pipeline, tool, toolkit, toolbox, artifact, interface, process, and package;
- **Business/organization** Client, agent, broker, procedure, server, export, import, and contract;
- **Office** Drawers, files, folders, paper, paper clips, stick-on notes, and attachments;

- **Social activity** Queue, pool, session, checkpoint, police, control, grant, authorize, utility, garbage collection, host, and protocol;
- **Human values** Trust;
- **Biology** Taxonomy, inheritance, tree, branches, leaf, web, virus, infection, and worm;
- **Deck of cards** Card and piles;
- **Documents** Books, chapters, bookmarks, figures, newspapers, sections, magazines, articles, newsletters, forms, and bind;
- **Geography/urbanism** Domain, landmark, pathway, place, site, location, region, and realm;
- **History** Trojan horse;
- **Traveling/Sports** Navigation and surfing.

In OO programming, most pattern names are also highly figurative: Factory, Bridge, Decorator, Facade, Proxy, Chain of Responsibility, Interpreter, Mediator, Observer, Strategy, and so on. As Erich Gamma and colleagues (1995) point out, finding good names has been one of the hardest parts of developing the catalog of patterns. In a pattern, the description of the problem, solution, consequences, results, and trade-offs of applying the pattern constitute the meaning of the named pattern. To a large extent, the meaning is determined in a constrained way from the external mental spaces that are unfolded by the name.

When Gerald Johnson (1994, 100) tries to explain—in his article about the difficulties of the computer discourse—the metaphoric word *application* (to apply: to use something for a given purpose) as "a set of instructions stored in memory," he is using three words with metaphorical origin: instruction, store, and memory. But the really interesting observation that he makes is about some examples of mixing metaphors for a given concept. He points out that the use of a metaphor makes abstract things concrete or solid; so concepts in a domain become objects in a software system.

Inconsistency is a key issue when treating the problem of using metaphor in computing science. The question is whether this inconsistency is a consequence of informal conversation or discourse, or whether such an issue is illustrating some deeper problem.

The first example cited by Johnson (1994, 100) explains that

IBM plans to announce its long awaited repository, or central data dictionary, for Systems Application Architecture (SAA) by early 1989 at the latest, according to industry consultants. IBM expects the repository to emerge as a storage facility for vital information across operating systems. But in its first implementation, the dictionary will act largely as an underlying foundation for a computer-aided software engineering (CASE) systems.

Johnson explores the inconsistent use of the term *repository.* We would normally think of this as a container, but in this statement it is also a *dictionary* and a foundation.

The answer to this frequently encountered phenomenon of multiple-metaphoric use for describing computing concepts is that computer science is a new species of science with a high degree of abstraction. As we deal with highly abstract and arbitrary realities (usually called virtual), we are obliged to give names to a large number of things that may not have obvious designations. When we read that a repository is a dictionary, a storage facility, and a foundation, we immediately recognize multiple metaphors where each one is contributing with a set of features that when joined in a blend, collectively describe the abstract thing we are intending to describe.

It could be argued that in this section we are sometimes considering a technical language, sometimes an everyday language, or sometimes a commercial discourse in which the use of words is not concerned with describing concepts but with selling ideas and products. We are, however, intentionally considering different types of language to show a general cognitive process, the construction of figurative language based on metaphors and blends. So, the question here is not of analyzing the suitability of language to a given purpose or the precision of its concepts but how it is built through some cognitive processes.

The inconsistency pointed out by Johnson does not exist if we read the list not as a heterogeneous set of literal meanings but a conceptual integration. From this point of view, we have each mental space contributing with its own frame to the conceptual integration:

- **Repository** A place where things are stored and can be found;
- **Dictionary** A book in which words are listed alphabetically, and their meanings, either in the same language or in another language, and other information about them are given;
- **Storage** The putting and keeping of things in a special place for use in the future;
- **Foundation** A support in the ground for a large structure such as a building or a road; the base of a belief, claim, idea, and so on.

Once all frames have been identified, we clearly see that a piece of software can be a container to store other pieces of software (things); these things are stored in a special place and order (so a physical device is also needed); these things can be accessed in a given order (for instance, alphabetically) like in a dictionary; and things have a description or definition in terms of a notation used for constructing such things. Finally, this new piece of software will be the base on which other applications will be constructed—that is, they will use the repository to perform their functions.

The blend receives partial structure from all input spaces, but we do not need to think that the new conceptual integration has to be consistent with each input mental space. It is the referential or literal conception of language that produces the effect of considering the emergent blend as inconsistent or contradictory with those input spaces. The conceptual integration has produced a new concept based on the raw material of the input spaces. It is not the supposed relationship to other preexistent concepts that make the conceptual integration useful, it is its suitability for the purpose at hand: to describe a new software application, which may be depicted using a new concept based on a set of different metaphors.

Another interesting example of conceptual integration is that of the computer virus. Fauconnier (1997) provides an extensive analysis of this in explaining the process of taking mappings, projecting them into new structures, and then using the new structures. When analyzing the conceptual system underlying the computer virus blend, we can see that the system is based on an integrated schema. This schema corresponds to the generic space we have already seen when portraying the general structure of a blend. Fauconnier (1997, 19) describes the following features of a computer virus:

x is present, but unwanted; it comes in, or is put in, from the outside; it does not naturally belong;
x is able to replicate; new tokens of *x* appear that have the same undesirable properties as the original *x;*
x disrupts the "standard" function of the system;
x is harmful to the system, and hence is harmful to users of the system;

The system should be protected against *x;* this might be achieved if the system were such that *x* could not come into it, or if other elements were added to the system that would counteract the effects of *x,* or eject *x,* or destroy *x.*

Instead of considering the analogical properties between computer programs of a particular type and species and biological organisms, we soon treat such computer programs as viruses in their own right. We don't just say that the harmful program is "like" a virus. We go ahead and say it is a virus. A metaphor unlike an analogy says A is B, not A is like B.

As a consequence of calling it a virus, we continue using the health vocabulary and apply it to the target domain of computer programs through terms such as infections, spread, vaccine, disinfectant, and so on. Once the blend is made, we would not necessarily have implemented the computer program called a virus. Even if we have already implemented such a program, we are not just conceptualizing an already-given domain in a certain way, we are actually building it so that it fits the mapping. The blend leads, manages, and pushes the implementation of new programs that fit the generic concepts of the health/computer domain.

Figurative Language in HCI

If metaphors and blends are at work in SE, so they are too in HCI. In HCI, we often use a spatial metaphor for describing situations and recognize that there are different levels at which we can consider the sociotechnical systems of HCI—the organizational level, the workplace level, and the individual level.

At the organizational level, there are at least two different perspectives that can be taken: the organizational view and the activity-based view (Sachs 1995). That is, we may embrace a vision based on the structural aspect or the dynamics of the organization. Adopting one or other of these perspectives leads to different visions of actors, relationships, skills, commitments, and so on.

The organizational view of HCI takes the vantage point of management—workers need training, working on tasks, with procedures, using techniques, and so on. An alternative point of view is on the activities of people—discovering problems, learning in informal conversations, creating communities of practice (Lave and Wenger 1991), and developing knowledge and skills. So, the spatial metaphor refers to a more general, social space in which people are located and from where the vision is necessarily different in different situations.

The analysis of all the metaphors that could build the core of the ideas of these different views goes far beyond the scope of this book. Lakoff (1996), however, points out that there are two different common metaphors for the concept of work, each of which uses moral accounting: the work reward metaphor and the work exchange metaphor. For Lakoff (1996, 54–55) the first can be stated as follows:

- The employer is a legitimate authority;
- The employee is subject to that authority;
- Work is obedience to the employer's commands;
- Pay is the reward the employee receives for obedience to the employer.

The second can be stated as follows:

- Work is an object of value;
- The worker is the possessor of their work;
- The employer is the possessor of their money;
- Employment is the voluntary exchange of the worker's work for the employer's money.

Both metaphors define work from the organizational point of view. It would be interesting to include some additional metaphors regarding other aspects of each perspective. A last example will show how a given problem (the "set-up-to-fail" syndrome) could be based on a metaphor: THE EMPLOYEE IS A CHILD (and hence lacks knowledge and skills). One consequence of the metaphor is the representation the boss has of the situation. Managers will often not blame themselves. Instead, it is the employee who did not understand, did not try hard enough, or did not follow procedures.

The main point about representations derived from an organizational view is the danger of failure produced by a poor vision of workplaces. Patricia Sachs (1995) describes a particular technology that was introduced in a telephone company to provide a "trouble ticketing system." This system, notes Sachs (1995, 39), replaced an old one that "allowed workers to talk to one another. In these conversations, they compared notes about what was going on at each end of the circuit. If there was a problem, they figured out what it was and worked on it together. These trouble-shooting conversations provided the occasion for workers to understand what was actually going on in the job, diagnose the situation and remedy it."

The organization took the view based on the metaphor EMPLOYEES ARE CHILDREN, abandoning their responsibilities and engaging others in conversation without any usefulness for the job. This view led to the apparently objective need and requirements for the trouble ticketing system, whose aim was to eliminate conversation. We would argue, however, that such views are not independent of any observer. They are derived from metaphors embodied in a given discourse and are suitable for some social interests—in this case, the organizational point of view. At this organizational level, just detecting and modifying the underlying metaphor should help to reorganize the whole domain of needs and requirements.

Another level of HCI is the workplace. Kim Halskov Madsen (1994) provides a summary of the use of metaphors in system design. One of the cases extracted from a set of five included in his article presents a design of a bank automated teller machine (ATM) taken from Allan MacLean and colleagues (1991). The authors tell us that the designers had personal experience of a bagel store that dealt with its lengthy lines by having an employee work along the queue, explaining the choices available and helping people fill out their order on a form. When they reached the counter, customers would hand over their forms, thereby enabling their orders to be processed more quickly. As Madsen (1994, 58) explains, "Their familiarity with the bagel store arrangement lead the designers to the innovative idea of having bank cards the customers could preprogram while waiting in line."

In the case of the ATM example, it is evident that we are not comparing two different existing systems (the bagel store versus the bank ATM) as the latter was not implemented yet. When we apply the metaphor (THE BANK ATM SYSTEM IS A BAGEL STORE) we create two mental spaces: one corresponds to the similar elements (the ground) and other to dissimilar elements (the tension). There is a dynamic relationship between both the ground and the tension that allows some elements of the tension to pass to the ground, giving this process its constitutive power to the metaphor. While considering that the employee working along the queue explaining the choices available belongs to the tension, there is no new conceptualization about the ATM system. It is when we move this idea to the ground (similar elements) that the new vision of the system appears: it is possible to replicate the employee task of helping to fill the form in its equivalent way of preprogramming the bank card.

The metaphor suggests some possible generic elements in the tension mental space. One of these possible generic elements is the employee working along the queue, but the equivalent in the ATM system is not immediately identified. Sometimes the generic space—with the common, usually more abstract, structure and organization shared by the inputs—will work as an intermediate phase before arriving at the final blend space. The generic space contains what both input spaces (the bagel store and the ATM system) have as equivalent abstract structures: the possibility of doing some task while waiting in line in order for the counter to speed up the process. Finally, the blend space will contain the actual form of speeding up the process as a programmable bank card. The blend space is built on structures coming from both input spaces and other spaces as well—in particular, that of the current bank card technologies. This last mental space is important, as it will allow the proposal of a programmable bank card to be actually evaluated and implemented.

What the metaphor has contributed is to envision new functionalities and, consequently, modify the requirements of the system being designed. The design process is a complex one, and there are well-known difficulties of completely defining the requirements of a system before beginning the design phase. During the design users uncover new possibilities, which may result in additional functionalities. One role of a metaphor is to anticipate what would normally be detected in the design phase. Not all new functionalities will necessarily be anticipated by metaphorical design, however. Some of the functionalities detected by a metaphorical design may not have been recognized by users, as the possibilities offered by new technology are not available to them. The designer will have different blends from the users.

We can conclude that metaphors are the original generative force, but we have to use blend (and generic) spaces as a way of making triggering concepts workable, or to elaborate these triggering concepts. The same way as general SE methods advocate documenting some critical design decisions through design rationale, we would advocate including in the ontology of HCI an additional issue about metaphors used in design with a trace to all triggering concepts and the resultant blend spaces.

At the organizational level, metaphors can help in generating needs and requirements. In the trouble ticketing system, such needs were inadequate to solve the (apparent) problem of employees engaged in time-consuming conversations. An alternative metaphor, EMPLOYEES ARE MATURE INDIVIDUALS, might make a difference. With this view, employees engage in conversation when they need to solve problems. It would have determined that troubleshooting conversations were not a problem but the solution. At the workplace level, metaphors can help us to envision new aspects and opportunities of the systems we are designing. Metaphors, in this case, are artifacts to produce new functions during design. But it is not a metaphor on its own that gives the design solution; different blends offer different design alternatives.

At the operational level, our focus is to consider the artifacts we use in constructing systems. We return to this in the next chapter.

SE Examples of Blends

The Layered Architecture

A frequently used concept in software design is that of a layered architecture: "the Layers architectural pattern helps to structure applications that can be decomposed into groups of subtasks in which each group of subtasks is at a particular level of abstraction" (Buschmann et al. 1996, 31).

In this case, the input space that projects its structure to the blend will be that of an architectural structure of layers, in the sense used in architecture or geology. That means that each layer is based on a lower level. Moreover, we observe that there is basically a spatial metaphor (SOFTWARE IS A SPATIAL STRUCTURE), a blend (the layered structure of the software), and a generic space in which there is a set of ordered elements, each element being supported by a previous one and considering support in a general sense—that is, resisting the weight of other layers built on it.

The connection between both input spaces (architecture and software) is quite deeply and generatively entrenched. Over the years, the software community has been using other similar connections as software and engineering, even if this last connection was established in order to project some characteristics of engineering processes to the software process. In the case of architecture and software, the connection is stated for projecting some design solutions from the former to the latter, considering that an abstract architecture means a structure with some functional relationships added.

In particular, in recent years, the concept *architecture* has become more and more broad to include the relationships with the environment as well as the principles guiding the design of the system and its evolution (IEEE Std 2000).

As the use of this type of conceptualization generalizes, it is the connections between the generic space and the software space that is directly established. The generic space of "architectural structures" becomes a new conceptual domain of its own. So it is the candidate to be one of the input spaces to a specific construction, as when we say, "This is a three-layer architecture with a first layer that contains . . ."

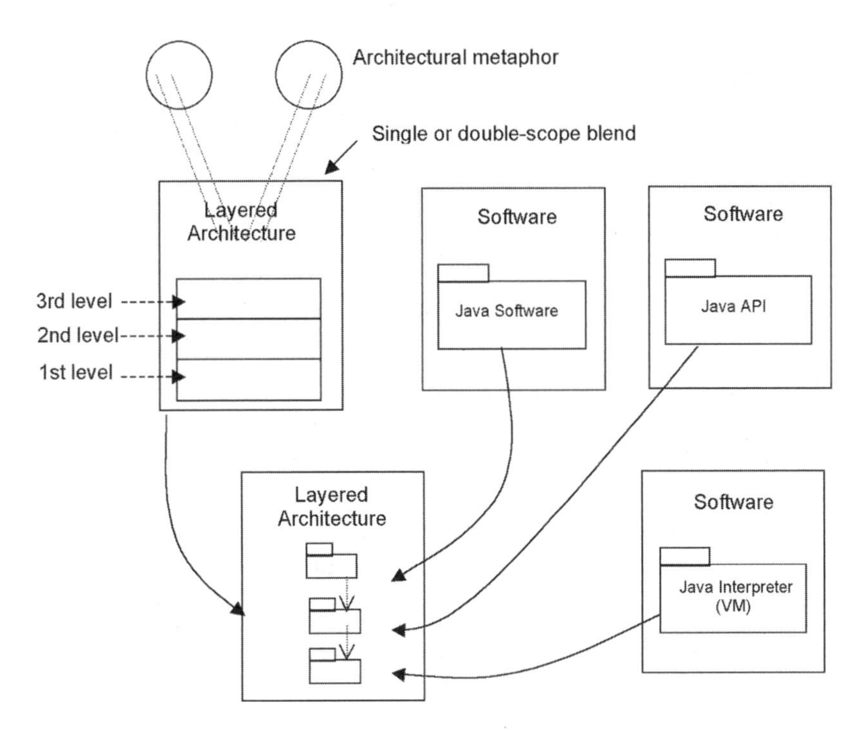

Figure 4.4
Domains of the Java example conceptual integration

Let us consider an example of a Java application, using the concept of package (from the UML) as a tool for grouping a collection of objects and with dependency relations with other packages. This blend is the result of various input spaces: a first input space of a layered structure (as we have seen, this is already a blend that projects its structure as a frame), a Java interpreter space (an application for executing Java instructions), one space of Java packages (which constitute the Java API software), and the application software space developed in Java (the Java software). This is illustrated in figure 4.4.

From the frame of the first space, there is a projection of the layered structure, which functions as a group of slots that are to be occupied by elements from the other input spaces. In fact, each of the other input spaces will transfer the Java Virtual Machine software, the Java API software, and the Java application software.

Depending on the input spaces, the meaning of the relationship between two successive layers will change. But the important issue is that the blend gives consistency and uniformity to the structure independently of the input spaces. This uniformity is a consequence of the general dependency relationship between the last three input spaces. In this sense, the blend allows a higher degree of categorization to a group of differently related chunks of software.

In figure 4.4, we observe the dependencies of each package on the next lower layer of the layered architecture. In the case of the software application (the third layer), the dependency means: "objects of a given package are built using elements of another layer (the Java API)." In the case of the second- and first-layer relationships, we can see that the dependency means: "the elements of the API are to be executed through the Java Virtual Machine." So there is a categorization of dependency whereby it can mean differently a construction or an execution.

The division of a given layer into further ones, tiers, is used to establish an ordered relationship in a given layer. The dependency between tiers means: "elements of the first tier use (or call) elements of the second one." The fact of categorizing different relationships using only one concept enables a uniform structure, such as the layered architecture. This has the advantage of smoothly categorizing things that would have been described differently, requiring a more detailed explanation with the inclusion of unnecessary complexity.

The Broker

Another example of conceptualization through a blend is that of brokers. A broker is someone who acts as an agent for others, as in negotiating contracts, purchases, or sales in return for a fee or commission. As this concept has been used to define a "Service Request Broker" and an "Object Request Broker," we would try to give a detailed description of the frame that such mental space projects into the blend.

The definition speaks of somebody who acts as an agent for others—that is, someone who can perform some type of negotiation and come back with the results. A broker may interact with a different organization in order to perform different kinds of transactions (contracts, sales, and purchases). It is a relevant feature that a broker could use different styles (or languages) as required by the context of the transaction. The broker adapts themself to the client who requests a service and may speak a language that the client can understand. Because of the broker's position as an intermediary—the definition speaks of "one who is in a middle position or state"—they may serve simultaneously each person (or company) asking for their services.

This frame has enough general structure to organize the software necessary to mediate between a set of pieces of software (clients) asking for services (functions to be performed in order to get a given result) from other pieces of software. We intentionally write a piece of software, and the name is derived from the context to recall that all additional names (client, server, or service) given to pieces of software are derived from the context, intentionality, and blend built with the input spaces.

We can build a representation of a broker in the input mental space and a different one in the blend to show that the general organization is applied to the specific context of software. It is possible that the representation used here for a broker may be influenced by the usual representation of a software broker or Common Object Request Broker Architecture.

In the context of a Service (or an Object) Request Broker, such specialized software is also known as middleware, which may be considered another spatial metaphor (because it is in a middle layer, between applications and operating systems) or projection from the blend of layered architecture.

As a real broker normally receives a fee or commission in return, in the blend there is an equivalent: something to pay. We need to pay an overhead since such middleware, as the intermediate software, is resource consuming and implies additional time to access any object of the context.

Figure 4.5 shows that when the role of an intermediate broker is added, what would have been a direct relationship between two objects in a piece of software turns into two objects communicating through the broker. In this way, for all possible differences of language, style, or whatever it may be, the intermediate software will solve the conflict. Similar to real brokers, the new middleware has to provide a list of different types of services.

This is the description of the blend, in which the depiction of a real-world broker is detectable. The frame of this last mental space projects a structure, so with only one word (broker), all the frame is automatically transferred, giving an immediate organization to the description of a group of applications that otherwise would require extensive commentary to give it a meaning.

We have already seen that when both input spaces come from apparently widely different specific conceptual domains, the result is typically judged to

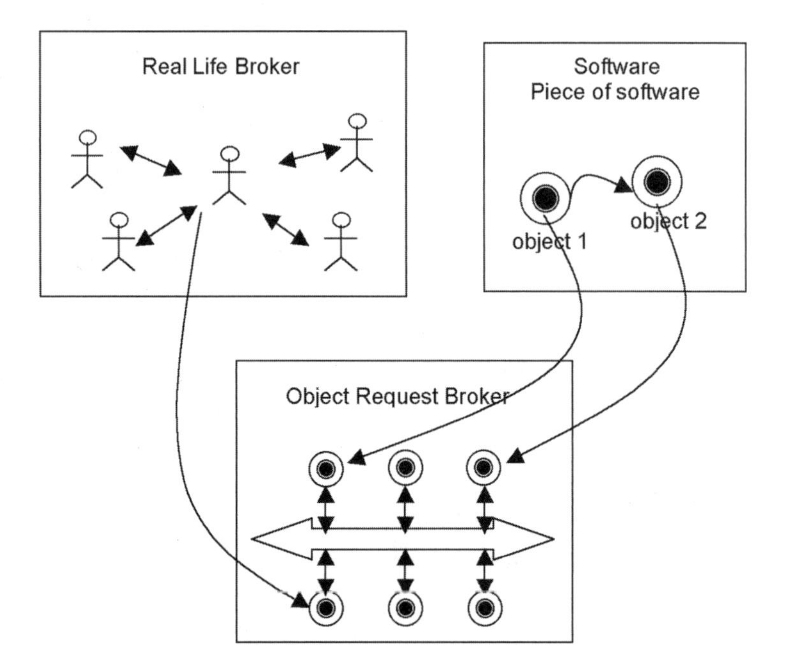

Figure 4.5
The broker conceptual integration

be highly figurative. As this concept of an Object Request Broker has a relatively long life of entrenchment, we are not aware of that feature being, in principle, highly figurative. From the point of view of our everyday language of computer developer, this expression is, on the contrary, quite literal. Moreover, when a new concept appears in the field of commercial software development, we try automatically to understand the meaning of apparently foreign concepts without even noticing the fact that it is a blend, which would be taken as highly figurative.

Let us look at another instance of this highly figurative language used in software development: the Java sandbox feature.

The Java Sandbox

We have already seen two examples, one taking its structure from the domain of architecture and the other from the domain of commercial brokers or stockbrokers. Now let's explore an example of a blend importing structure from the domain of children playing in a box of sand.

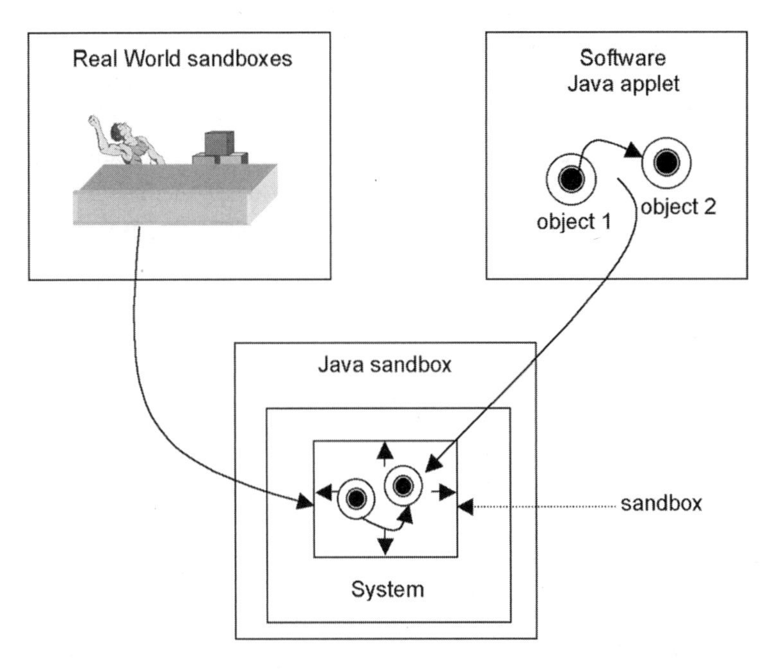

Figure 4.6
The sandbox conceptual integration

The source input activity is that of playing without dangerous effects or a lot of trouble as a consequence of such playing. Such a goal is met by getting into means of a box (a container with limits), so the consequences of the children's actions are limited to the extent of the box's sides. The potentially annoying children's actions are associated—in the blend—to the consequences of executing an imported applet beyond some imposed limits.

The sandbox: Java's security allows a user to import and run applets from the Web or an intranet without undue risk to the user's machine. The applet's actions are restricted to its "sandbox," an area of the Web browser dedicated to that applet. The applet may do anything it wants within its sandbox, but cannot read or alter any data outside its sandbox. The sandbox model is to run untrusted code in a trusted environment so that if a user accidentally imports a hostile applet, that applet cannot damage the local machine. (Fritzinger and Mueller 1996, 4)

What has been achieved with the blend is to give coherence to a set of characteristics of the Java language in order to guarantee the security of environments where downloaded applets are executed from the Web or a local area network.

Once again, the blend would appear as highly figurative, but the fact of using more and more figurative language in the domain of software determines an acceleration of the process of generative entrenchment. The domain of software development (commercial products and definition of standards) determines an increasing use of figurative language as a literal one. There is not even an intermediate period when such new expressions are considered as figurative; they are immediately associated with the "objective" world of software and so considered as literal.

5 Software Engineering

Software engineering is the term currently used to describe the activity of understanding, specifying, programming, testing, and implementing computer programs. It employs a range of methods and notations to help programmers in their activities. The aim of this chapter is to show how the constructs employed by the methods are built on image schemata, metaphors, and blends, which are manipulations in mental spaces. In particular the use of metaphors for building new blends is important, as they offer an endless source of new meaning and therefore the possibility of creating new concepts. This is especially so in HCI, but also true in SE.

One key aspect of conceptual integration is the relations, or relationships, that pertain between the elements of the input spaces. We have seen that single-scope blends (when the organizing frame of one of the input spaces is projected into the blend space) appear to be more literal than double-scope blends. It is also true that the relations between input spaces get compressed into the blend space. This may occur to the elements within a space (inner-space relations) or those across the spaces (outer-space relations). In SE, we tend to find simpler single-scope blends.

Concepts and Notations

In SE, the UML is a notation for specifying object-oriented programs. This notation has tended to supersede previous notations such as data-flow or entity-relationship diagrams. These other notations were part of an approach to SE called "structured methods." Structured methods were themselves formulated to supersede the "unstructured" methods of the 1960s that focused on the flow of physical objects and the "spaghetti code" that resulted from the overenthusiastic use of the "Go To" programming construct.

In SE methods and notations, the historical order in which the concepts of a given method appear is the opposite of the order in which we use them. The historical development of concepts moves from programming to design to analysis. This is then inversely applied when constructing new applications. We undertake analysis, design, and programming. It is also the case that model elements are defined on concepts already in existence. For example, the concept of "class" in OO languages was already available as a programming construct when the corresponding construct for it was developed.

A notation, in SE, plays the same role that a schema or frame does in everyday language. We know that for concepts to have a meaning, we need a previous frame, defined in a larger social and economic organization. For example, to understand concepts such as "sale" or "vendor," we need the "commercial event" schema. As we saw, this is the meaning of frame according to Charles Fillmore's ideas (1977), but other researchers have also suggested a similar concept of frame. Marvin Minsky (1975), for one, proposed the term frame for a data structure used to represent commonly encountered, stereotyped situations. In Minsky's proposal, a birthday party frame includes slots—such as food, games, and gifts—that specify general features of the event, and these slots are bound to fillers or particular representations of a situation.

We are using the word frame in its widest sense, covering a simple data structure, or the more general meaning of cultural or social schema. A given notation has the function of frame. Sometimes, as in the case of UML, the meaning has been previously defined in a metamodel, which offers a definition to all the constructs of the notation.

SE has employed a number of different methods for the analysis, design, and documentation of programs over the years. Once a given method or methodology has been established, we are able to use it in order to build new models. What we usually do is to produce new instances of constructs based on the general one we have previously defined. As we will see later, two important constructs are entities (things) and the relationships that exist between them. An instance of the entity construct might be "Customer" and other might be "Order," and an instance of a relationship might be "sends": "a customer sends an order" (figure 5.1).

In figure 5.1, we have used the UML style (for example, U2 Partners 2003) to indicate that there are two different levels (model and metamodel) and that the involved operation is instantiation. This is the production of a model element from a construct defined in the metamodel level. This instantiation operation is a blend.

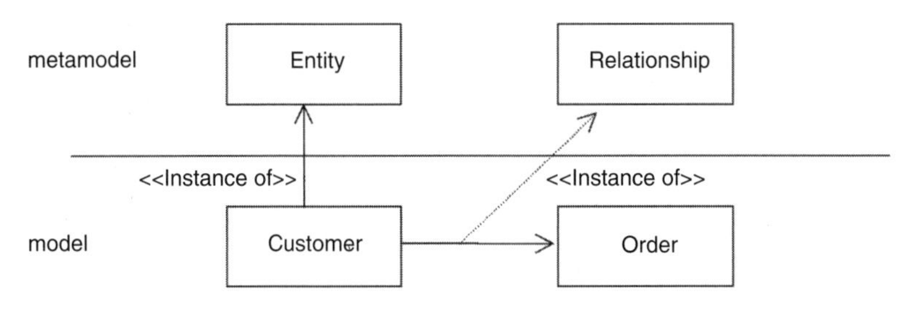

Figure 5.1
Producing new instances from constructs

Nili Mandelblit (2000) analyzes the integration operations underlying English cause-motion sentences (formerly studied by Fauconnier and Turner [1996] and Goldberg [1995]). Let us explore an example of such types of sentences: "Peter threw the ball into the basket."

Here, we observe that it integrates a whole causal sequence of events. Peter, acting on the ball, causes the ball to move into the basket. The verb throw itself specifies both Peter's action and the ball's motion, and the fact that they are causally related. Mandelblit analyzes such integration as a blend between an abstract representation of the cause-motion construction and a novel cause-motion event sequence. One of the input domains to the blend is not a representation of any actual sentence in the language but rather a representation of the "construction form and semantics—a schema abstracted from all instances of the construction. It is only through the linguistic blending operation that an actual sentence is generated" (Mandelblit 2000, 240).

There is an abstract schema, which has been abstracted from all instances of the same type, and is used as one of the input spaces. The syntactic form of the construction is [NP V NP' PP], where NP is a nominal phrase to indicate an agent, V is a verb to indicate an act producing a motion, NP' is an additional nominal phrase that refers to the patient of the action, and PP is a prepositional phrase to indicate a trajectory and a reference point. The other input space is that of a new perceived event. The graphical representation of such a blend would look like figure 5.2.

The important fact in this example is that *threw* specifies simultaneously Peter's action and the ball's motion. It is this integration—compression—that is reflected by the blend in the new sentence.

In the same way, an instantiation of an entity (metamodel) into an entity in a specific model (Customer) is a blend from two input mental spaces. The

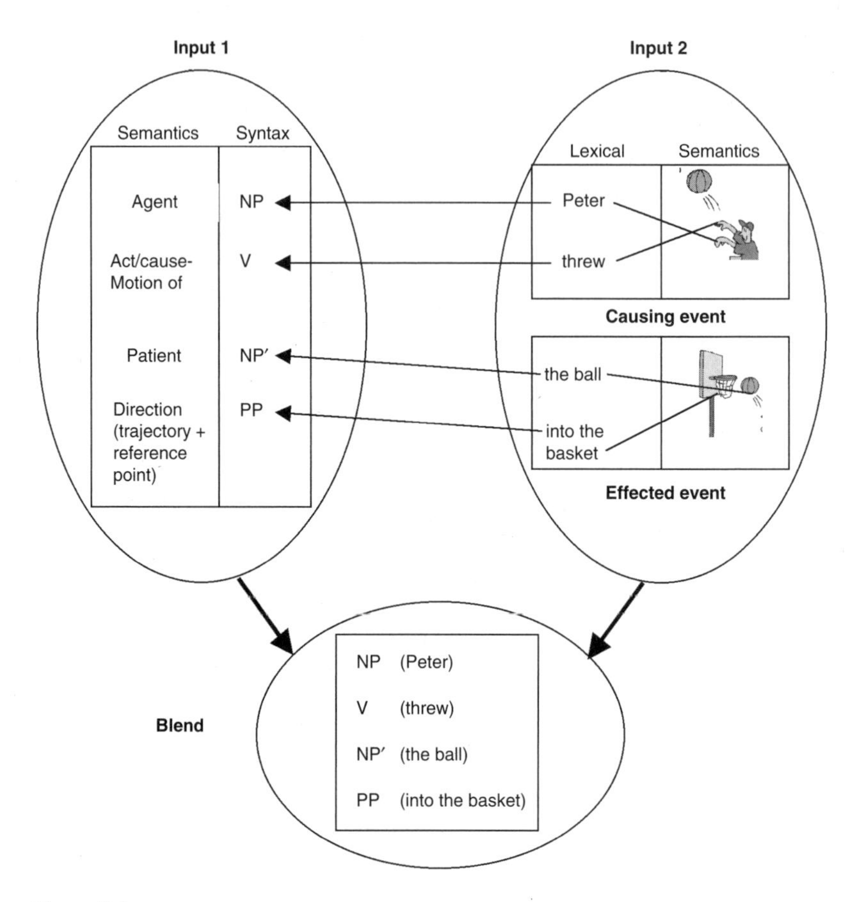

Figure 5.2
A cause-motion sentence as a linguistic blend

first input is the frame, the construct to represent entities. The second is the specific requirements of the model. The difference between this and the linguistic blend of figure 5.2 is that the Customer entity has a richer Input 2 mental space. A systems analyst has to search for and detect the collection of attributes of Customer in a complex world of activities and relationships. Moreover, the usual case is that of finding only some of the attributes intended for a given activity and leaving other possible attributes for a future search. The problem with this gradual uncovering method is that of changing the implementation of such entities (usually implemented as a database), but this is more a technological problem than a cognitive one. The instantiation cognitive operation represented in UML as shown in figure 5.3 corresponds to the blend illustrated in figure 5.4.

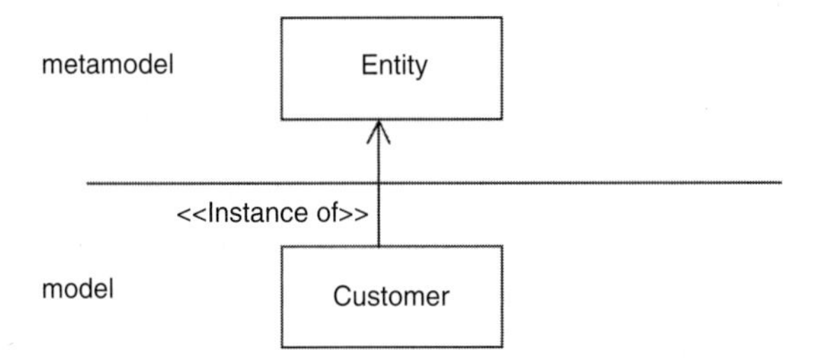

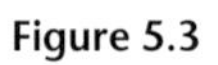

Figure 5.3
Instantiation of the entity construct

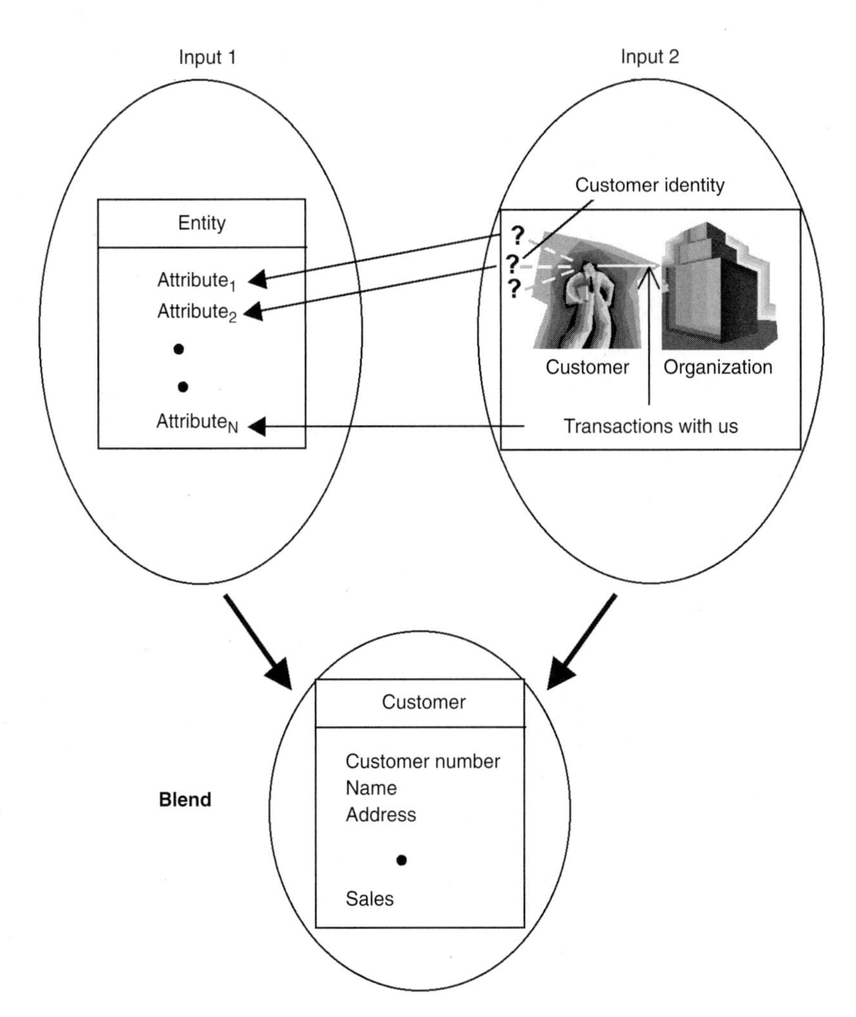

Figure 5.4
The customer entity as a blend

Entity-Relationship Models

Entity-relationship models are based on two metaphorical projections: the entity is a container, and the relationship is a link image schema. The entity contains attributes with different characteristics (such as key, alternate key, foreign key). Such attributes are properties of real-world things, taking into account that a "property" is not something objectively existent in the world independent of any being. It is what Lakoff (1987, 51) calls an "interactional property." Properties of entities arise as a result of our interactions in a social and cultural environment given our human bodies and cognitive capabilities.

As we continue interacting with the model and the entities, it is quite likely we will find new attributes that need to be added to the current version of the model. This is something that every software engineer has experienced in their everyday practice, and shows the veracity of considering properties as emerging from the interactions and goals of the system at hand.

The relationship, as a link, has only the function of relating two different entities without any sense of direction. Relationships are relations between an element A and an element B to which we assign a name (usually a different name from that assigned to the relation between the element B and the element A). This means that another type of metaphorical projection has to be established: the path. In order for a relationship's name to have a meaning, it is important to know where the relationship originates from and where it goes. The name is associated with a given direction of the path image schema on which it is based.

So we can differentiate two cases: the first one using a container and a link image schema for the metaphorical projection, as shown in figure 5.5.

The second case, with a container and a path image schema, is aimed at producing a difference between both possible directions. Depending on whether there is only one or two names associated with the path image schema, it could be thought of as one or two path image schemata, each one going from one entity to the other (figure 5.6).

When using two names, each one corresponds to one of the path image schemata, but it is more usual to represent the model with only one link and not including an arrow to indicate the direction. The situation in which we need to show all the involved relationships is represented in figure 5.7.

The final conceptualization is the result of superimposing four metaphorical image-schema projections: two from a container and two from a path.

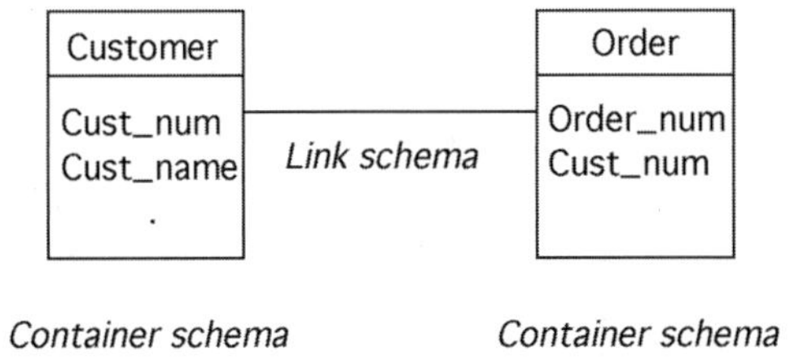

Customer
Cust_num
Cust_name
Link schema
Order
Order_num
Cust_num
Container schema
Container schema

Figure 5.5
Entities as containers with link schema (relationship)

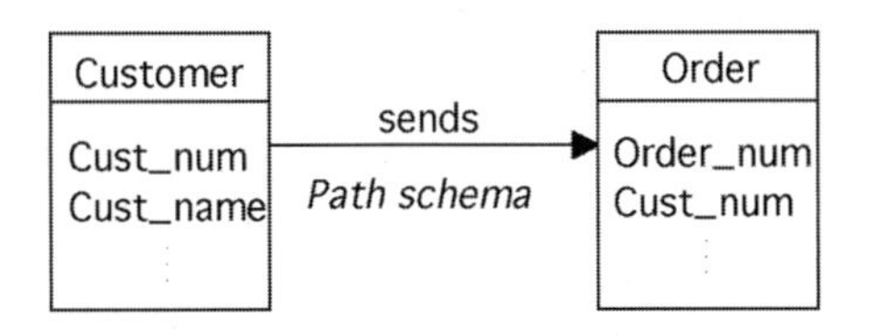

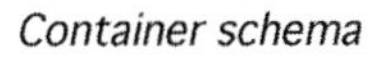

Customer
Cust_num
Cust_name
sends
Path schema
Order
Order_num
Cust_num
Container schema
Container schema

Figure 5.6
Entities with a directed relationship (path schema)

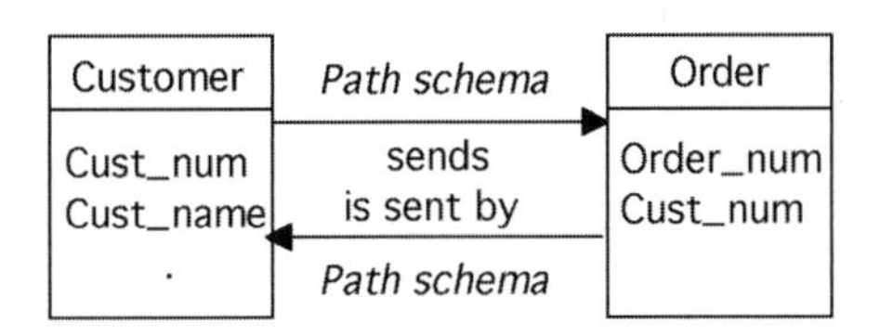

Customer
Cust_num
Cust_name
Path schema
sends
is sent by
Path schema
Order
Order_num
Cust_num
Container schema
Container schema

Figure 5.7
Entities with two directed relationships

Strictly speaking, one might only say that a source-path-goal image schema is represented as in figure 5.8.

The direction is deduced from both source and goal locations. The arrow is the addition of a metaphorical projection from real-life artifacts—hunting instruments that clearly indicate the direction they were thrown or fired.

It would be interesting to say that the path image schema just indicates the direction of an action; it differentiates who is the actor and who is suffering the actor's action. The direction, which has been defined on a path image schema, refers to the graphic representation and means the sense of the path in reading the relationship: Customer sends an Order.

An alternative meaning would correspond to paths that actual orders (or customers) might take—a question not considered in models of this type. So, it is clear that the path image schema is only used to indicate a direction of reading of the entities related by the relationship—a separation between a sentence's subject and object, and not a direction in a geographic or procedural sense.

When defining the container image schema, we have seen that the structure of such schemata implies a direct logical fitting of other containers into the original one and in this way structuring a container by others. This is the usual logic of sets, whereby if container A is put into container B, all elements of A are also elements of B, so X belongs to A and as A is in B also belongs to B (figure 5.9).

In SE, when using an entity A containing another B, the usual meaning is just the opposite to that used in set theory, indicating that all attributes of A are also attributes of B. The reverse is not valid, however. Sometimes, the representation used is that of one container in another, and the meaning is that of a subordinate or progeny in a genealogical tree, where the contained entity possesses all attributes of the container as shown in figure 5.10.

Figure 5.8
A representation of source-path-goal image schema

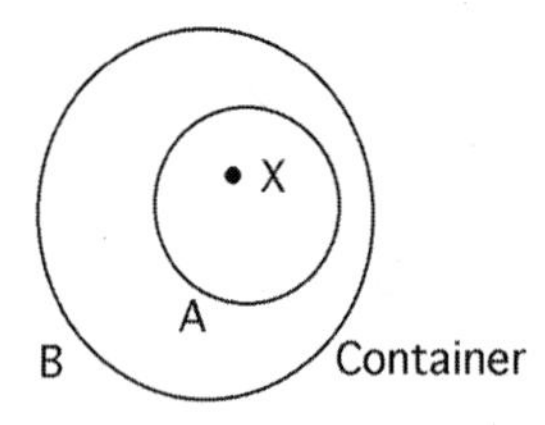

Figure 5.9
The logic of containers

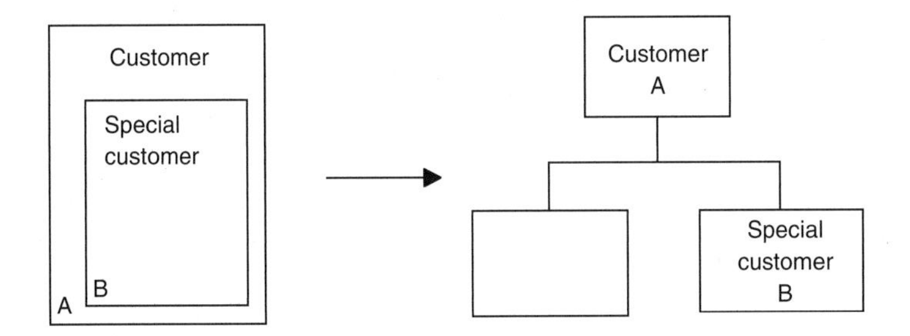

Figure 5.10
A contained entity is a subordinate entity (subentity)

From a cognitive point of view, entity A (ancestor or superordinate) has been built from a collection of basic-level categories and generalizing all common attributes to the superordinate. From a set point of view, all attributes contained in B would also be contained in A. But in this particular case, what figure 5.10 is intended to mean is that B contains also some attributes not contained in A. So, the representation on the right of figure 5.10, as used currently in OO SE, is more intuitive as there is a clear separation of both entities, indicating that special customer B is inheriting from customer A.

State-Transition Diagrams

A typical state-transition diagram (STD) is built by means of a composition of path image schemata. The end or goal point of a path may be the origin or source point of yet another path. There are indeed some places that are both an origin and an end point at the same time, as state B in figure 5.11.

In a state-transition diagram, we need to indicate where the path comes from and where it goes. Each node represents a state or location, and is usually conceptualized as a point. But if in place of a point we use a container, such a container could contain (as in the case of entities) a name and a set of attributes. In such a case, and interesting from a cognitive point of view, a state is conceptualized as a thing (an entity), in the same way that events of everyday life are also conceptualized as things.

A change in conceptualizing the node to a container from a point offers the opportunity of transforming any state-transition diagram into a state chart where the structure of each node might be represented as another state-transition diagram at a lower level (figure 5.12).

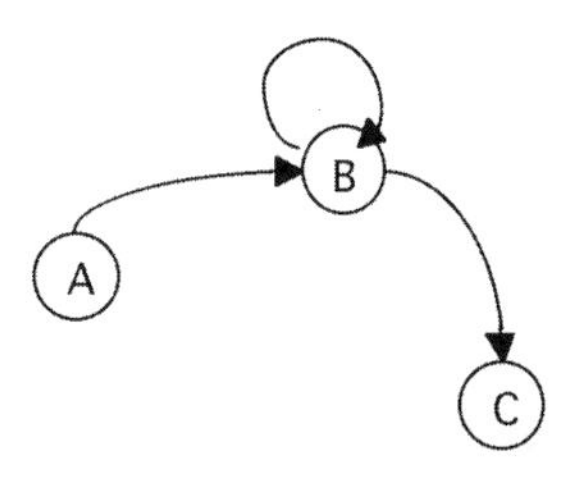

Figure 5.11
State-transition diagram as composition of path image schemata

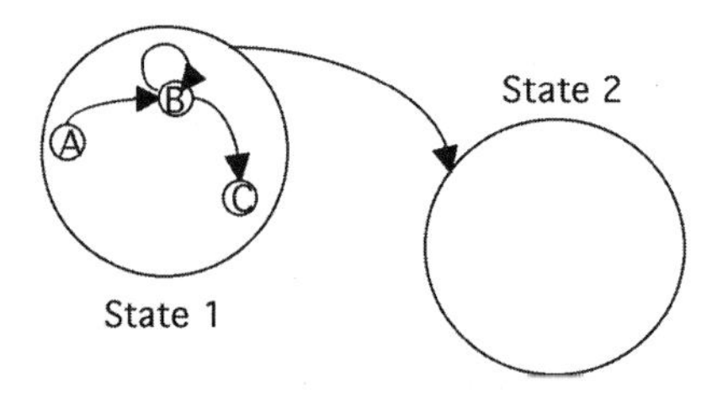

Figure 5.12
Superstates as containers

The Top-Down Method

This frequently used representation (for entities or processes) is based on the container image schema as well as a spatial metaphor; there is a set of levels or layers, each of them being successively selected for representation. We can think of these levels as being equivalent to mental spaces; we pass through different levels as if we were constructing new mental spaces. This special way of categorizing—like nested Russian dolls—can be called categorization by container, and corresponds to the well-known top-down analysis and design method. The problem with this way of categorizing is that it depends on which levels we are looking at (see figure 5.13).

Starting at a high level, we conceive a whole large system implying composition by other subsystems. We are a long way from basic-level categories. It is at this level where there is a risk of losing one's way, as Ed Yourdon (1989, 360) has pointed out in relation to the top-down problem: "analysis paralysis," the "six analyst" phenomenon, or the "arbitrary physical partitioning." Yourdon's proposal is to use a middle-out method, in which the middle is closer to basic-level categories, and from where to go down and up looking for concepts that fit the analysis purpose better (see figure 5.13). Moreover, somebody who successfully applies the top-down method is a person who has sound skills in the specific domain that one is working on.

The successive structuring of a container in terms of a collection of other containers leads us to ask about the validity of this way of categorization. The scalability problem concerning Edsger Dijkstra's (1972) original idea is clearly stated by James Martin and Carma McClure (1988, 103):

> The one programming problem of paramount concern in the 1970s was complexity. This is the problem of programming in the large. It became possible and necessary to develop large, highly interrelated systems of programs. When the same heuristic programming practices used to develop small, stand-alone applications were tried in this new environment, they failed miserably. It soon became obvious that the problem of scaling up was indeed very difficult.

As pointed out by the authors, top-down programming is a popularized version of Niklaus Wirth's (1971) stepwise-refinement method. It represents an important advancement over earlier, ad hoc programming methods because it is an orderly way of attacking large programming problems. Nevertheless, it is an informal, nonrigorous method.

There is another crucial issue regarding the top-down approach. Even if a pure top-down approach offers a "false sense of security," though not necessarily being a coherent and rigorous method, it could be used as a clear one for the exposition of the design results. What we mean is that the top-down approach shows its limitations when applied as a design method, but this limitation does not disqualify it as an excellent exposition method. A top-down

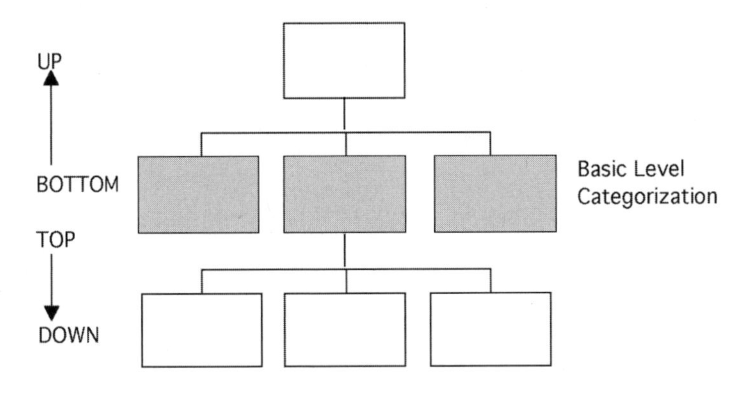

Figure 5.13
The middle-out method

explanation to show the design of a system previously done using other methods can often be clear and concise.

The neat and well-structured documentation obtained as a result of applying a top-down method has likely determined that the same approach was used for designing systems. The method of categorizing used in design is not necessarily the same as the method of explaining the results in a comprehensible way aimed at training or the discussion of results.

Therefore, once the design has been finished and has to be presented to an audience, the top-down approach is an excellent way to explain the characteristics of such a design. Applying the top-down method can be thought of using a travel metaphor, where we first fly over a territory identifying the main cities and towns. After landing at each of the cities and visiting them, we continue to fly to the next one. The same travel metaphor might be applied to visiting the town with another transport such as bus and stopping to see some places in detail. In order for the metaphor to be applied in the appropriate manner, all we need to have are cities already existent to visit; the flight, on its own, can only give us some general guidelines, but not precise information in order for us to plan a new city.

This excellent method, when used for an exposition purpose, is not necessarily a good methodological tool for building new designs and models. What is needed is an approach based on some known cognitive pattern. We will return in a later chapter to this issue, when considering user requirements and after presenting some additional ideas, like scripts and stories.

Data-Flow Diagrams

As we have already said in the previous chapter, an important fact to be taken into account is that metaphors are not only used to build new user interfaces but also to elaborate new theories or paradigms. In this sense, a new metaphor has a constitutive power, and a whole theory or method may be brought into being when a new metaphor is used. It is not just a new light that is shed on already-existing notions—features offered by analogies—but an act of creation that only metaphors generate (Sfard 1997, 344).

This was Michael Reddy's argument. The same idea is clearly expressed by Richard Boyd (1993, 486):

> Nevertheless, it seems to me that the cases of scientific metaphor which are most interesting from the point of view of the philosophy of science (and the philosophy of lan-

guage generally) are those in which metaphorical expressions constitute, at least for a time, an irreplaceable part of the linguistic machinery of a scientific theory: cases in which there are metaphors which scientists use in expressing theoretical claims for which no adequate literal paraphrase is known. Such metaphors are constitutive of the theories they express, rather than merely exegetical.

Data-flow diagrams (DFD) are based on a metaphor. Even if one process is also categorized as a container and its structure is determined by another data-flow diagram at a lower level, the main metaphor on which the model is based is THE SYSTEM IS AN INDUSTRIAL PLANT. In such a plant, there is a collection of processes interconnected by pipes or assembly lines. The raw material for one process originates from other processes, external sources, or stores containing by-products of yet other processes. Data-flow diagrams are concerned with transforming data.

The lines connecting two processes (data flows) have a direction, but they are thought of as containing data elements that move from the source process to the target process. So, data flows correspond to equivalent pipes or assembly lines containing elements to be processed in the next production step. An alternative point of view is to consider data flows as an instance of the CONDUIT metaphor, whereby a message is an object in a container; communication is transferring an object spatially from the speaker to the hearer and so on (Turner 1996). We prefer the metaphor of the industrial plant (figure 5.14) because it unifies conceptually the whole diagram, avoiding the use of individual image schemata like containers and conduit metaphors.

The idea of giving structure to a process by means of a submodel (another data-flow diagram) contained in it is a projection of the concept used in

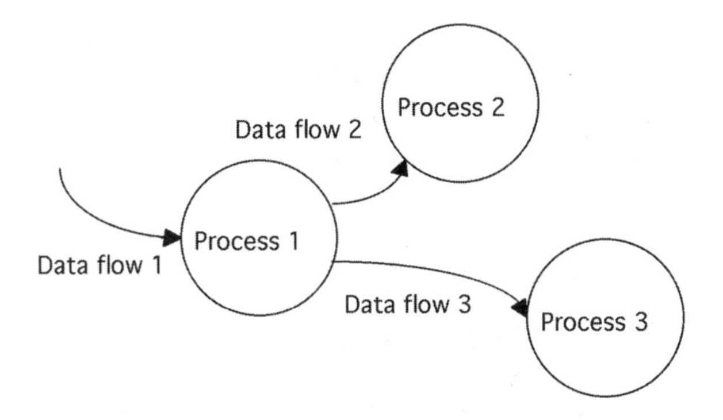

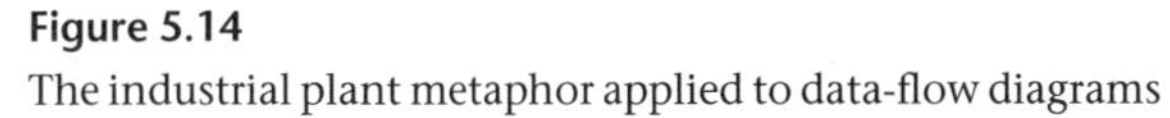

Figure 5.14
The industrial plant metaphor applied to data-flow diagrams

structured programming (stepwise refinement), but subsequently renamed as the top-down approach. It is not surprising that this metaphor has been the constitutive one that has ruled most of our SE methods since the mid-1970s, as the concept of SE is already an expression that reveals such an implicit metaphor.

This is the main characteristic of methods used from the mid-1970s, where the constitutive metaphor was that of THE SYSTEM IS AN INDUSTRIAL PLANT, where processes use entities as raw material or semi-elaborate products to produce new entities as subproducts. That means also that the constitutive metaphor determines the type of elements we employ in such a paradigm: processes and material. There has been no need to use any additional metaphors when building constructs, as all of them are based on the same constitutive metaphor. Therefore, constructs representing material are built using a frame, the entity, as one of the inputs and compressing into the blend concepts of the considered domain as a second input.

The OO Paradigm

The structured methods that prevailed in SE from the mid-1970s until the mid-1980s, gradually gave way to object orientation. The new paradigm had its own constitutive metaphor: THE SYSTEM IS A SOCIETY OF PEOPLE. Object orientation is full of expressions based on this metaphor. Objects have *responsibilities,* they *collaborate* with each other, they *have acquaintance* of other objects, they *communicate,* they have a *defined behavior,* and so on.

Structured methods are mostly built using metaphorical projections from image schemata and blends from "business stories" that compress the properties of things into entities. We will see how a typical OO construct like class has a relatively higher complexity than the entity construct, and how we will need to consider it as a blend from richer business stories than entities.

In order for an element of the real world to be used in an OO construct, it would be necessary to project to a blend space a complete business story—that is, the whole set of transformations a real-world element (thing, entity, event, and so on) may undergo at different stages of its "life." Sometimes, it is not a transformation suffered passively but an active initiative that the object takes: "print me," "copy me," "transmit me," and so forth. (It is evident that this approach is just the opposite of Dijkstra's ideas. Dijkstra, a well-known computer scientist, blamed the computing research community for thinking about computing systems in anything other than strictly mathematical terms and particularly what he called "anthropomorphization" [Colwell 2003, 11].)

In object orientation, a class is a compact construct of different elements. For most writers, there are three main containers used to build the concept of class in the UML:

1. The container of name;
2. The container of attributes;
3. The container of methods.

Some authors include an additional fourth container, called responsibilities, where they include another type of description (Booch, Rumbaugh, and Jacobson 1999; Rumbaugh, Jacobson, and Booch 1999). This new container could be an interesting place in which to reflect on the main highlights of the business story. We return to responsibilities later in this chapter.

Each container is built using an image schema (container) and elements of other mental spaces. In particular, the properties of the thing are selected from these mental spaces, as we have seen with entities. Supposing that a class will be used to represent something in the real world, and most of the elements contained in the first container are projected from the mental space of the real-world thing. But in general, a class is used to represent any type of entity: of the real world, culturally or socially invented, or even specially created to participate in the computer model we are building. These latter entities that are specially created to participate in the computer model are *design entities,* included in a later phase than analysis.

Each one of these containers will be filled through some external relations—outer-space relations into the class. Some outer-space relations will be compressed into inner-space relations, while others will be projected without compression. Blends often compress the relations from the input spaces. Some of these are relations between the two input spaces (outer-space relations) and others are relations internal to a space (inner-space relations).

In figure 5.15, we observe an agent starting its business story. We have intentionally used these mannequins to suggest that the objects are humanoids—that is, something like human beings with a limited intelligence and learning capacity. During their travels, the objects will encounter other objects, which they will interact with. Each interaction will be compressed as an operation and eventually implemented as a method into the appropriate part of the class construct. At the end of the business story, all the

Figure 5.15
An object's successive interactions

object's interactions will be compressed in the blend, so that an instance of the class would be able to reproduce the whole business story. This is illustrated in figure 5.16.

Consider the domain of invoicing. When speaking about that domain we begin to unfold a set of mental spaces: the space of invoices, the space of customers, the space of staff that create, modify, or delete invoices, the space of printing invoices, and so on. From each space, we may abstract a set of properties and operations that will eventually be compressed into the class as attributes and operations.

The space of invoices focuses on characteristics of the entity invoice—in particular its properties. An invoice is a cultural creation and usually implies a piece of paper with appropriate information to reflect a commercial transaction. All properties of an invoice are of type "data."

So the first mental space to be taken into account is that of the entity invoice—an entity that cannot initiate any type of behavior by itself. In other domains entities have a behavior—for instance, a car—and this might imply a need to project properties and operations from the input mental space. This is the case when we need to make simulations of real-world entities. But in the

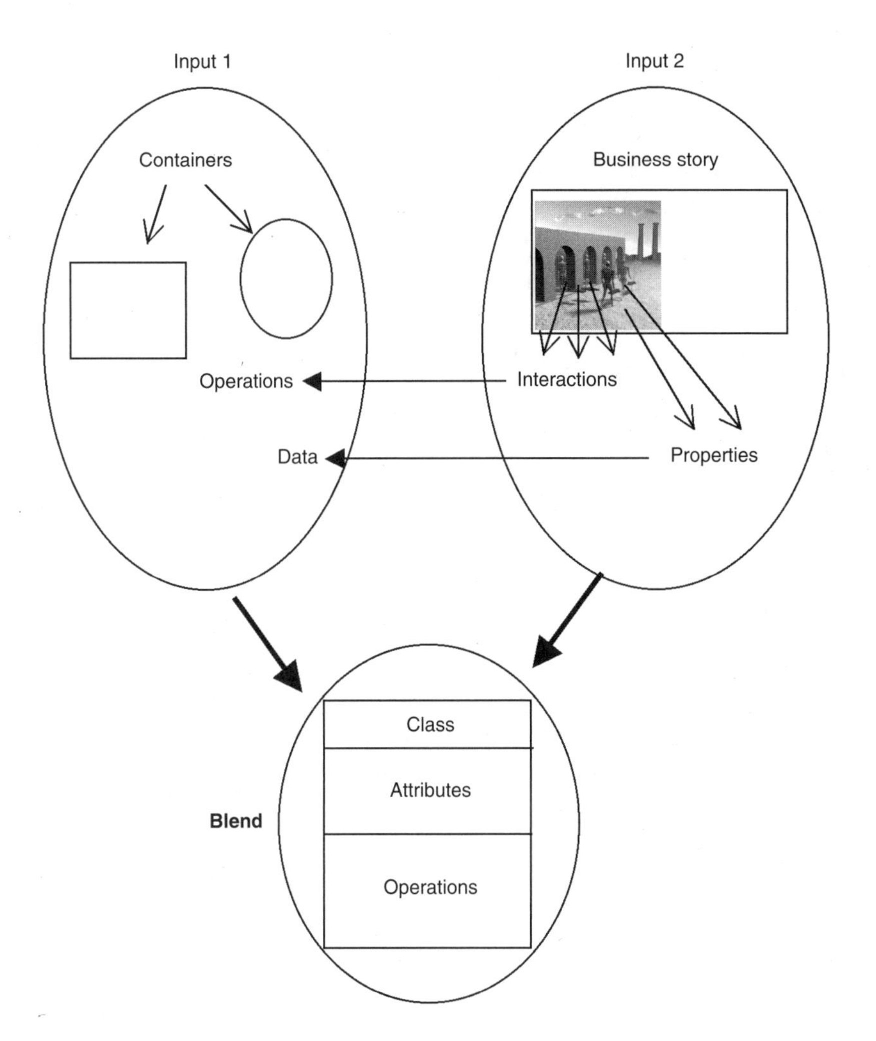

Figure 5.16
The class construct as a blend

general case, even if the entity is capable of autonomous behavior, we are not usually interested in modeling such capacities. A car is usually only represented in a structural way, as ordinarily it is considered as something constructed, stocked, or sold, as merchandise. Only in the case of simulating the features of a car would it be necessary to include its behavior.

What we really incorporate into the blend is behavior that some agents will perform on the entity we are modeling. In order to get a complete set of mental spaces, we need to analyze the different stages of the invoice in its whole business story or life cycle. So in general, there may be several other mental spaces that provide a source of behavior in terms of operations.

Looking at figure 5.17, we may imagine each mannequin as a real person or machine acting on the invoice and transforming it (writing or printing the invoice, including the delivery date, archiving it as paid, and so on) as it goes through the life cycle. Each working action done on the invoice is projected on the class "Invoice" as a compressed operation:

These outer-space relations between mental spaces of different activities (operations) to carry out a given business process and the mental space of the entity on which the operation is performed will be compressed into the blend (the class). These outer-space relations are transformed—compressed—into inner-space (the blended space or class) relations as methods of the class. Each operation corresponds to an outer-space cause-to-effect link between an agent and an entity. The cause, the agent, determines that a given attribute is created, modified, or deleted, the effect. The corresponding compressed inner-space relation is a method capable of applying the same transformations to attributes of the class.

Figure 5.18 shows how the outer-space relations between agent 2 in activity 2 and task 2.1 applied to some attribute of the real-life invoice (for example, writing a name) is compressed into an inner-space relation: operation

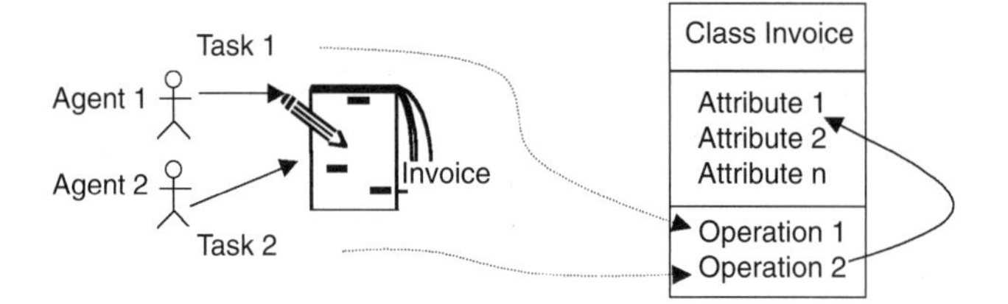

Figure 5.17
Agents operating on an invoice

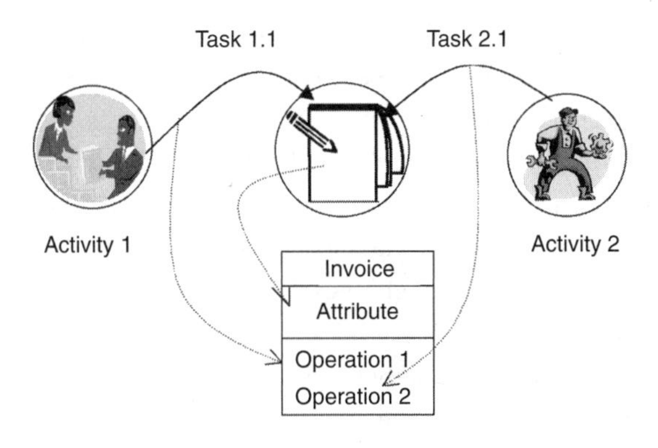

Figure 5.18
Outer-space relations compressed into an inner-space relation

2 applied to attribute 1 of the Class Invoice. The transformation of an outer-space relation into an inner-space relation is normally carried out when entities of other mental spaces perform some type of activity over the entity of the mental space we are considering, like the invoice entity. Not all types of outer-space relations are transformed into inner-space relations, they are just represented as attributes-link (references or pointers) in order to capture such connections between different mental spaces.

As a consequence of creating the blend, there will be an emergent structure in a class regarding the input mental spaces. We may see that an invoice class—in contrast to a real-world invoice—will generate objects capable of producing events or sending messages to other objects. This behavior is something that real, inanimate invoices cannot do.

The folk theory of object orientation argues that OO concepts are close to real-world situations. Clearly this is not quite true. It is evident that the name of many classes along with some of their attributes and methods refer to real-world circumstances in the usual sense. But the concept of class itself is a complex blend, an imaginative creation made by software engineers. In many cases, it has no direct referent in the real world. Some tasks of real-world activities are selectively projected to the blend (class), but a class usually includes other operations not directly derivable from real-world activities: they are projected from the interaction of a given class with other classes.

There are classes that are included in the model, typically in later stages of the blend, because they are needed to optimize the model, and usually they are called helpers. They are elements of the model we need to help solve a given problem. For example, between the class Hotel and the class Customer, there is a relation to indicate that the customer is accommodated at the hotel. This is an outer-space relation between two mental spaces referring to a situation in the real world. But this is an abstract relation between both classes, and we will soon need to further refine it if we are to implement a suitable computer system. For instance, an additional class such as a transaction class will be needed in order to model the different charges the customer may generate while staying at the hotel.

A general pragmatic clue to determine whether a given mental space may project a relation in a compressed way over the blend is considering if such mental space corresponds to an actor that directly performs a task over the entity we are considering. Let us explore the example of the invoice by adding two new mental spaces: a clerk that modifies the invoice and a customer that sends the invoice (figure 5.19).

This example shows that the mental space of the clerk modifying the invoice will project a compressed relation, so the operation of modifying will be incorporated into the blend, while the mental space of the customer will also project some structure over the blend: the representation of its identification in order to maintain the outer-space relation between both mental spaces.

As we mentioned briefly in chapter 3, Fauconnier and Turner (2002) define some vital relations. These are the types of outer-space relations that may be compressed into inner-space relations, and include cause-effect, role, change, time, identity, intentionality, representation, and part-whole, among others. When constructing classes, the cause-effect relation is the most frequently compressed one from external spaces. Another relation that is projected, but

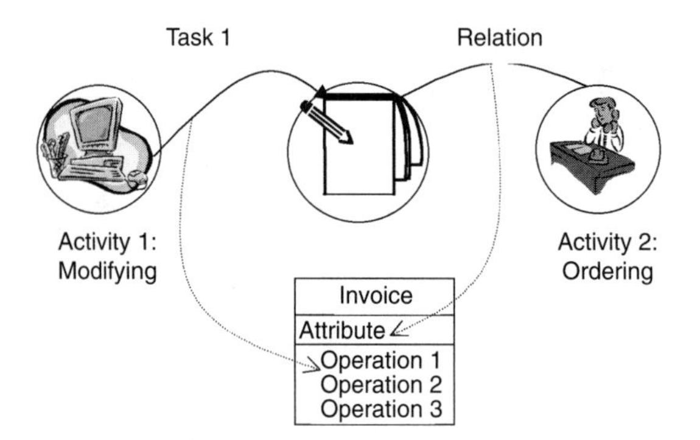

Figure 5.19
Adding new mental spaces to invoice example

not compressed, into the blend is the role relation. For example, a customer owns orders. We project the relation between both mental spaces (of the customer being an owner—that is, their role) into one of the classes by including a representation of it. We say that the role is not compressed into a class because usually both classes remain as individual ones (the class Customer and the class Order) and the relation is projected into one of the classes as an attribute; in this case, it would normally be the Order class, which includes a reference—attribute—to the Customer class.

In the example of figure 5.19, we observe that the relation of modifying the invoice is a cause-effect relation as the clerk may be the cause of some modifications to the invoice. This external relation between two spaces is compressed into the blend.

To sum up, some outer-space relations from the domain are compressed into the blend. The type of relation usually compressed is the cause-effect relation in the form of operations. Some outer-space relations from the domain are projected into the blend. The type of relation usually projected into the blend is the role relation in the form of an attribute. Not all outer-space relations of the blend come from the input mental spaces of the domain—that is, they are provided by additional classes of the model, not necessarily derived from the real-world domain.

All we have seen concerns the analysis phase—that is, the first draft of an OO analysis model. The next phase—design—refines the abstract model to produce a design model that only adds classes derived from the required solution and is not related to any type of real situation.

Just as we instantiate a class, such as the Invoice class, from the class construct, so concrete invoices are instantiated from the Invoice class, each one with the same characteristics of the others. The difference between both processes is that the first one is a manual, imaginative process, while the second may be automated as the class from which an object is an instance is a highly framed one (all attributes and operations are perfectly defined).

The fourth container of the class blend will contain a list of responsibilities of the class. This concept has been taken from the mental space of social obligations, particularly those derived from a collaborative activity such as jobs at work. As we have seen, the use of such mental space implies that we are employing an underlying metaphor: OBJECTS ARE PEOPLE.

In particular, each object has a general goal, its responsibility, in its interactions with other objects. The concept of responsibility is a way of specifying at a high level the goals that an object is designed to achieve. From a list of general responsibilities, we will be able to derive most of the operations a class may be required to have.

In line with the underlying metaphor, one of the first methods used to analyze a system in terms of object orientation was the cards, responsibilities, and collaborations method (Booch, Rumbaugh, and Jacobson 1999). When using this approach, a group of designers begin by taking a card and writing the list of responsibilities and collaborations on it. A responsibility corresponds in general to a set of operations. The concept of collaboration is also important because it is the way of conceptualizing the set of classes that must interact with each other in order to produce the whole system behavior. In this way, the responsibility is the starting point, while the collaboration is the whole consequence—the set of events triggered by the initial point—of such responsibility.

The container of responsibilities is aimed at those participants in design who may use the cards, responsibilities, and collaborations method, or that need an initial list of responsibilities, which are later to be refined as operations. The problem with the concept of responsibility is that it is closely associated with that of collaboration, and in order for us to specify a given collaboration we need to have previously defined the participant classes. As it has been pointed out in the previous sections, the process of creating models implies some interactions in which further classes are included in the model, so a collaboration may not be completely specified until all participant classes are already defined. It is also true that collaborations may be gradually refined, even if we do not have all the participant classes.

A Basic Ontology for SE

Taking a cognitive semantics perspective, we view the domain of ontologies as, in fact, the realm of epistemology. It is not a question of knowing what is out there; it is how we come to our representation. Another issue concerns finding a minimum set of ontological elements in order to build an ontology. (As the use of the word ontology is so ubiquitous in software, we continue using it even if it would be preferable to use the term epistemology.)

As Johanna Seibt (2001) points out, there is more explanatory power in an ontology with fewer basic notions than there is with many. Dov Dori (2002, 82) argues similarly, criticizing the size of the UML alphabet—150 symbols and 9 diagram types: "Since UML has evolved bottom-up from OO programming concepts, it lacks a system-theoretical ontological foundation encompassing observations about common features characterizing systems regardless of domain."

Therefore, the need for an available minimum set of concepts to be used as the ontological foundation of SE notation (in particular UML) becomes increasingly compelling. Our proposal has the following notions:

- Class;
- Relationship;
- Instantiation;
- Time;
- Event.

Class

A class is a blend that describes structural and behavioral features. This concept may be used to define other, derived concepts. In UML, there is an equivalent concept, that of classifier, but the difference between class and classifier is not clear, as both are defined as encompassing structure and behavior. The class is a general frame or schema used to instantiate more concrete classes belonging to a given domain (as order, invoice, bill, picture, or money).

Relationship

This concept is based on the link image schema. It is a general connection between other modeling elements. It is clear that neither classes nor relationships are things that exist in the real world. Classes are blends—existing as conceptual elements—that may be eventually implemented in a computer in order to build up a software system. Relationships emerge from our interests, goals, or desires regarding elements of the external world (these "external" elements may be physical, cultural, scientific, and so on—that is, elements different from the "cognitive" ones).

Instantiation

Instantiations are blends applied to the general class concept (or to particular classes to produce objects) in order to get specific ones. Unlike the definition proposed by Wolfgang Degen and colleagues (2001), our definition allows us to iterate the instantiation process. Some instantiations are blends from different mental spaces and others are processes occurring on the computer, as when instantiating a specific class to produce objects. Note that, in fact, before occurring in the computer, the latter instantiation occurred in our minds when writing a program or an object's method where the instantiation takes place.

Time

Time cannot be observed as something in the external world. All we can do is to observe events and compare them. As Lakoff and Johnson (1999, 138) remark, "In the world, there are iterative events against which other events are compared. We define time by metonymy: successive iterations of a type of event stand for intervals of 'time.' Consequently, the basic literal properties of our concept of time are consequences of properties of events."

It might be shocking not to have an objective metaphysics (or ontology) of time. All we have is a concept defined by metonymy and multiple metaphors. Time is one of the concepts analyzed at length by Lakoff and Johnson (1980).

- TIME IS A RESOURCE You have some time left, I've got plenty of time to do that, and so on.
- TIME IS MONEY I have to budget my time, I've invested a lot of time on this project, and so forth.

There is simply no literal definition for time.

Event

As in the case of time, the concept of event and others associated with it—like causes, changes, states, actions, and purposes—are not just reflections of a mind-independent reality. They are fundamentally human concepts. They arise from human biology and are essentially metaphorical concepts.

As Lakoff and Johnson (1980, 178–179) explain: "Our most fundamental understanding of what events and causes are comes from two fundamental metaphors, which we shall call the Location and Object Event-Structure metaphors. Both make use of the primary metaphors Causes Are Forces and Changes Are Movements." That is, one conceptualizes events in terms of locations, while the other sees them in terms of objects.

- EVENTS ARE LOCATIONS You're in a deep depression, we're far from safety, and so on.
- EVENTS ARE OBJECTS Things seem to be going with me, things took a turn for the worse, and the like.

What Lakoff and Johnson call the "Event-Structure" corresponds to a whole structure of concepts integrated in the same metaphor. Such concepts are states, changes, causes, causation, actions, purposes, means, difficulties, freedom of action, external events, and long-term purposeful activities.

This is the basic SE ontology from which other concepts can be developed. And we can see that herein lies a fundamental problem for HCI and SE: there is no conceptualization of people in the ontology.

6 Human-Computer Interaction

In the previous chapter, we showed that SE methods have undergone a transition in their constitutive metaphor: from THE SYSTEM IS AN INDUSTRIAL PLANT to THE SYSTEM IS A SOCIETY OF PEOPLE. In fact, while there has been a transition regarding the dominant constitutive metaphor, the final result is a situation where both metaphors are employed simultaneously. Although object orientation may be considered as the dominant paradigm (based on the second metaphor), concepts such as component, plug-in, or framework illustrate the industrial plant source. This superposition of different metaphors reveals that one approach is rarely enough to create a valid and exhaustive discourse regarding any scientific or technical domain.

In HCI, we have seen similar issues moving from HCI IS A DIALOGUE to HCI IS DIRECT MANIPULATION. Ben Shneiderman coined this phrase in the late 1970s to characterize the new interfaces of the time that had windows, icons, menus, and pointers. He noted that one aspect of direct manipulation was a visual representation of the world of action, adding that objects of interest and the actions of interest were shown on the screen, continuously. It was direct manipulation because just like door handles, there were small rapid, reversible actions and immediate feedback. Direct manipulation interfaces avoided the complex syntax of the previous generation of language-style interfaces.

In fact, there are many competing views on the best way to conceptualize HCI. Jenny Preece, Yvonne Rogers, and Helen Sharp (2002) describe various "conceptual models" that we might characterize as HCI IS INSTRUCTING THE SYSTEM, HCI IS A CONVERSATION, HCI IS DIRECT MANIPULATION, HCI IS NAVIGATION, HCI IS BROWSING. These different conceptualizations coexist across the many different types of devices we now interact with.

David Benyon, Phil Turner, and Susan Turner (2005) provide a framework for HCI based on four key components; people, activities, contexts, and

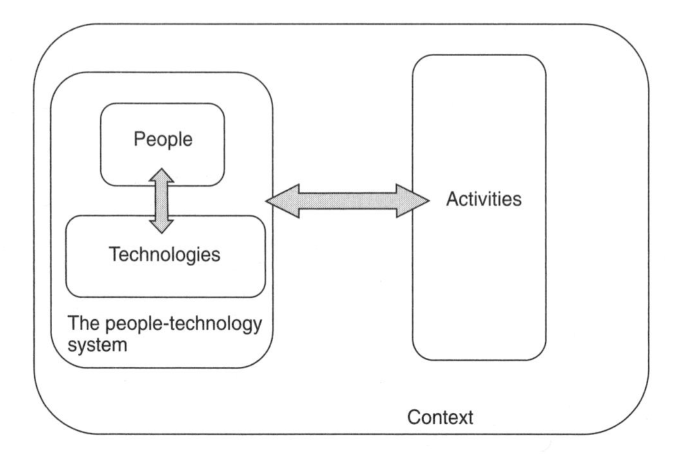

Figure 6.1
The people, activities, contexts, and technologies framework for HCI

technologies (see figure 6.1). HCI is about harmonizing these within some domain. Nevertheless, one problem HCI faces is that no sooner has some technology (such as software, or a combination of hardware and software) been developed to support some activity, than the technology will change the nature of the activity. This, in turn, will create new requirements for technologies. Consider how the domain of watching movies has changed as the technology has gone from cinema, to television, to video, to CD, to DVD, to mobile devices.

Another way to look at the relationships between people, activities, contexts, and technologies is to see it as a series of blends—a conceptual integration network. People coming together with a context leads to some activities. These activities make use of technologies creating a new context within which people undertake activities, and so the process continues. In particular taking people, activities, and contexts on one side of a blend and technologies on the other characterizes the HCI problem nicely. These two input spaces have different organizing frames. Human activities are concerned with achieving human goals, but technology is ultimately constrained by having to be instructed through a series of actions. The tension between these two frames means that most HCI is concerned with what Fauconnier and Turner call double-scope blends.

We have seen that single-scope blends are those in which both input spaces may have a different organizing frame, but one of them is projected to organize the blend. When both input spaces partially project their organizing frames to the blend, we refer to it as a double-scope blend. The organizing frame of the blend includes parts of each of those frames and has an emergent structure of its own. Another aspect of a double-scope blend is that "both organizing frames make central contributions to the blend, and their sharp differences offer the possibility of rich clashes. Far from blocking the construction of the network, such clashes offer challenges to the imagination: indeed, the resulting blends can be highly creative" (Fauconnier and Turner 2002, 131).

In chapter 3, we provided a first example of such clashes when a surgeon is equated to a butcher: THE SURGEON IS A BUTCHER. The incongruity of a butcher's means with a surgeon's ends leads to the central inference that the surgeon is incompetent, then offering an imaginative emergent structure that could have hardly been foreseen in advance.

In HCI, one double-scope blend is the desktop interface. The two principal inputs have different organizing frames: the frame of office work and the frame of traditional computer commands. The emergent properties of the blend include a number of physical features such as dragging, clicking, double clicking, and so on. Once the blend has been established through the first graphical user interfaces and become entrenched, we no longer see the original input spaces. New examples, however, such as the Macintosh OS X, based on a kernel of the UNIX OS, show us that the blend continues being valid, as one of the input spaces (UNIX) is a space of commands.

HCI focuses on accessibility, usability, acceptability, and engagement, aiming to achieve a harmony of the four components; HCI is getting people, activities, contexts, and technologies to sing in tune. HCI is difficult and complex, and in order to equip ourselves with the necessary conceptual tools to understand and design for HCI, we need to explore some more ideas and concepts from conceptual integration—principles for developing good blends.

If we look at figure 6.1 as the organizing frame for thinking about HCI, we can see that there are several levels at which we can consider HCI. Between people and the technologies are the actions that people have to take, such as pressing buttons, pointing with a mouse, or selecting items from a menu. If we take the people-technology system as our unit of analysis, we can consider the relationship between this system (sometimes also called the work system) and the activities of the domain. This is the task level of description. We can also consider the overall objectives or goals that this system has. Following a discussion of the principles of blends, we then look at HCI at the detailed level of actions, the intermediate level of tasks, and the high level of goals. We conclude with a look forward to a harmonized whole of future interactions.

Principles of Blends

Fauconnier and Turner (2002) devote a chapter of their book to the principles required to define the process of blending. To be useful, a theory must deal with constraints. It is no good trying to explain something if you finish up explaining everything. What, then, are the principles underlying the process of blending? For a game like football there are "constitutive principles," rules that constitute the activity and distinguish it from other activities, such as shopping, boxing, or watching television. The rules of football determine how each player in the game must behave, indicating what is valid and what is prohibited, what is necessary and what is not. But these general constitutive principles will not tell us what we will see in a particular game. There are multiple additional rules, strategies, and concepts developed in different cultural contexts that will also be employed, but that go far beyond the "rules of the game." Some behaviors, even if they are not prohibited by the rules, are never applied. Other behaviors would just be strange—such as sitting and watching your opponents when playing football with them. These behaviors do not contribute to an important feature of playing football—namely, winning a game. These additional rules, which are emergent from the previous constitutive ones, are called "governing principles."

In terms of blending, constitutive principles are concerned with the rules of blending, with the legitimate processes of integrated networks of mental spaces. We have described these in chapter 3. Governing principles are concerned with understanding the optimal strategies for developing effective blends. One significant observation is that these two levels of constraint (constitutive and governing principles) will not determine the final result. They will tell you many things that will not happen, but will not tell you exactly what will happen. In the case of blending, constitutive principles place constraints on the process, while governing principles provide strategies that further limit their scope.

The key aim in applying principles is to arrive at a blend "at a human scale." The embodiment notion that underlies experientialism, embodied cognition, and so on, argues that we think as we do because we are human and live in human societies (chapter 2). Our cognition is fundamentally embodied; we feel knowledge and understanding. Accordingly, we should aim for blends that describe activities at an appropriate level of perception and action for people, and that use familiar background frames. The blend needs to tell a good story that engages the imagination. It should avoid unnecessary clutter and detail, ensuring that the key issues, the vital relations, stand out. Although there are times when these different principles will conflict, the adept designer will get to know and understand them, developing the skill and tacit knowledge of when and where to apply them.

Compression

One of the main features of blending is that the relations between the input spaces are compressed into relationships in the blend. Two sets of relations need to be considered: relations between elements within a single space (inner relations) and those across the input spaces (outer relations). It is vital that the appropriate relations are preserved in the blend. One key principle, then, is "Borrowing for compression." Fauconnier and Turner (2002) explain that when one input has an existing tight coherence on a human scale but the other one does not, then we should project the one that operates at a human scale. They use the desktop interface as an example, contending that office work is more humanly scaled than computer commands and so this is rightly projected into the blend.

"Single-relation compression by scaling" is a governing principle that refers to the fact that some inner- or outer-space vital relations can be scaled to a more compressed version of the same vital relation in the blend. When considering object classes (chapter 5), we have seen that classes compress outer-space vital relations belonging to a business story into operations that objects will be able to perform.

"Single-relation compression by syncopation" is a principle that relations with a diffuse structure can be compressed into the blend by dropping out all but a few key elements. For instance, this type of compression would convert a whole business story to only two possible crucial elements or states. Taking the trash can as an example, it is represented as either empty or not empty. None of the intermediate states are shown because they are not important for the blend.

"Highlights compression" applies when a set of elements in a whole story can be compressed into a simultaneous arrangement in the blend. This is the

Figure 6.2
Highlights compression applied to the trash can story

case when we take, for example, an everyday story of throwing documents into the trash can. In the desktop interface, this icon can have only two possible states: empty and full. The full state means that the trash can contains at least one document, but it does not change if it contains many documents.

Besides the principles of compression, certain other characteristics of blends are desirable. These are addressed through the principles of topology, pattern completion, integration, web, and unpacking. As we will see, it is often not possible to satisfy all of these at the same time, so designers need to make decisions informed by these principles, rather than governed by them.

Topology

Topology concerns the logical arrangements of the elements of an input space. When considering both input spaces, it is useful to analyze relations within and between input spaces. The first are called "inner-space topology" and the second "outer-space topology." There are various possibilities for projecting inner- and outer-space topologies to the blend. In the example of the desktop interface, we can see that topology has been relaxed since unlike real-life offices, the trash can is on the desktop. According to the topology principle, the trash can would have been placed off the desktop in the desktop interface blend, but this decision would destroy the internal integration of the blend.

Even if we can think also that this decision is the result of projecting geometrically a three-dimensional space onto a two-dimensional one (the screen), it is easier to have the trash can at hand, and not to perform an intermediate step in order to show it and then move the desired documents into the trash can. This optimization derives from the principle of integration. Another argument may point out that the original input space is a desktop, but the resulting blend is not necessarily a replica of the original desktop, so we may talk of a generic work space in which different items appear: folders, documents, sound and video devices, applications, and even a trash can. Indeed, as the collection of elements contained on the desktop increase more and more, we would better speak of an office or work space and not of the traditional desktop surface.

This issue shows an interesting aspect of blends: using the same metaphor of running the blend, we may consider the blend as a nonstop running application executing in a detached manner. That means that blends evolve as biological beings—they are running in a background status—so what initially could be considered as a desktop surface needs later to be approached as a generic three-dimensional space.

Principles for Integration

Integration may be considered as one of the main principles of blending; "integrated blends is an overarching principle of human cognition" (Fauconnier and Turner 2002, 328). The aim of blending is to achieve an integrated conceptualization so that it can be manipulated as a unit, as a whole structure. A well-integrated blend is easier to memorize. People can run the blend without having to remember where the inputs have come from and without having to take into consideration other aspects of the integration network.

Pattern completion is a principle that seeks to bring background knowledge to the blend in a systematic way. If there is an existing integrated frame that can be recruited to complete the blend it should be used. One attempt at completing the desktop interface blend is the Magic Cap interface (Gentner and Nielsen 1996). The office frame is brought into the blend in order to make additional functions available at the interface (figure 6.3).

Web is a principle concerned with recognizing the connections between the blend and the input spaces. A good blend will have appropriate connections. Whereas topology is concerned with projecting appropriate aspects of the input spaces into the blend, web is concerned with projecting back from the blend to the input spaces. Although our focus is on the blend, the whole integration network is still there, in the background. Web concerns ensuring these backward connections are at a human scale and appropriate for people to make use of.

Related to the web principle is the unpacking principle. One important feature of blends is that they carry with them the germ of the entire network. The unpacking principle concerns designing blends so that their construction, or

Figure 6.3
An example of a pattern completion recruited to the blend

their derivation, can be understood. If there are appropriate connections from the blend to the input spaces, and from these to their input spaces, and so on, then unpacking the blend becomes easier. It is not just a question of structure, however; it is one of communication and connotation.

Fauconnier and Turner (2002) use the example of an antismoking poster in the United States. The poster shows a cowboy smoking a drooping cigarette with the caption "smoking causes impotence." The blend can be unpacked to reveal the use of the cigarette as the penis in the input space of sexual prowess and as a regular cigarette in the other input space of smoking. This process of unpacking is reminiscent of Roland Barthes' (1957) analysis of images. Indeed, it is a familiar characteristic of much advertising that key ideas from two domains are brought together into a blended image.

Fauconnier and Turner (2002) also point out that the unpacking principle helps the blend to be employed as a mnemonic device. If you see an image or an icon on a computer screen, or the screen of a mobile phone, and can unpack the blend, it reminds you of what the function of that icon is.

Relevance and Recursion

Elements in the blend should be relevant to the purpose of the blend. There should not be unnecessary elements in a blend. The relevance principle relates to the integration network, and elements should be relevant to the business of being able to unpack the blend. Of course relevance is a subjective issue, and we should not be overly dictated to by the network structure. There may be important emotional or aesthetic relations in the input spaces that need to be projected into the blend. Elements may be included in a blend to promote the feel of the blend over its logic.

A blended space from one network can often be used as an input to another network. This is what Fauconnier and Turner (2002) call the principle of recursion. By employing blends as input spaces in new blends, a further level of compression is achieved. If the first blend is at a human scale and captures the essential relations, then when it is reused, these benefits can be projected into the new network.

The Principles in Action

The governing principles (though we prefer the term "guiding principles") for blends interact in complex ways, as we will see when we return to designing with blends in chapter 8. For example, the classic historical example of the failure to achieve the integration principle is the use of the trash can to eject some external devices, such as floppy disks on early Macintosh computers. The current version of the Mac operating system has modified the design to remove the problem. As an external storage device is moved toward the trash icon, the icon changes into an eject button icon (figure 6.4). The user may choose to click directly on an eject icon or drag storage devices toward the trash can to eject them, but at least they no longer have to put them in the trash can.

Figure 6.4
Replacement of the trash can sign for ejecting or dismounting

Even if this design problem has been overcome, it is worth analyzing it, and discussing Fauconnier and Turner's (2002) analysis, in order to see the interplay of the governing principles. They argue that in the old trash can design, there are failures of integration, topology, and web. The solution provides good compression, but compression may not be employed when there are two functions that should have been kept separate in the blend for other reasons, such as to preserve topology or integration. In this case, we should speak more specifically of cohesion as a particular aspect of integration.

Fauconnier and Turner (2002, 341) suggest there are violations of integration in three ways:

1. There is a contradiction in the dual role of the trash can, as one of them is used to keep (maintain) the external device rather than discard it.
2. Any operation of dragging one icon to another has the result that the first is contained in the second, with the exception of dragging external devices to the trash can.
3. For all other manipulations of icons on the desktop, the result is a computation, but in this case it is a physical interaction at the level of the hardware.

We would object to the second and third arguments above. Dragging one icon to another may have a result other than containment—for example, opening a document when dragged to the appropriate application. Some other manipulation of icons may result in a physical interaction at the level of hardware, such as writing a CD or DVD, printing a document, and so on. Moreover, there is no "pure hardware interaction" as even a simple function such as ejecting a floppy implies some computation.

Thus, there is fundamentally only one contradiction in the dual role of the trash can when considering violations—the integration principle. We have seen that the trash can violates topology because it is on the desktop rather than under the desk. In the input space of offices, putting an object in a folder or the trash can results in containment, and this topology is projected to the blend with the exception of dragging an external device to the trash can when it is ejected. Another violation of the topology principle derives from the fact that in the input space of offices, items transferred to the trash can are unwanted and destined to become irretrievable.

Another example discussed by Fauconnier and Turner is the competition among the governing principles applied to select-copy-paste used in word-processing programs. Fauconnier and Turner (2002, 341) argue that:

it violates Topology because in the input where text is actually copied by scribes or Xerox machines, copying (after selection) is a one-step operation. There is no pasting and no clipboard. Properties specific to the Integration in the blend make it convenient to decompose this operation into two steps, but they do not map topologically onto corresponding operations in the input of "real copying."

If one of the input spaces here is a photocopy machine, we may break the process down into three steps:

1. *Select* Taking the documents to be copied;
2. *Copy* The process of being read and transferred to the roll;
3. *Paste* The process of being printed into n copies.

There is even a clipboard: the roll where the document is kept electronically during the whole document-copying session.

If the process is performed by a scribe, we may observe similar steps:

1. *Select* Taking the papyrus to be copied;
2. *Copy* The process of reading a phrase or paragraph, and storing it in immediate memory;
3. *Paste* The process of writing the phrase/paragraph.

There is also a clipboard: the short-term—and capacity—of the scribe's memory used to memorize phrases and paragraphs. (If, however, we believe one of the spaces heralds from the domain of journalism, then we might interpret things differently, as discussed briefly in chapter 8.)

It may be argued that we are using the structure from the word-processing programs and projecting it back to "real copying," but this mapping of structure from blends to input spaces is quite likely, and it helps to see the hidden structure that was already out there. Another point is the dissimilar use of the same word, copy, applied to both whole processes of copying a document and a step in the process (reading and storing in memory, or some electromechanical device). What we need to take into account when analyzing topology is the isomorphic mapping between both structures: the word-processing and real copying processes independently of using similar words for different purposes.

Of course designs change over time. In the case of the current word-processing programs, some modifications have been introduced that allow moving text directly by selecting and dragging it, or copying text by selecting and dragging it while clicking a key to differentiate both operations (so-called drag-and-drop editing). While dragging the selected text, it does not actually "move" to the new location until the mouse is unclicked, but there is a "clone" or "ghost" of the text that physically moves as the mouse is dragged on. It is possible to copy text the same way, by clicking at the same time the Alt key. We recognize that it is a copy and not a move because there is a ⊕ sign added to the clone of the text.

Principles of blends are useful for understanding the difficulties with existing designs and guiding new designs. Yet as we have seen, they are not foolproof. There are assumptions as to where the input spaces originated and this drives how the network is unpacked. As blends become more entrenched, the web becomes more difficult to see and unpack. It is not necessary to remember all the principles individually as many of them are concerned with general issues of good design. What is important is to be a good software critic able to reason about designs. Digital literacy is about recognizing that the blends in HCI need to be at a human scale if they are to be successful at fitting in with people's lives.

Actions in HCI

The basic actions for interacting with computers have evolved over the last twenty to thirty years. They can be seen as blends between the input spaces of the characteristics of input devices as one space and the basic manual actions as the other. These basic actions are subsequently given some meaning, as they are themselves used in more complex blends.

In this section, we look at how the conceptual integration network for working with a mouse and a graphic user interface works. Of course as new devices proliferate, new and different actions and meanings are created. The rocker switch of a mobile phone or the click wheel of an iPod are new methods of input that are blended with the actions of a particular domain to create new interactions, such as "select a track," "answer a message," and so on. Figure 6.5 shows the manipulation or handling blend, which takes a new device as input space 1 (mouse, joystick, or trackpad) and manual usual actions as input space 2.

In the blend, we also have composite units built on the basic three elements and the emergence of new meanings:

- *Click* = press + release, which also may mean "select";
- *Double click* = click + click, which means "open";

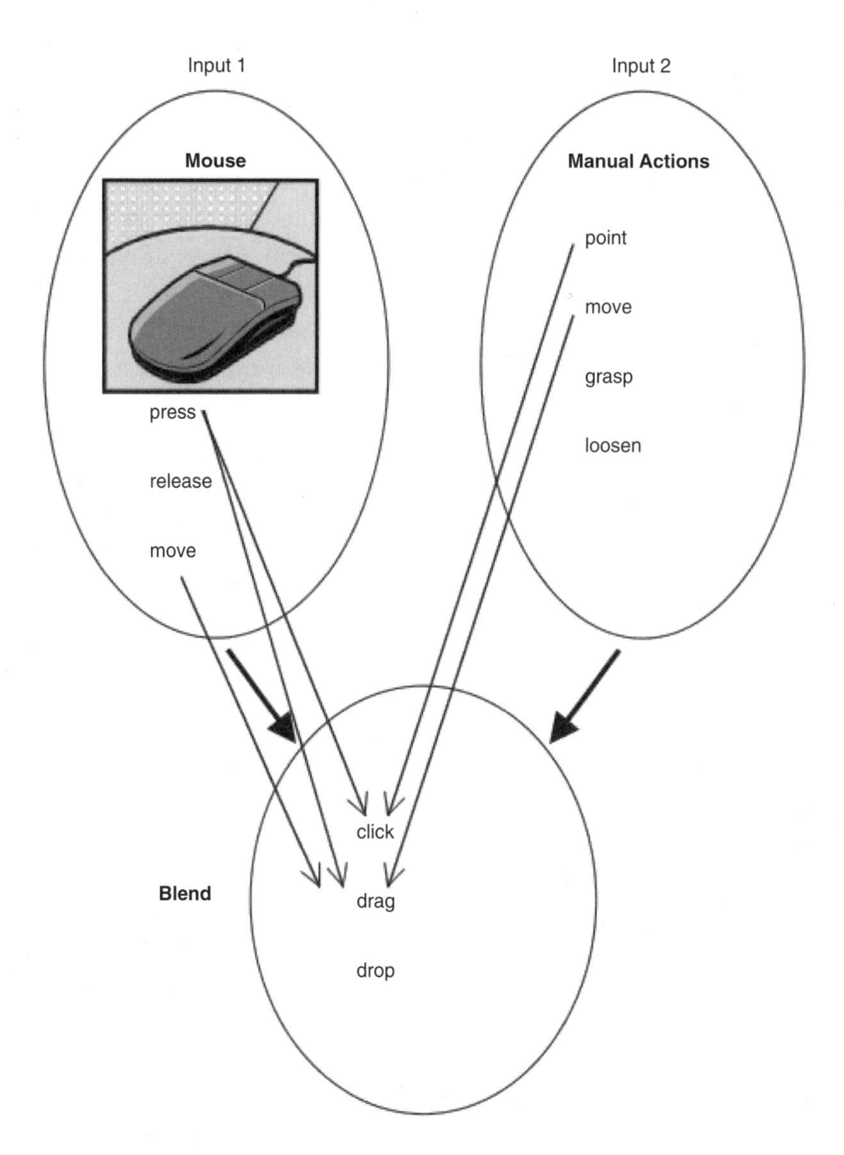

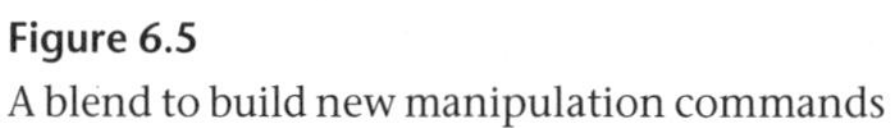

Figure 6.5
A blend to build new manipulation commands

- *Drag* = press + move, meaning “moving something”;
- *Drop* = release (after dragging), meaning “stopping dragging.”

The recursion governing principle tells us that there are chains of blends where some of them take the blend resulting from previous conceptual integrations as the input space. Once the manipulation blend has been built, it can be used as input to various subsequent blends. For example, it may be taken as input to build the folder blend as illustrated in figure 6.6. Here, we can see the blend of the basic graphical user interface actions with the second input space of real-world folders. This results in the operations described in the blend.

This process of blending results in a set of computer-based signs. Thus, we see the icon above and we recognize it as a folder. Different computer-based signs have different handling features. A folder sign, for instance, has:

- *Select* = click on the sign;
- *Open* = double click on the sign;
- *Drag* = drag on the sign to change its position on the interface;
- *Move into* = drag and drop an object on the sign.

On the other hand, a button normally has only one (click) meaning—in this case, activation or triggering. On the personal computer, different meanings can be attributed to a left click and a right click.

In the case of current Mac OS X folders, they can have various different colors, various sizes, and one of two shapes indicating open or closed. Both the size and shape are permanent characteristics of a folder. In the case of the color, there are two possibilities, each indicating a different state of the folder: normal state (light blue), selected (dark blue), and opened (open shape and dark blue). The state of opened has two substates: one is the open shape and dark blue; if another object is dragged on the folder and held there, the folder is actually opened and seen as a new window.

The trash can sign has properties similar to those of the folder sign plus a new emergent one: delete. A trash can sign has the following features:

- *Select* = click on the sign;
- *Open* = double click on the sign;
- *Drag* = drag on the sign to change its position on the interface;
- *Move into* = drag and drop an object on the sign;
- *Delete* = click on the appropriate option in the main menu.

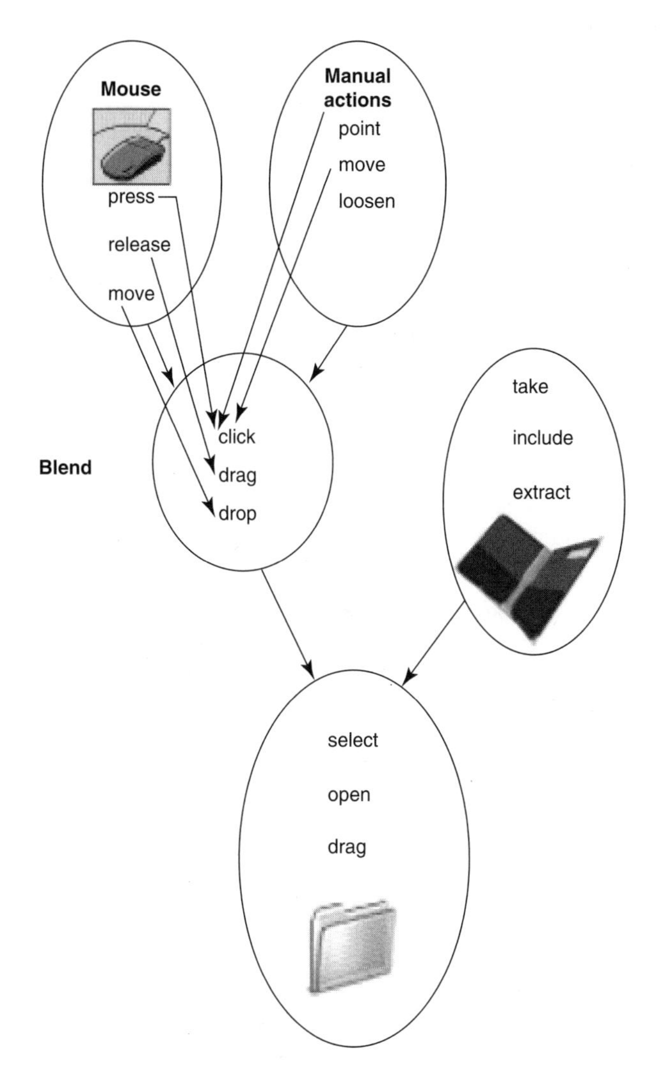

Figure 6.6
The folder blend

The blend is built the same way we produced the folder blend: using the previous blend of manipulation or handling blended with the usual actions performed on everyday trash cans and the space of computer commands (figure 6.7).

If we do not want to violate the topology governing principle of the second input space (real-world trash cans) while at the same time using as much generic-level structure from the third input space (computer commands) as is consistent with this preservation, it is evident that the resulting sign will usually perform a transition from an *empty* to a *half-full* state, but will never achieve a *full* state. This is a consequence of the new created image-schematic structure where there is no limit to the amount of objects to be deleted. The virtual full state could be reached as a consequence of an exceptional operating system or hard-disk condition, but it is not an inherent trash can state. That is, it is not a state resulting from the blend; quite the opposite, the obtained result is an *unlimited* container.

The structure of "unlimited capacity of the trash can" is emergent when contrasting both input spaces, where the trash can belongs to the category of containers, and hence objects of a limited capacity. The idea of limit derives from the finite capacity of a real trash can when taken as a source domain for projecting structure from such an input space.

The implementation details of a command such as *delete* is in fact a "logical deletion." It only assigns to the object (document, folder, or whatever) a state indicator to show that it has been logically deleted. The physical deletion, on the other hand, will imply the "real" deletion of the object, but even this action may be performed using a second indicator in order to suggest that such space could be used for other objects. Thus, the structure of the trash can with limited capacity is projected from real-world trash cans and not from implementations of folders. This implementation strategy clearly shows that the trash can does not need to be implemented—for example, as a type of folder—nor is its capacity the entire unused capacity of the system, as Fauconnier and Turner (2002) mistakenly suggest. The emergent structure cannot be anticipated and is not necessarily deducible from the input spaces.

Another example of an emergent structure is dragging icons with the mouse. This operation belongs to neither moving objects on a desktop nor giving standard symbolic commands. It is a consequence of the operation for moving an object onto another in order for the latter to contain the former. In

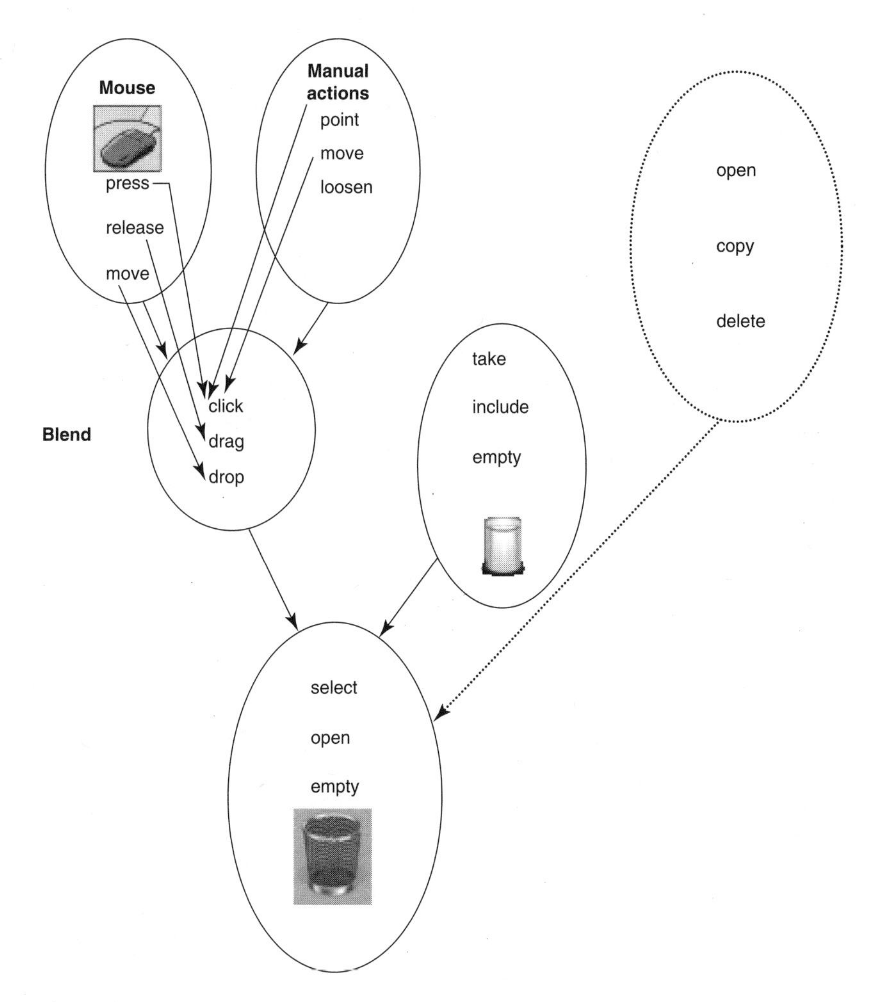

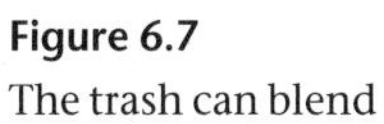

Figure 6.7
The trash can blend

the desktop interface, there is an integrated context with its own coherent structure. It could happen that while moving an object onto another, we accidentally release the button of the mouse. In such a case, we would have to produce an aborted moving, but the resulting operation must be preserved to guarantee the integration of operations. The new emergent haptic operation is a pure dragging one.

It could be asserted that the drag operation is already present in the use of the mouse. As the device used to interact with the user interface may vary from a joystick to a trackball to a finger moving on a surface (is the finger dragged or moved?), it can be considered a function of the original device used. The blend contains a structure that is not calculable from the inputs. We think this is a fundamental argument against the idea of using any calculable—or algorithmic—approach for studying conceptual integration.

Although we have focused on traditional graphical user interface actions in this analysis, it should be clear that any new interaction method will be blended from previously existing input spaces. The click wheel of the iPod blends a menu with a trackpad with a button, producing a new interface device. As haptic and gesture-based interfaces emerge, we will see more novel interactions. For example, there are already mobile phones that include a potentiometer enabling movements such as waving, scanning, and pointing to be used as input to remote systems. As more sensors become part of the interface, more possibilities will arise.

Tasks in HCI

A key concept in HCI since the earliest days is the notion of "task." The concept of task derives from a view of people, or other agents, interacting with technologies in an attempt to achieve some change in an application domain. Taken together, the people-technology system (figure 6.1) constitutes what is called a *work system* or *joint cognitive system,* which is separate from the "application domain." John Dowell and John Long (1998) emphasize that the domain is an abstraction of the real world—that is, some abstract representation of some sphere of activity. Importantly, task analysis is concerned with some aspects of the performance of a work system with respect to a domain. This performance may be the amount of effort to learn or reach a certain level of competence with a system, the time taken to perform certain tasks, and so on. This conceptualization is shown in figure 6.8.

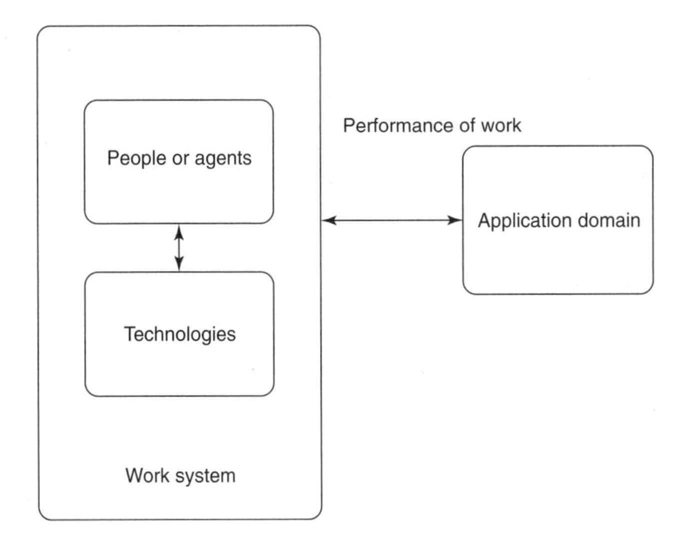

Figure 6.8
Tasks are concerned with the performance of work by a work system

Dan Diaper (2004, 15) sums up the situation as follows: "A work system in HCI consists of one or more human and computer components and usually many other sorts of thing as well. Tasks are the means by which the work system changes the application domain."

This particular view of HCI employs the underlying metaphor HCI IS THE PERFORMANCE OF WORK. One can see tasks as the blend resulting from the two input spaces of the work system and domain. Unless the work system has been carefully crafted to fit the characteristics of the domain (such as where specialized instrumentation has been developed, for example), this will be a double-scope blend with the two input spaces having different organizing frames.

The fundamental difference between the two spaces is that the work system expresses its wants and desires in terms of goals: a state of the application domain that a work system wishes to achieve. This definition allows for artificial entities such as technologies, agents, or some combination to have goals. It is not just people who have goals; the work system as a whole may have them. For this reason, the term agent is often used to encompass both people and software systems that are actively and autonomously trying to achieve some state of the application domain. The term technology is used to encompass physical devices, information artifacts, software systems, and other methods and procedures.

A task is seen as a structured set of activities. It will often consist of subtasks, where a subtask is a task at a more detailed level of abstraction. The structure of a task may include selecting between alternative actions, performing some actions a number of times, and the sequencing of actions (Benyon, Turner, and Turner 2005). The task is broken down into more and more detailed levels of description until it is defined in terms of actions. Actions are simple tasks. Whereas a task might include some structure such as doing things in a particular sequence, making decisions as to alternative things to do (selection) and doing things several times (iteration), an action does not.

A task-based view of HCI derives from the source-path-goal schema and the metaphor HCI IS A SEQUENCE OF ACTIONS. This view results in a number of task-analysis methods. Diaper (2004) makes an important observation regarding many task-analysis techniques—namely, that they are usually monoteleological. That is to say that they assume the agent or work system has a single purpose that gives rise to its goal. In reality, of course, people and work systems may be pursuing multiple goals simultaneously.

Task analysis is an important part of systems development, but it is a term that encompasses a number of different views. It is undertaken at different times during systems development for different purposes. During analysis, for example, the task analysis should aim to be as independent of existing technologies as possible for the aim is to understand the essential nature of the work in order to inform new designs. During the design and evaluation of future tasks, task analysis focuses on the achievement of work using a particular technology (that is, a particular design) and hence is device dependent.

During analysis, task analysis is concerned with the practice of work, the current allocation of function between people and technologies, existing problems, and opportunities for improvement. During design and evaluation, task analysis is concerned with the cognition demanded by a particular design, the logic of a possible design, and the future distribution of tasks and actions across people and technologies.

Because tasks are seen as consisting of subtasks that may themselves consist of subtasks, and so on, a structure chart notation is often used to represent tasks during analysis or design. Structure charts represent a sequence of tasks, subtasks, and actions as a hierarchy, and include notational conventions to show iteration, selection, and the sequencing. Paths through the hierarchy are described that aim to achieve particular goals. For example, making a call using a mobile phone has two main routes through the hierarchy of tasks and subtasks. If the person's number is in the phone's address book, then the caller has to find the number and press call. If it is not, the caller has to type the number in and press call.

Tasks are prescribed by the design of the technology and hence are often not considered at a human scale. They are described by the sequence of actions—button presses, mouse clicks, and so on. Yet rarely do people have goals of pressing buttons or clicking mouse buttons. A person's goal is perhaps to talk to their son on the phone. The tasks are thus to select the address book (press X, press Y, press Z), select the name (press A, press B, press B again), and select call (press the green telephone icon).

Goals and Personae

Another key concept in HCI is people or a "user." Users have goals—that is, things they want to achieve in the domain. In the early definitions of computer science, the user was included in more general phenomena. Allen Newell, Alan Perlis, and Herbert Simon (1967, 184) say that computer science is "the study of computers and the major phenomena that surround them." More recent definitions (Denning et al.1988,) consider that computer science is "the systematic study of algorithmic processes that describe and transform information: their theory, analysis, design, efficiency, implementation, and application," leaving us to think that those algorithmic processes must evidently include interaction with users.

For a long period, the user has been hidden or even forbidden. John Carroll (2000) has commented that it has been commonplace for large corporations to keep their designers away from their users, and Liam Bannon (1991, 25) writes: "To my astonishment, I was informed that not only could I not proceed in this fashion [go out and talk with users], but—ultimate irony—I was not allowed, for political organizational reasons, to meet with even a single user throughout this process!"

The user has been hidden in definitions of computer science where the computer was the totem and users were prostrated before it. This history of the unknown user leads us to look for a solid foundation to elaborate a more scientific concept of user. We will base our discussion on the concept of user elaborated by Alan Cooper (1999). He takes the term user as a construct in much the same way that we have seen when analyzing software objects or computer-based signs.

Cooper's (1999, 123) definition of a "persona"' is profoundly simple: "Develop a precise description of our user and what he wishes to accomplish." He continues arguing for a description that is sufficiently concrete, in the sense of a rich network of traits and relationships. It should also be a description that is verisimilar—that is, an analogue to any real or physical user.

Persona is an Etruscan origin word, meaning *mask,* which is a quite suitable way to design a prototypical person. Cooper speaks of hypothetical archetypes and not real people.

In chapter 3, we saw that basic-level categories play an important role from a perceptual and functional point of view. When considering real-world objects, the functional analysis involves a general motor program and cultural functions as well. That is why we have mental images and general motor programs for using chairs and tables, but not for a generic piece of furniture.

The same consideration may be applied to users, with the difference that they have no general motor programs to be associated with, but significant social and cultural traits that distinguish each other. So the term concrete, when applied to users or personae, must be taken as involving a richness of traits and personal characteristics in order for us to easily create mental images or mental spaces associated with any particular user (figure 6.9).

This approach of taking concrete and verisimilar characters to derive scenarios, features, and specifications is coherent with the results of cognitive semantics or embodied interaction. The problem is that we are inclined to confuse things, thinking in terms of a generic user because it is difficult to think about a concrete one. What Cooper offers us is precisely a method to construct a concrete and verisimilar user, a persona.

A persona is not a real, physical person. The fact that the actual user is immersed in the real activity does not mean that they could be a good candidate to clearly see solutions to problems. Even if real users do see solutions, they

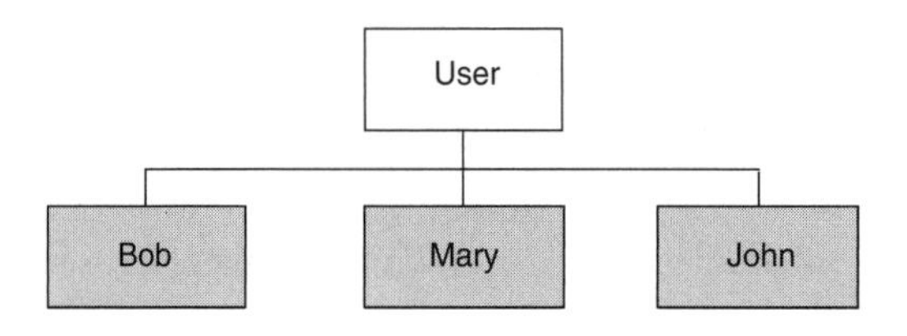

Figure 6.9
Using basic-level users or personae

do not necessarily know how to talk about what they do. Sometimes, people provide answers that they think will please the interviewer or try to project an attractive image of themselves (Carroll 2000).

So selecting a reduced group of personae will help in the process of designing a product that will satisfy a large group of actual users. When intending to create a product that must satisfy a broad audience of users, this decision will lead us to try to include a broad specter of functionalities into the product.

One of Cooper's recommendations is to be specific in order to lose the usual elasticity we assign to the word user. A first step in this direction is to assign a name to the newly created persona and perhaps a photograph. This is important in order for us to consider the persona as a basic-level entity and not take it to a higher level of abstraction. If Cooper (1999, 128) chooses a persona named Emilee, he will articulate her with singular detail and precision: "As we isolate Emilee with specific, idiosyncratic detail, a remarkable thing appears: She becomes a real person in the minds of the developers. As a real person, we can refer to her by name. She assumes a tangible solidity that puts all of our design assumptions in perspective. As she loses her elasticity, we can identify what her skills are, what her motivations are. And what she wants to achieve."

Other concepts that Cooper uses are precision and accuracy. He points out that it is more important that a persona be precise than accurate. By precision, he means concreteness. He considers it critical to define the persona in great and specific detail, in order to make this persona as concrete as we can. When Cooper speaks of accuracy, he refers to selecting the most suitable persona for the purpose.

The introduction of a cast of characters will help to solve many discussions about the introduction of new features or functions to the application to be developed. For example, consider the following discussion (Cooper 1999, 133):

Programmer: "What if the user wants to print this out?"
Interaction Designer: "Rosemary isn't interested in printing things out."
Programmer: "But someone might want to print it."
Interaction Designer: "But we are designing for Rosemary, not for someone."

The temptation to reason in terms of logical possibilities is strong for programmers, so the use of personae forces the team to reason in terms of concrete characters and stop endless discussions about users imagined in the abstract. During interviews of actual users of the future software, a new persona is created including their story. After a reasonable number of personae have been collected, a detailed analysis usually shows similarities between actual users that allow us to collapse them into one persona.

Another key issue is to make personae intentional characters, with purposes that move them into actions and explain most of their behavior. In Cooper's (1999, 149) terms, "'Good interaction design' has meaning only in the context of a person actually using it for some purpose. You cannot have purposes without people. The two are inseparable. That is why the two key elements of our design process are goals and personas; purpose and people."

When taking into account people's goals, we are better positioned to understand their needs and the meaning of their actions. This is the only way of understanding artifacts and actions, and it brings us back to the importance of looking at embodied cognition. As Dourish (2001, 207) observes, "The artifact, and the actions that people might engage in with that artifact, have meaning, both for the people engaged in those actions and for members of the community of practice. Interaction with physical artifacts, as has been explored, often also implies a reaching through those artifacts to a symbolic realm beyond."

We also think that goal-directed design helps in devising interactions that let users achieve their aims. The key aspect is to differentiate between goals and tasks: in terms of the source-path-goal image schema, a goal is an end condition or state of affairs, while tasks are the path or the intermediate stages to achieve the final result. While goals are relatively stable, tasks are transient and dependent on technology, and that is why a solution based on goals is more appropriate and, at the same time, quite likely a satisfactory design.

The same ideas are shared by Martin Fowler and Kendall Scott (2000) when they explain that a problem may happen with employing use cases. A use case, according to Fowler and Scott, is a set of scenarios tied together by a common user goal. They add that when focusing on the interaction between a user and the system, one can neglect the possibility of changing the business process where such interactions occur in order to get a solution that better fits the problem.

According to this analysis, use cases are associated with a user's goals, while business use cases are associated with business goals or business processes. Among personal goals there is the need not to be humiliated or made to feel stupid by the system. Considerations such as these are left out when taking into account only the technological aspects of the interaction.

Cooper provides an example that shows clearly how goal-directed design works and how goals may be different from the usual task analysis performed under such circumstances. He imagines Jennifer, an office manager of a small company. Her goal is to make her office run smoothly, so she must get her computer network to run smoothly. To achieve this involves:

- Setting the network properly;
- Monitoring its performance;
- Modifying its configuration periodically to maintain its peak performance.

Cooper (1999, 151) notes that "in Jennifer's mind, her job is a seamless blending of these three tasks, contributing to her one goal of smooth running. From Jennifer's point of view, there is no really difference in the three tasks. She doesn't sense a big difference between initial setup and subsequent reconfiguration of the network."

A first issue in Cooper's description corresponds to the blending of three tasks. There are two input mental spaces: one from goals, and the other from the domain of the means or tasks to be performed in order to get the goal achieved. The domain of tasks implies a sequence of execution, derived from the fact that tasks are a way of breaking the goal down. In the resulting blend the specific goal, such as the smooth running of the office, does not dictate an order in which to perform the tasks. All tasks may appear simultaneously as necessary, and Jennifer can execute them as and when required.

It is apparent that the meaning of the smooth running of the office is variable, and dependent on the activities and tasks needed to achieve such an end. Cooper's idea of considering goals as stable is correct when seen as a general intentionality of a user. The goal is a final state of a process, but the process continues performing and is dependent on the activities, which compounds the process as a whole.

As we saw in the previous section, tasks are dependent on the technology and goals are more independent. We say "more independent" because people will only form their goals given some idea of what is technologically possible. Cooper offers the example of a journey from St. Louis to San Francisco in 1850 and 1999. When considering the goals—speed, comfort, and safety—they seem to be the same, as we are using the same words, but the meaning has much changed from 1850 to the journey to Silicon Valley in 1999. The word speed remains the same, but there is a huge gap between the ten kilometers per hour of the former to the nine hundred kilometers per hour of the latter.

The same is valid for both comfort and safety, as Cooper points out, which may imply just the opposite as in the case of safety.

So what does it mean to say that the goals remain the same, when it is evident that the meaning of the three concepts associated with the new technologies has radically changed? Maybe we could say that we are seeking the best speed that fits the conditions of the time, and the same goes for comfort and safety.

The domain of tasks is technologically dependent, and their description and conceptualization results from an analysis intended to implement a system. That is why a software engineer would consider such tasks as the origin of functions to be implemented as different chunks of software. In this reasoning, it seems likely that each function has also its own chunk of interface. This is the traditional approach whereby the interface has a hierarchical list of components, and when selecting a given component from the list, it is possible to show the details in other areas of the interface.

We would call this traditional approach a task-directed one, in opposition to the previously defined goal-directed solution. The problem is that tasks are defined in terms of the needs of the software engineer and not of the user (or persona). In place of presenting a pattern of elements where it is possible to see simultaneously different aspects of the functioning of the network, the user needs to choose between a list of elements presented hierarchically and continue looking for new components in other windows until they can find all the information necessary to make a decision.

The opposition between task-directed and goal-directed approaches is the origin of the "cognitive friction," a term employed by Cooper. It is also the origin of the HCI-SE problem. The friction derives from the fact that frequently, interfaces based on components, functions, and so on (useful concepts for developing software systems) are not suitable for a user's goals.

Another example may help to understand this issue. For a long time, the idea of using the hierarchical representation of folders and subfolders has been criticized as not being appropriate for the user's goals and needs. The tradition dates back to the first operating systems and is the main solution adopted by all file systems. It is the mechanism used by the operating system in order to classify and allocate all folders and documents into the system. But this solution produces many inconveniences to users, who usually need to navigate through various levels of depth in order to find their documents. A

Figure 6.10
A goal-directed design of a browser: on the left are all the folders we need

new goal-directed solution has been implemented in the new releases of Mac OS X, which has a browser with all the folders needed by the user presented as if they were in the same higher-level folder independent of their hierarchical locations (figure 6.10).

Cooper divides goals into four categories: personal, corporate, practical, and false goals. Personal goals consist of things like not feeling stupid, not making mistakes, and having fun. Much of the research done on task analysis has reminiscences of Taylorist assumptions. These include performance measured in terms of keystrokes per minute, transactions per hour, and so forth. This emphasis on the "performance of work" does not take into account that boring activities may determine low levels of productivity, or that a system that projects a feeling of stupidity also creates the conditions to lower the level of productivity or increase mistakes.

Corporate goals include increasing profit, increasing the market share, and defeating the competition. Even if these goals are important from the corporation's point of view, it is clear that as the corporation is not doing the work—people are—the dominant goals are the personal ones. More significant for the user are personal goals. Goals such as to increase profit or defeat the competition are quite abstract and do not affect the user directly.

Practical goals include avoiding meetings, handling the client's demands, and recording the client's order. Cooper calls corporate and practical goals "hygienic goals," adapting the term from the "hygienic factors" defined by Saul Gellerman (1963). Such hygienic factors, according to Gellerman are necessary but not sufficient, or "prerequisite for effective motivation but powerless to motivate by themselves" (Cooper 1999, 157).

False goals include such things as saving memory, saving keystrokes, making the system easy to learn, safeguarding data integrity, and so on. Each of these features needs to be analyzed individually and in the context of a given software system, as their relative weight depends on the system and the additional features to be taken into account. As Cooper explains, even a target like "being easy to learn" isn't always a primary goal. For the fighter plane pilot, safety and winning are more important than devoting time to learning the system.

Future Interactions

The contradiction between the sequential, procedural, task-based approach to design and the goal-directed activity of people is a central part of the HCI-SE problem. On the SE side, classical algorithmic solutions seek to break down the problem into steps—in this case, tasks. When considering interactive solutions or systems, however, we observe more powerful problem-solving methods and devices. The difficulties noted when goals are translated into tasks may be conceptualized as an opposition between algorithms and interactions. The traditional solution to computing problems has been developed in terms of algorithms, while it is evident that we need new paradigms to cope with the problem of everyday physical, cultural, and social interactions.

The embodied interaction approach argues that the "design and analysis of systems based on tangible interaction needs to encompass more than simply their 'tangible' characteristics, and to understand how they are caught up in larger systems of meaning that connect the physical to the symbolic rather than separating them into two disconnected domains" (Dourish 2001, 207).

We may deduce that the symbolic are the goals, embodied as human needs and intentions, while the physical are the tasks we may observe in the workplace or elsewhere. The main problem of confronting two separate worlds remains: one is the world of sequential thinking, each step in turn producing a transformation that will be used in subsequent steps; the other is the world of the symbolic, with rather complex structures not necessarily represented as linear or sequential steps but as whole patterns we deal better with as interactions.

Peter Wegner (1997) and Wegner and Dina Goldin (2003) contend that classical algorithmic solutions provide an output completely determined by the input, while interactive systems provide history-dependent services over time that can learn from and adapt to experience. They point to some interesting antecedents in Alan Turing's papers. Turing machines (which Turing called automatic machines or *a-machines*) could not provide a complete model for all forms of mathematics. In his 1936 article, Turing also defines *c-machines* or choice machines as an alternative model of computation. Here, he added interactive choice as a form of computation and later even *u-machines* (unorganized machines) as another alternative that modeled the brain. Unfortunately these machines were not formalized by Turing, and in the 1960s were considered as unnecessary, as "it was assumed Turing machine models could completely describe all forms of computation" (Wegner and Goldin 2003, 101).

Since the 1960s, a-machines have been considered the only model for all types of computation, even when there are interactions added to the system, in which case it should be analyzed in terms of what Turing defined as c-machines. Wegner and Goldin (2003, 102) end their article pointing out that "the assumption that all computation can be algorithmically specified is still widely accepted."

Wegner (1997, 82) explains that "algorithms are metaphorically dumb and blind because they cannot adapt interactively while they compute. They are autistic in performing tasks according to rules rather than through interaction. In contrast, interactive systems are grounded in an external reality both more demanding and richer in behavior than the rule-based world of non-interactive algorithms."

One could ask, What are the differences between interactions and other approaches already used in SE, like parallelism, distribution, and openness? The main differences, as pointed out by Wegner, are:

- Interactive systems interact with an external environment they cannot control—that is, the output of the interactive system may modify, but not determine the external world (modify means a transformation not foreseen by the interactive system).

- Parallelism or concurrency occurs when computations of the system overlap in time.
- Distribution occurs when components of a system are separated geographically or logically.

Both parallelism and distribution can be expressed by algorithms in the absence of interaction. The third concept—openness—implies interactions with the environment, so open systems can be modeled by interaction machines, while closed systems are modeled by algorithms.

HCI has changed over the years as generic methods have evolved when technology permits and the complex blends of concepts have become entrenched in new approaches to interaction. Yet fundamental issues remain. The most notable is that people think and act in terms of goals, but machines do not. This often forces people into behaving at the technology scale, rather than at a human scale. Tasks are dictated by the design of technology, rather than technology being designed to suit goals.

Dourish (2001) provides some high-level design principles for future interactions based on embodied interaction:

- Computation is a medium.
- Meaning arises on multiple levels.
- Users, not designers, create and communicate meaning.
- Users, not designers, manage coupling.
- Embodied technologies participate in the world they represent.
- Embodied interaction turns action into meaning.

Unlike the ephemeral interactions of screen-based technologies, embodied technologies participate in the world they represent. In research into telepresence (or presence, as it is usually abbreviated), there is a topic known as "the book problem." This characterizes the problem that we can feel really immersed and involved when reading a book. The medium though which we are interacting is apparently very impoverished compared, say, to the cinema or virtual reality, and yet the feeling of presence we experience can be quite considerable. You can really get transported to another place through the skills of the storyteller—the medium through which we interact with the significances that the story has for us.

Designing for presence is about designing the illusion of nonmediation. When you put on a head-mounted display, you are immediately transported into the computed world beyond the headset. You are not aware that there are two tiny displays sitting close to your eyes; that part of the interaction is apparently unmediated. For the remote teleoperation of vehicles and tools, a feeling of nonmediation, or embodied interaction, would be an advantage. The person controlling the Mars Lander wants, ideally, to feel that one is really picking up the rock to examine it. The headset, the gloves, the transmitters, and the robot arms all need to disappear into a single medium so that the controller feels the interaction is unmediated—that it is embodied.

HCI is changing in the light of new media and a future of pervasive digital artifacts. We need to find ways of measuring the "amount" of mediation in an interaction on various dimensions such as fidelity, interest level, concentration level, and so on. Recalling briefly the book problem, we suspect that there is a correlation between the fidelity of representation and the opportunity for connotation. The book is rich at the connotative level because it is low fidelity and the reader has to fill in so many details. As things become more visually truthful, the opportunity to explore the connotations becomes less feasible.

HCI needs to explore the new information spaces that are being created through pervasive, distributed computing environments and rise to the challenge of new forms of interaction. Here, Benyon (2001) has already characterized a new HCI, concerned with the navigation of information spaces. Looking to lessons from architectural semiotics, interior design, and garden design, we are looking to the design of physical environments with many embedded information and communication devices. The information space is built into the environment, and people are in a very real sense inside an information space. Theirs is a medium that they will shape and form into an environment within which they can engage in activities.

This new medium needs new approaches to assist designers, and embodied interaction is such an approach. People create meanings, and couplings of action and meaning in an environment, so rather than designing for simple, functional use, we should be designing for the appropriation of media.

As an alternative to traditional design approaches, we can consider the design of interactive media as a critical process, creating experiences drawing on fundamental human abilities and looking to architecture and other design disciplines of physical interactions. Goal-directed design aims at removing the task level of HCI that is determined by technology-focused designs. It aims at providing the illusion of unmediated interaction in which people feel they are operating directly on the elements of a domain—inside an environment.

Embodied cognition recognizes that cognition takes place in a physical and social world, and so needs to draw on philosophical foundations such as cognitive semantics. This leads to designing for a directedness of experience, a coupling of actions and meanings, and an interaction experience that focuses on presence.

7 Understanding Requirements

Software is generally developed to meet some requirements. These requirements may be initiated as a result of an existing problem, a new service, an idea for a product, or to update some business process. Requirements need to be understood, and they need to be packaged and presented in a way that all the various people involved in the production of software—the people who will interact with the system, the people who will program it, managers, customers, clients, and so on—can understand.

It is a fundamental problem with software that several different sorts of people are involved. The people who will use the system do not know what technology can do for them. They may not even want to change, but some other stakeholder (for example, the management in an organization or, in general, any part that has an interest in the application to be developed) may want to bring in technology to make things more efficient. The systems analyst has to try to understand requirements and then represent that understanding to the programmers. HCI people have a different set of interests than do programmers. In this chapter, we explore issues concerned with understanding and representing requirements.

Perspectives on Requirements

The discourse used to refer to requirements in SE is embedded with expressive metaphors. People talk of requirements *extraction, construction, capture,* or *gathering.* These metaphors offer particular points of view about requirements. Sometimes, a requirement is the equivalent of extracting or mining some mineral from a geologic stratum. The systems analyst, or requirements "engineer," will have to dig down, clearing away the mess and rubbish until the requirement is located. The requirement can then be pulled out and presented. At other times, requirements are seen as the process of gathering, like wild mushrooms or firewood. The metaphor suggests that requirements are lying around the place and the analyst's job is to find them, pick them up, and dust them off a bit.

When speaking of requirements capture, the metaphor REQUIREMENTS ARE ANIMALS IN MOTION is being employed. There are some changing aspects of requirements to be taken into account. Requirements might slip away if we do not grab them. They need to be trapped.

The constructionist viewpoint, on the other hand, suggests that requirements consist of elements that need putting together. Unlike the ideas of capture, or gathering, in constructing requirements, the analyst is creating something new that did not exist before. Yet another view is that of requirements *generation.* This is also a constructionist view, but it is more sensitive to the needs of people. The requirements are generated from some understanding of a raw material, working with that material and the people who have the material. The requirements are not simply bolted together as in a mechanical construction.

The detailed analysis of figurative language used in relation to requirements shows that the simultaneous use of different metaphors is an advantage and does not represent any contradiction or a shortage of precision. Moreover, when trying to define a concept using only one of a few available metaphors, we are restricting the meaning and richness of the definitions.

A statement of requirements is usually called a "requirements specification," indicating that a process of elaboration has been applied to the requirements. In such a document, there is a description of what a system should do (functional requirements) and what properties it should have (nonfunctional requirements). A requirements specification document is often part of a contract between a customer and a supplier (Lauesen 2002).

However requirements are presented, and however they are arrived at, there are two main ways of focusing on what they tell us. In a traditional SE approach, requirements are expressed in terms of functionalities and features of the systems. In HCI, requirements are expressed as scenarios and user stories focusing on the tasks the user will have to undertake to achieve their goals when using the system to be created.

In the development of human-computer systems there are these two differing views. Software engineers may have a view of the object classes of the systems as a class diagram, or how objects interact with each other in sequence diagrams. HCI people may view the system as a black box, with no idea of object structure and interaction, but instead attending to the activities that people want to undertake by using the system. The concept of "view" is based on the familiar visual metaphor of a system architecture and the metaphor is: SOFTWARE IS A BUILDING. An architect may produce floor plans, elevations, and other representations that show the system from a particular viewpoint or perspective. In the definitions taken from the IEEE standards (2000), the visual metaphor becomes more abstract, and the view is held by "concerns and issues," leading to another concept, a viewpoint: "A view is a representation of a system from the perspective of related concerns or issues"; "Viewpoint is a template, pattern, or specification for constructing a view."

Here, then, a view is the equivalent of a scope—the scene on which we focus our sight. The position from which the observation is made—the viewpoint—becomes a template or pattern for constructing the view.

Ronald Langacker (1987), in his consideration of cognitive grammar, discusses cognitive abilities in chapter 3. The concepts outlined by the author turn out to be relevant to the current section. He examines cognitive abilities in terms of four main headings that look quite different from a standard view of cognition: mental experience, autonomous processing, focal adjustments, and transformations. Langacker explores how we experience and come to know about events in the world—something a requirements engineer surely has to do. For our purposes, the cognitive abilities of "focal adjustment" concern different views and will help us set up the ground to define more accurately some SE concepts.

Langacker is another part of the movement away from the literal in linguistics, and his theory includes some important concepts and positions for our view of exploring the cognitive foundations of HCI-SE. His interest is in grammar, which he labels a description of the structure of a language. Moreover, Langacker argues that semantics is language specific and based on conventional imagery. For the problem of HCI-SE, this is critical as all the various stakeholders involved in the development of software speak different languages. The end users speak the language of their work. Managers speak the language of corporate objectives, programmers the language of programming, and HCI people the language of usability and engaging interactions. Trying to find ways to bridge these gaps in meanings is central to the problem of HCI-SE.

Although in the following discussion we focus primarily on the requirements engineer, we must not just consider the immediate users of a system when developing it. There are many interested people, stakeholders, with different concerns—some political, some organizational, some managerial, and so on. There are people who will be used by the system as much as they use the system. Some people may just be providers of data to the system, while others will change their jobs as a result of the system and may have to get to know new ways of working or new facts and procedures. Ian Alexander and Suzanne Robertson (2004) describe the "onion" model of stakeholders with rings covering stakeholders with a direct relationship to the system, the "functional beneficiaries," and the "political beneficiaries." For them, it is the stakeholders who have viewpoints.

Recall figure 5.15, where we conceptualized an object in the OO programming sense. We observed that the main character—an object or agent—is performing a journey, during which it interacts with other objects. The object's story is then compressed into a blend, which will make up eventually a software object. Yet this story is considered as composed by a set of interactions or scenes, each one needing a particular way of focusing it. A first concept that we will need is called by Langacker (1987) *selection.* This determines which facets of a scene are being dealt with. A second concept is that of *perspective,* which points to the position from which a scene is viewed. The third one refers to *abstraction* to indicate the level of specificity at which a situation is portrayed.

In figure 7.1, we note an external observer—in this case, the software engineer—in a given perspective: the observer is in a location internal to the system. There are two more specific notions subsumed in the concept of perspective: *vantage point* and *orientation.* A vantage point is the position from which a scene is viewed, and in this case the vantage point would be internal to the system. The orientation refers to the alignment with respect to the axes of the visual field and is something necessary when used in real-life situations. In our case we are dealing with abstract concepts, and it would be useful to use this concept as a figurative one (note that all these notions are used figuratively), meaning, for example, different orientations of observations (the security orientation, the quality orientation, and so on).

Selection subsumes, in turn, other notions. One of them is the *scope,* related to the portions of a scene that it specifically includes. In the previous ex-

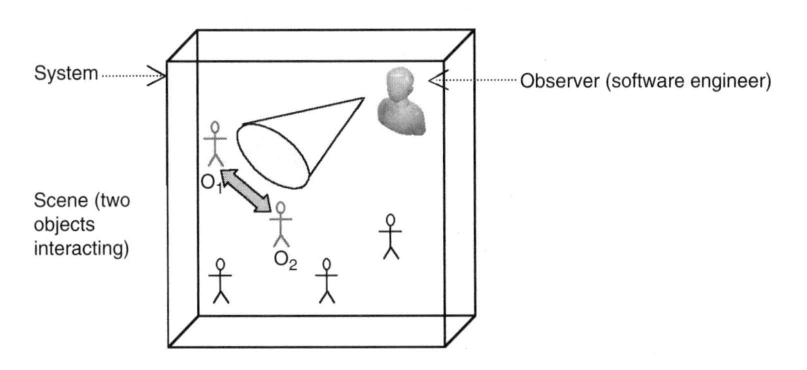

Figure 7.1
A scene observed from a perspective

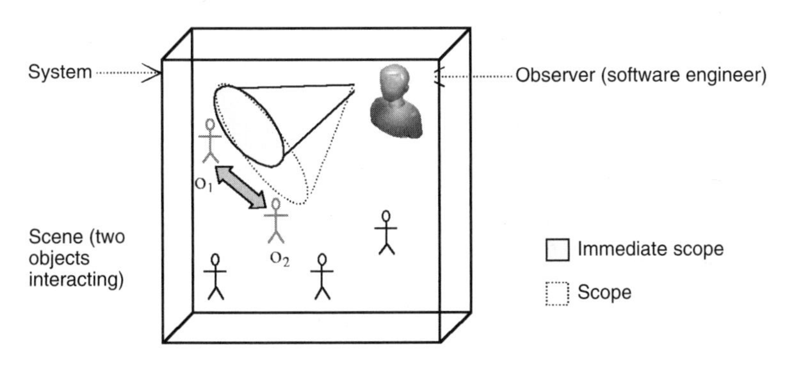

Figure 7.2
The same previous scene with an immediate scope

ample, the scope is the set of two objects (object 1 and object 2) and the interactions between them. Sometimes, it is necessary to identify an innermost region within the scope, as when we observe object 1 and its interactions with object 2. The scope is the same—both objects and interactions—but one of the elements has a highest degree of relevance and we call it an *immediate scope.* This concept is useful when we are designing object 1 (considering attributes and operations) to carry out its interactions with object 2. On the other hand, we take object 2 as an immediate scope to design its interactions with object 1.

Objects are not isolated individuals but social entities. They are conceived to participate with other objects to produce a higher-level behavior (we say higher level compared to the behavior that an isolated object usually performs). So, in fact, the first place a software engineer has to occupy is one external to the system, from where they may observe the functionalities or features a system will incorporate. The software engineer may select—in turn—each one of the functions and increase or decrease the scope, shifting from an immediate scope to another, and so on. This case may be represented in the following figure:

Selection subsumes another important notion, that of *scale*. We need to take into account the granularity of concepts we are using: objects, subsystem, system, or networks of systems. The example of figure 7.3 shows an external vantage point and a given system's external behavior, a system function, as the scope. We have moved from the scale of objects to the system's scale. The

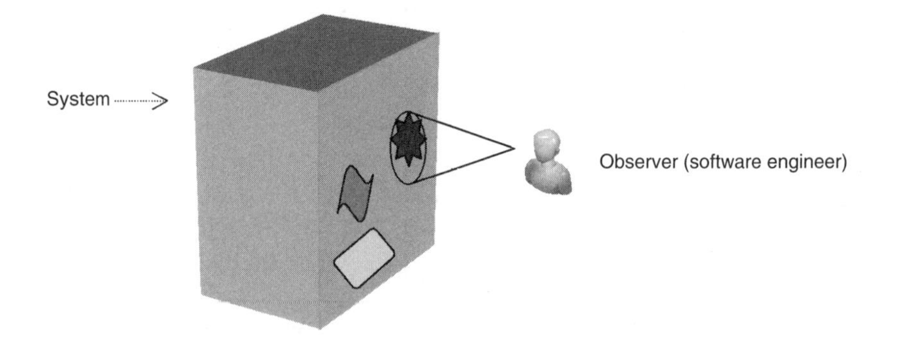

Figure 7.3
The system observed from an external vantage point

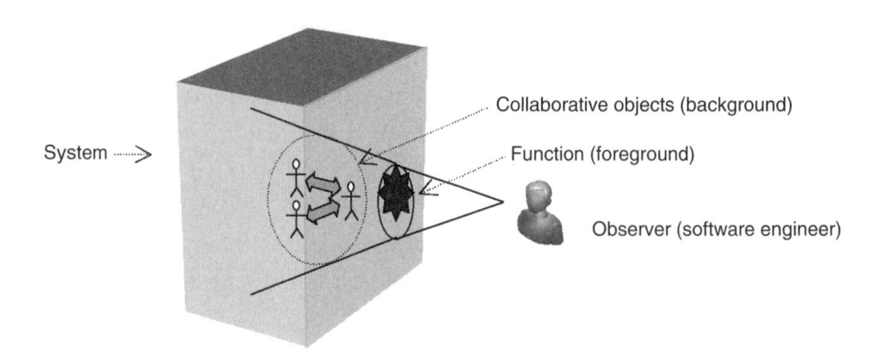

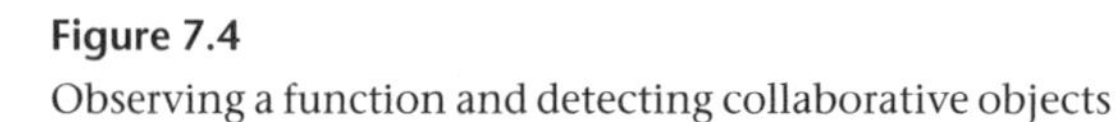

Figure 7.4
Observing a function and detecting collaborative objects

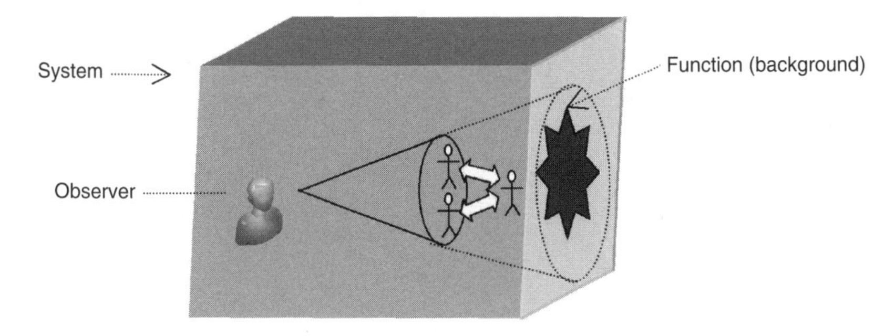

Figure 7.5
Analyzing objects to produce a function

scope may vary and include more than one function in order to aggregate them into categories, which will be put into menus as different options.

Sometimes, it is useful to focus simultaneously both on a function and the collection of objects that perform such a function. In order to perceive this mapping between a given behavior (functionality or feature) and a set of collaborative objects, we need to include an additional notion: *foreground* and *background*. Clearly, things in the foreground are more easily perceived.

Even if the foreground is closer to the vantage point, it is quite possible to *focus* attention on the group of collaborative objects in order to detect the role each object will play in the collaboration. It is also possible to put the vantage point inside the system, thus getting the group of objects as foreground and the resulting function as background in order to help design collaborative objects.

In the same way, we may consider an external observer with a scope covering both the user interface and the user. This scene implies considering a typical HCI approach, even if it is possible to enlarge the scope and also take into account the wider context of the task or activity that the user is included in. We might also focus on the user's end goals, the business process the user is performing, and so on, or we might add other users, such as the idea of interacting through the interface may suggest.

It is clear that we adopt, in turn, different vantage points with different foregrounds and backgrounds, changing the scale, focus of attention, and scope when designing a piece of software. This is a highly dynamic process, but trying to identify these parameters of focal adjustments will prove useful in defining more carefully many of the concepts used in HCI and SE.

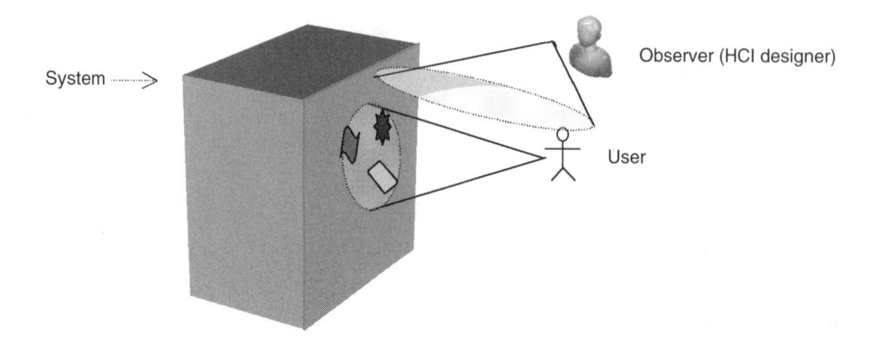

Figure 7.6
Observing the system from an HCI vantage point

A third notion required to define the focal adjustment is *abstraction.* It is interesting to observe how Langacker points out three different usages of the term abstraction. One of the meanings is equivalent to what has been previously called selection, and involves just omitting from consideration certain domains or properties. It is one of the golden rules of software modeling: to take into consideration only those features that are relevant for our purpose and keep apart from the model any other nonpertinent feature.

Our focus will be on the abstractness of a schema relative to instantiations, in the sense we have previously defined (both schema and instantiation). As we have defined them, a schema is abstract relative to an instantiation, as the latter is characterized by a high degree of specificity. An instance, compared to its schema or type, offers more details, precision, or specificity along one or more parameters. Langacker uses a similar concept for schema and instance. What Langacker calls an *elaboration* is defined, in the UML, as a realization, but the process of instantiation for an object to provide more information than the schema from where it derives is essentially the same.

When dealing with structured methods—especially with structured programming—we noted an equivalent term, that of refinement (or stepwise refinement), whereby each successive step provides additional information. The process of increasing information is not limited to instantiation, as the implementation of operations shows that the later steps in software development also contribute to a decrease in abstractness.

For example, the class construct has a higher degree of abstraction than a Customer class, the same way that a Customer class is abstract in relation to object Smith Inc. We are introducing, then, a viewpoint while describing requirements. As we are talking about functionalities and features, it would be useful to say that features are merely one or more product functions and related data, so it is again a question of levels of abstraction when describing requirements.

In the next two sections, we are going to see the differences—in terms of viewpoints—in traditional requirements and scenarios. In particular, traditional requirements would be an algorithmic approach applied directly to describe functions and features, while scenarios is an attempt to describe more general elements, such as human needs and goals at the same time as interactions between human beings and software systems.

When considering the system as a bundle of functions and features, this approach leads to describing such elements as observed from a neutral, aseptic point of view. This is the *dry* discourse we need in order for us to specify requirements in terms of more formal languages (diagrams, tables, and formal languages). The description of requirements as scenarios allows us to sustain a *wet* discourse where it is possible to hold important aspects of human intentionality needed to optimize the design of interactions, such as we have already seen in chapter 6.

The representation of figure 7.8 shows Cooper's ideas about personae, goals, and interactions that we encountered in chapter 6, but it also maps onto the ideas expressed by Matthias Jarke and Klaus Pohl (1994), cited by Jawed Siddiqi and M. Chandra Shekaran (1996, 17), when they point out that "the juxtaposition of vision and context is at the heart of managing requirements. . . . Jarke and Pohl partition context into three worlds: subject, usage

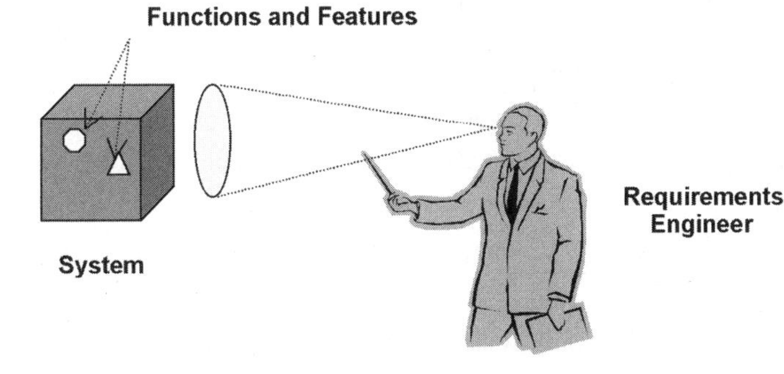

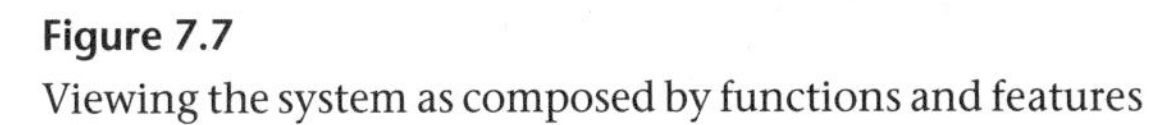
Figure 7.7
Viewing the system as composed by functions and features

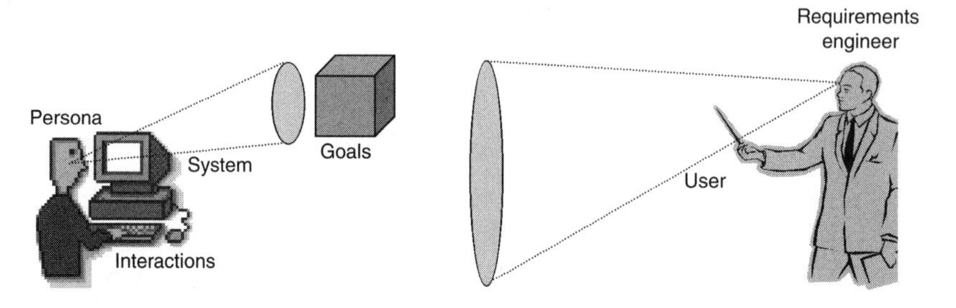

Figure 7.8
A description of interactions as scenarios

and system. The subject represents a part of the outside world in which the system—represented by some structured description—exists to serve some individual or organizational purpose or usage."

Requirements in SE

The classical metaphor in SE considers THE SYSTEM IS AN INDUSTRIAL PLANT. This focus is clearly on function and results in a functional decomposition of the system. As a result, the functional requirements specify the system. When the dominant viewpoint focuses on functions, the final result will be a list of functions together with a textual description of each function, additional activity diagrams, and a detailed user interface. The consequence of such an approach is that the user interface is built on underlying functions, with an implementation-driven user interface.

The way we describe functions and features in this case is in plain text. Lauesen (2002) discusses requirements through the example of a hotel system because most people have some idea what the application is about. The hotel system will be designed to support the hotel reception, and the tasks of booking rooms, checking in, checking out, and so on, and recording services such as lunch on a guest's bill. The typical list of features will be described, by Lauesen (2002, 85), as follows (R1 = Requirement 1):

R1 The product shall be able to record that a room is occupied for repair in a specified period.
R2 The product shall be able to show and print a suggestion for staffing during the next two weeks based on historical room occupation. The supplier shall specify the calculation details.

R3 The product shall be able to run in a mode where rooms are not booked by room number, but only by room type. Actual room allocation is not done until check-in.
R4 The product shall be able to print out a sheet with room allocation for each room booked under one stay.

There have been many attempts to use a linguistic background to explain the derivation of analysis models from requirements and trying to use this derivation in automated methods (Buchholz, Düsterhöft, and Thalheim 1996; Juristo, Moreno, and López 2000; Naduri and Rugaser 1994). These attempts are based on two main underlying assumptions:

1. The folk theory of language;
2. Most cognitive processes are formalizable.

The use made of linguistic instruments normally implies a folk theory of language, which usually means to consider that we "say what we mean" or "put the meaning into words" (Fauconnier 1997). This folk theory derives, first, from the classical conduit metaphor (Reddy 1993; see chapter 2) whereby words contain and hence transfer meaning. The second underlying assumption is that the computer and the brain have a similar behavior, so each one is a model to explain the other. Therefore, if the computer may translate a given language (COBOL or Java) to machine code, then it is also valid to translate requirements sentences (expressed in natural language) to analysis models.

This approach leads to constructing a set of selected sentences to form the requirements—a process that could, eventually, be automated. The background to this automation of the analysis process is in the underlying assumption that the meaning of requirements is already contained in the set of sentences used to capture them. As we have already seen, most metaphors used to refer to the requirements engineering process suffer from the same syndrome. Requirements are "things" (like "animals") to be captured in sentences, or ideas to be elicited from the mind of users and transformed into statements.

To justify the use of formal or semiformal methods of translation from natural-language sentences, some of the arguments employed state that OO analysis "is now performed unsystematically and depends highly on the software engineers' experience" (Juristo, Moreno, and López 2000, 80). One answer to this is that requirements as well as analysis and design do depend highly on the software engineers' experience. Another answer is that once the object model is built using the proposed semiformal method, it will still need immediate refinement in order to add attributes, methods, and other classes that are derived from the context of the domain. This again requires the software engineers' experience.

In the context of cognitive linguistics, Fauconnier (1994, xxxviii–xxxix) has maintained that

> the important feature to bear in mind is the extraordinary underspecification of cognitive mental space configurations by language. There is no algorithm that would yield the space configuration corresponding to some linguistic form. Rather, the linguistic form will constrain the dynamic construction of the spaces, but that construction itself is highly dependent on previous constructions already effected at that point in discourse.

In the context of requirements, the written sentences that specify requirements can only represent an underspecification of cognitive mental spaces activated when eliciting and writing such requirements. This is one of the reasons to state that requirements are essentially incomplete. Much of the mental space configuration has been generated by earlier discourse—that is, the context where such a sentence has been elicited. The interaction between the requirements engineer and the users, and the context of that interaction, is not completely reproducible when a different developer reads the requirements.

Another argument runs that we need a more formal, propositional style for representing requirements if they are subsequently to be translated to more formal languages used to implement the requirements. That is correct, because implementation is a gradual translation to more formal ways of representing requirements up to the stage where the representation is executable by the hardware. What we are asserting is that an immediate translation of requirements performed by the requirements engineer from a natural language to a propositional style implies a possible loss of meaning that may eventually produce a limited or defective system. For example, R1 above suggests that there are only two states a room can be in: a free state, meaning that the room can be allocated to a guest; or an occupied state, with the room waiting for repair or allocated to another guest. The reality is probably far more complex, as Lauesen (2002, 90) remarks: "Sometimes a room may be waiting for repair, but not all repairs mean that the room is not able of being allocated to a guest (depending on the guest and the type of repair it would be possible to allocate the room for a lower rate)."

What we need are valid frameworks in order for us to be able to master the process of requirement engineering. As requirements engineers, we do need a previous understanding of the requirements. In particular, we need to be aware of the process of creating and transforming them. We are not intending to say that requirements in the form of textual sentences are not useful in modeling the different views of analysis. What we mean is that these sentences are necessarily incomplete. They are incomplete in the sense Alan Davis (1993) has explained, arguing that it is impossible to produce a perfect requirements specification. They are also incomplete in the sense that sentences can only be general guidelines to get their whole meaning in an ongoing process that takes into account the context. Davis also points out that incompleteness refers to a future evolution of requirements. We can never get to a final state of requirements as they are continually evolving.

Often, the nonlinguistic knowledge required to completely define the meaning of requirements is not available to analysts, as some ethnomethodologies have shown (Jirotka and Goguen 1994). Sometimes, the users themselves are not capable of clearly stating which actions are associated with their task, and at other times they are not able to imagine what the interactions with the new system may be. Meaning develops in an ongoing process that implies feedback from later phases and iterations. It is not directly derivable from reading a set of sentences. As we have seen, the folk theory of meaning, the conduit metaphor (chapter 2), ignores the fact that language does not carry meaning but only guides it. Cognitive activity mediates the relationship between words and the world. The study of meaning is the study of how words arise in the context of human activity, and how they are used as incomplete information to perform the cognitive constructions for the purpose of constructing meaning.

Even the case of the seemingly simple structure "is_a" is open to question. Most writers equate this with inheritance hierarchies, but Fowler and Scott (2000) have shown that "is_a" may mean a generalization relation between a subclass and a class ("a car is a vehicle") or a classification—that is, a relation between an instance and a class to which it belongs (like in "a Border Collie is a breed"). It is not allowed to chain generalizations and classifications in order to deduce some fact, as can be seen in the following example:

1. Fido is a Border Collie.
2. A Border Collie is a breed.

but (1) and (2) do not imply

3. Fido is a breed.

As Fowler and Scott point out, it is better to use expressions like "Dogs are a kind of animal" and "Every instance of a Border Collie is an instance of a dog." So there are semantic language traps that it is necessary to avoid in order to get valid models.

If the automated derivation of an analysis model from requirements written in natural language is impossible, we may consider how to manually derive an abstract model from requirements. This can show how some additional model elements that were not included in the original list of sentences are needed. We are going to use an example taken from Alexander Egyed (2002), but we will include some requirements in propositional style that correspond to the model. What we are trying to show in this section is how such an abstract model may be refined as a concrete model by adding new elements that will be used in a later stage of designing the system.

Let us consider a collection of sentences that might represent the requirements:

1. A guest may either stay at a hotel or have reservations for it (the *or* is not exclusive, as the guest may stay and have reservations for later dates).
2. A hotel employs employees.
3. A hotel has expenses.
4. A guest causes the hotel a set (collection) of expenses.
5. A guest makes payments (for their expenses).
6. There are guests who have to be considered as groups (collections).
7. A guest requires a security deposit.
8. A guest may produce a set (collection) of payments.

The abstract model corresponding to the previous sentences might be represented using an OO notation such as a class diagram. As the list of requirements sentences are already expressed in the traditional logical form, whereby they are based on logical propositions with a truth-conditional value and a minimum—reduced—context, it is possible to make a quite direct translation to the equivalent classes and relationships.

If we apply a standard notation such as the UML, we easily get a diagram as in figure 7.9:

The point is that this model cannot be automatically derived from the initial requirements, as new issues emerge in the context of producing the abstract model. The refinement is possible by means of additional knowledge of the hotel management system domain, asking additional questions to users or previously knowing how such a domain works. This is the ongoing process

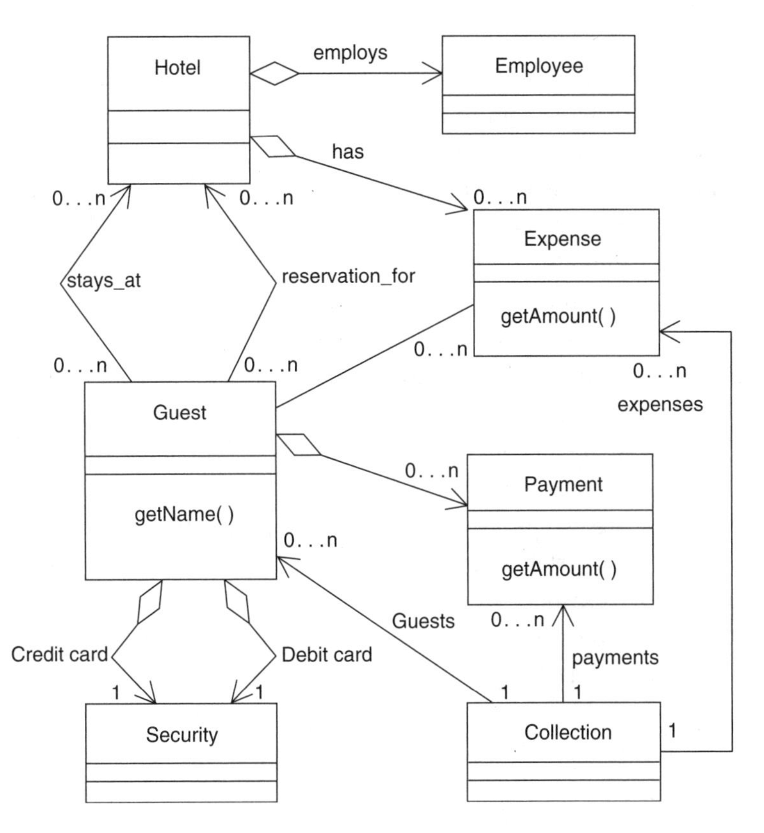

Figure 7.9
Hotel management system: Abstract model as a class diagram

that leads to producing additional meaning in a concrete model not previously available in the abstract model.

For example, in the new concrete model, there are some new classes such as Reservation, which may be considered as a conceptual combination of two previously available classes: Guest and Hotel. The clue that leads to the new class is the relationship "reservation_for" between the classes. Historically, it might be considered that the concept of a reservation is originally a blend—a concept already available in the domain of hotels—from two previous mental spaces: the mental space of the guest arriving and staying at the hotel, and the mental space of the hotel. A current relationship between both mental spaces is projected to a new mental space, that of reservation.

The previous discussion allows us to consider a class like reservation as a blend (like any other class, as we have seen in chapter 5) recruiting structure from mental spaces corresponding to other already-defined classes as well as future dates. From the point of view of analysis, it means that reservation will be composed of attributes coming from both input mental spaces: guest and hotel. But there is also an additional mental space that participates in the blend: the calendar, from which a range of future dates will be selected.

It could be argued that the class Reservation is not necessarily a new class resulting from combining other classes (Hotel and Guest) of the abstract model and the calendar mental space, as reservation is an everyday concept in the hotel domain. So the concept reservation would have been included in the initial requirement sentence without needing to wait until the first draft of the abstract model. The important fact is that new classes appear in the context of any abstract model, most frequently as a design or technological need, and without a direct relation to the domain under consideration.

The type of things we use in requirements are propositional sentences, which were originally stated as natural-language sentences, but have lost most of their characteristics, "wetness," because the context has been reduced to a minimum. The propositions we eventually get after refining and specifying requirements are of the type "A verb B," such as "The client sends orders," and so forth.

As names have been traditionally translated in SE to entities and later to classes (in OO methods), propositions of the A verb B type are represented as two entities or classes linked by a relation between them.

The typical case of a general relation between two classes corresponds to a sentence of the following type:

A verb B (the customer sends orders).

We are not taking into consideration the special cases of inheritance or aggregation. This kind of sentence is quite directly represented as both classes A and B, and the verb indicating the relation is associated as a role with a segment, which represents the relation itself.

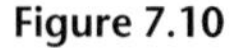

Figure 7.10

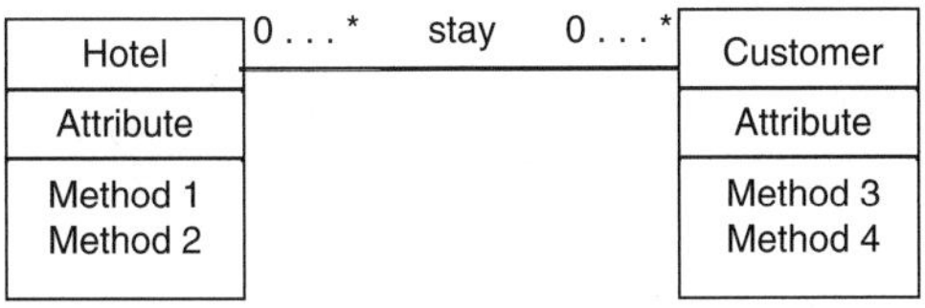

Figure 7.11

As both mental spaces (customer and order) are quite heterogeneous, there is no compression of the outer-space relation, but it is projected into one of the classes as an attribute (this point has already been discussed in chapter 5 when analyzing how the class blend is constructed).

But there are also other cases when the inclusion of a relation in the form of an attribute does not solve the problem we are facing in the model. The classical standpoint in entity-relationship diagrams is to consider the multiplicity associated with the studied relation and determine whether there is a many-to-many mapping between both classes.

In such a case, we must include a new class (entity) in order to solve the problem of the many-to-many multiplicity. But this solution is tightly associated with a relational model, in which a many-to-many multiplicity violates the first normal form (the multiplicity would imply including a repetitive group to represent the multiplicity in each one of the entities).

It is interesting to observe that in fact, what we do in such a case is to modify the analysis model forced by the technological restriction of the relational model. It is a design restriction rather than a consideration of the domain and the analysis itself.

As a final example, Turner (2001) uses the "ditransitive" construct, explaining that such a grammatical structure is associated to a conceptual integration network. The typical sentence is as follows:

A verb B C, where A, B, and C are names.

Some examples provided by Turner are:

- Mary poured Bill some wine.
- She denied him the job.
- She told me a story.

Instead of being led by the technological framework of many-to-many, what we need here is to investigate the domain at hand in search of relations for additional roles between two given classes. In the example of the hotel

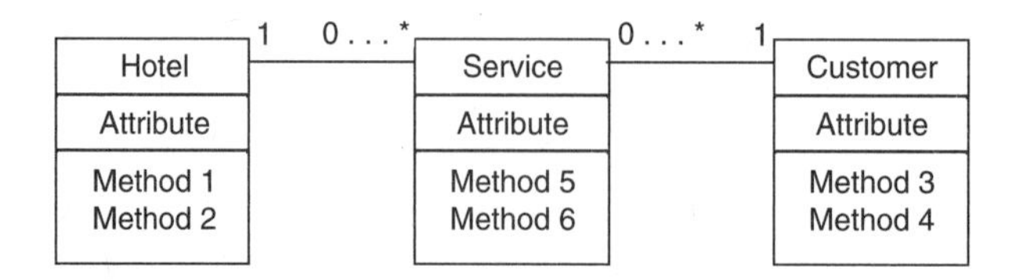

Figure 7.12

and the customer, it may be found that in addition to staying at the hotel, the customer has other relations with it. For instance:

- The hotel provides the customer services.

The mental space of staying at the hotel leads us to detect what events happen while staying there. The reason for searching for these types of ditransitive constructs is that the first part of the sentence shows a direct relation between both classes (Hotel and Customer) with the inclusion of the third element we were looking at: services (figure 7.12).

Most texts on software requirements would prefer the process of understanding and representing requirements to be a more rigorous and well-defined affair. Since the 1970s, the discipline has been trying to establish itself around the metaphor CREATING SOFTWARE IS ENGINEERING. For some more technical systems—such as network controllers—and other systems that do not involve people—such as the embedded systems in cars, elevators, or power plants—this is the case. There are many safety-critical systems that must have precise expressions of requirements that can be demonstrated to be the equivalent of the final program code. But for systems that involve people, directly or indirectly, creating software is not engineering; it is a craft. To deal with these issues, another approach to understanding requirements has been proposed: Scenarios.

Scenarios

Making Use is the title of John Carroll's (2000) book on scenario-based design. Carroll has made a huge contribution to the study of HCI and information systems through his work on scenarios, but even he admits that he is not in a position to demonstrate exactly how they work. Scenario-based design, he argues, is simple and powerful, and a general method for all design. But unlike SE's desire to specify requirements in a manner that is unambiguous, correct,

Alexander	Dreyfuss
Simple set of components	Ergonomic handles and controls
Easy assembly of components	Headlight for recess illumination
High cleaning power	Low profi le for occluded access
Low cost	Protective rubber bumper
	Carry handgrips
	Kink-resistant cord
	Multipurpose packing materials
	Accessory rack
	Easy-to-use disposable dust bag
	Easy-to-clean surface
	One-piece construction
	Pleasing and elegant lines

Figure 7.13
Alexander's and Dreyfuss's requirements for a vacuum cleaner

traceable, modifiable, and so on, Carroll's interest is to help designers make sense of things. In the design of interactive systems there is no stable practice (or at least not much). Design practice varies when applied to new designs, and of course new technologies are constantly coming along that require new practices. Interactive systems design practice is a continuous process of learning for all the participants, users, and designers.

We can take up the example used by Carroll (2000, 36) where he shows the difference between two styles of requirements: abstract versus concrete. This is a comparison of two designers, Christopher Alexander and Henry Dreyfuss, and how they specify the design requirements for a vacuum cleaner:

After having a look at figure 7.13, we may deduce that while Alexander's requirements are the equivalent of the furniture category—that is, a superordinate category—Dreyfuss's are the equivalent of basic-level categories—these requirements are formed by entities we physically interact with, thus determining basic elements of perception and function. Dreyfuss's requirements are more humanly scaled than Alexander's. We could write a scenario describing a cleaning activity performed by a persona (chapter 6), and clearly stating the goal, the needs, the concerns, and the likes. The scenario could be something like this:

Mary is a forty-three-year-old clerk at the local post office. She lives in a two-story Victorian house just around the corner from her elderly mother, who has her own bungalow. On the weekends, Mary usually vacuums her mother's house as well as her own. Her mother is very fussy about ensuring that all the corners of her house and right under the bed are cleaned properly, and she is very protective of her furniture, which she cannot bear to see scratched. Mary is quite stylish and house proud, and hates to see any dirt or other marks on things.

From this brief scenario, we can see that Mary's requirements of a vacuum cleaner are close to those specified by Dreyfuss above. She has to carry the vacuum up and down stairs and around to her mother's house. The buttons and controls should be ergonomically designed. Mary is concerned about damaging the walls and furniture, and needs to have a light to illuminate when she should clean under the bed or sofa. She is stylish and house proud, and so does not like to clean the dust bag or unkink the vacuum cord.

The scenario in this case is a description that highlights the requirements. Some of them are needs such as the ergonomics of the handles and controls, or the ability to illuminate recessed locations. Others are concerns such as not damaging the furniture, and still others are preferences of objectives.

Scenarios come in a variety of forms and can be called many different things. Indeed, Larry Constantine and Lucy Lockwood (2002) present something of a tirade against the lack of clear definitions of both the terms scenarios and use cases. Alistair Sutcliffe (2002) lists visioning scenarios, scenarios of use, context and use scenarios, usage scenarios, and problem-statement scenarios, and we distinguish user stories, conceptual scenarios, concrete scenarios, and use cases (Imaz and Benyon 1999). But whatever form they take, scenarios are basically stories. As Carroll (2000) writes, citing Vladimir Propp's (1958) *Morphology of the Folktale,* a story implies a setting, includes agents or actors each typically with goals or objectives, and has a plot, which is a sequence of actions and events. This view considers scenarios as stories about people and their activities.

Storytelling, as a mental activity, is a constant activity of human beings. In *The Literary Mind,* Turner (1996) develops his theory of the centrality of stories to human thought. We are constantly constructing small stories and projecting them to other stories. Our capacity to categorize is tightly associated with small spatial stories in which we partition the world into objects. This partitioning into objects depends on the typical stories in which they appear: we catch a ball, sit on a chair, and take a drink from a glass (Turner 1996). Categorizing is associated with stories, as we do not just recognize a collection of particular objects involved in particular events but also a set of objects that belong to categories and events that belong to categories as well. Both human capacities, storytelling, and projection from some stories to others are the cognitive foundation of scenarios that, in their turn, inform requirements from informal stages to more formal ones. As Turner (1996, 12) observes, "Story, projection and parable do work for us; they make everyday life possible; they are the root of human thought; they are not primarily—or even importantly—entertainment. . . . We might therefore think that storytelling is a special performance rather than a constant mental activity. But story as a mental activity is essential to human thought."

The simplest story's structure includes an agent, an action, and an object. In this basic abstract story there is an animate agent that performs a physical action on an object. Moreover, in a general sense, we can consider this basic abstract story an interactional story: the agent interacts with an object. The conceptualization of reality derives from interactions with objects: interactions are the basis of stories and the categorization of objects involved in such interactions. The focus of stories on interaction is important for understanding what people are doing and what they might want to do. Also crucial is the notion of parable. If a metaphor is a cross-domain mapping, then a parable is a cross-story mapping—understanding one story through another.

When we have a human agent in the story, we can observe additional aspects such as intentional acts and the human-scale categories of events. If we watch someone sitting down on a chair, we can also see that sitting involves an agent's act with intentionality and an object like a chair. We immediately project features of animacy and agency onto it from stories in which we are the actors.

Another significant aspect of stories is that they represent a basic-level categorization, as we conceptualize reality at this basic level when interacting with objects. We have already defined basic-level categories in chapter 3 as formed by entities we physically and perceptually interact with, thus determining basic elements of perception and function. The communication aspect and knowledge organization are based on both perception and function. In fact, "basic-level categorization is defined not merely by what the world is like, but equally by how we interact with the world given our bodies, our cognitive organization, and our culturally-defined purposes" (Lakoff 1988, 134).

We also pointed out in chapter 3 that we can form a general mental image of some objects or biological beings, like chairs or dogs. But we cannot form a mental image for superordinate categories like furniture or animals. What we have are mental images for individual elements of the furniture category: chairs, tables, armchairs, beds, and so on, but not for a generic piece of furniture.

We have already seen the importance of stories and parables in the Buddhist monk tale (chapter 3), and in Turner's 1996 book we can see the beginnings of *The Way We Think* (Fauconnier and Turner 2002), with its central ideas of conceptual integration, or blending and the principles that apply to blends. Turner (1996) again emphasizes image schemata in stories, and how stories are projected onto other domains and thus provide real insight. He argues that stories are highly effective as prediction, planning, evaluation, and explanation. Pattern completion is one of the principles of blends that we utilize in interpreting stories (chapter 6); we can predict, explain, and imagine what is going to happen in some familiar circumstance.

What we assert in this section is that in order for analysts to understand and make sense of situations, it is useful to employ scenarios as the basis of this process. Scenarios are rooted in the conceptual foundations of cognition—image schemata, basic categories, imaginative projection, and blending. In the early stages of requirements it is important that all the ambiguities, changing factors, needs, and concerns of the stakeholders are understood from a variety of perspectives. Carroll (2000, 37) points out that

> a design process in which scenarios are employed as a focal representation will ipso facto remain focused on the needs and concerns of prospective users. Thus, designers and clients are less likely to be captured by inappropriate gadgets and gizmos, or to settle for routine technological solutions, when their discussions and visions are couched in the language of scenarios, that is, less likely than they might be if their design work is couched in the language of functional specifications.

The problem inherent in HCI-SE, however, is that at some point the blends produced by the designers (the objects, user interfaces, interactions, and so on), when they bring together requirements and new software, become more and more technological, and finally the system will be specified in terms of classical SE artifacts. Our overall approach to scenario-based design is illustrated in figure 7.14 (adapted from Benyon, Turner, and Turner 2005, 204). As noted earlier, we distinguish four different types of scenarios: user stories, conceptual scenarios, concrete scenarios, and use cases. At different stages of the design process, scenarios are helpful in understanding current practice as well as any problems or difficulties that people may be having in generating and testing ideas, documenting and communicating ideas to others, and evaluating designs.

User stories are the real world, or imagined experiences, of people. Conceptual scenarios are more abstract descriptions in which some details have been stripped away. Concrete scenarios are generated from abstract scenarios by adding specific design decisions and once completed these can be represented as use cases. The lines joining the types of scenario indicate the relationships between them. Many user stories will be represented by a few conceptual scenarios, yet each conceptual scenario may generate many concrete scenarios. Several concrete scenarios will be represented by a single use case. Figure 7.14 also illustrates three critical processes involved in design and how they interact with the different scenario types. Designers abstract from the details of user stories to arrive at conceptual scenarios. They specify design constraints on conceptual scenarios to arrive at concrete scenarios. Finally, they formalize the design ideas as use cases. The second and third stages are essentially what is usually termed design work. Our approach to this is discussed in chapter 8.

Both Carroll and Lauesen (as well as Cooper and many others) base their scenarios on personae—stereotyped characters who will use the system.

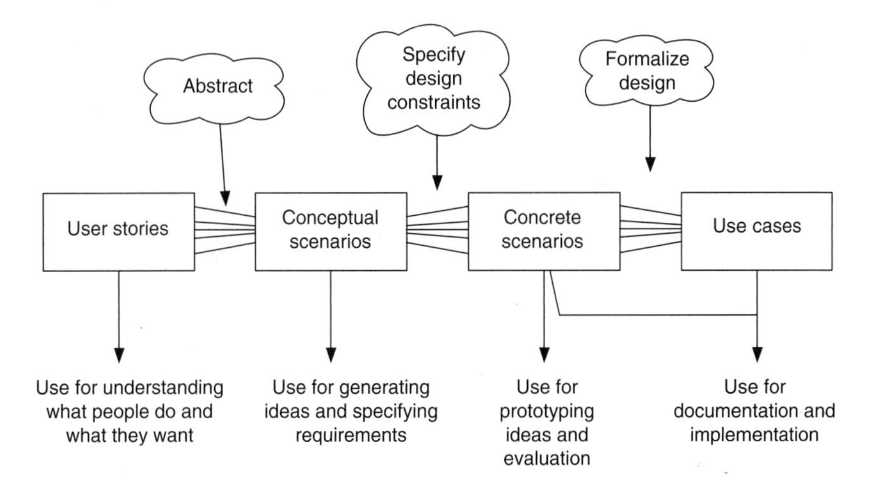

Figure 7.14
Scenario-based design

They call these types of scenario *contextual scenarios.* These correspond to the conceptual scenarios in figure 7.14, and are produced by abstracting the features of a number of user stories.

Benyon, Turner, and Turner (2005, 316) provide the following example, based on the usage of a new device, the Home Information Center (HIC).

Scenario: What shall we do now?

Jan and Pat are a couple in their mid thirties. Pat is a university lecturer in Cultural Studies and Jan is an accounts manager at Standard Life insurance. They live in the Stockbridge area of Edinburgh, Scotland in a two-bedroom flat overlooking the river. It is 12.00 noon on August 15th. Jan and Pat are sitting in their large, airy kitchen/dining room. The remains of pizza and mixed salad mingle with a pile of newspapers on the kitchen table. Jan and Pat have recently returned from a holiday on the island of Zante and, apart from checking their e-mail, they have not gone back to work. They decide that they would like to go to see one of the events that are happening as part of the Edinburgh Arts festival.

Jan activates the HIC and chooses "Edinburgh Festival." The HIC connects to the different content providers who are registered as providing content about the festival. The display shows five categories of information—Times of Events, Specific Artists, Specific Events, Specific Venues, Types of Events—a catalogue and a query facility.

There is also a rationale attached to the scenario, which explains that

this scenario has been developed as part of the first prototype. It is intended to provide a rich description of a general context of use of the Home Information Centre (HIC). The scenario is deliberately vague with respect to a number of features such as input and output media and modalities, how the content is provided, etc. in order to stimulate discussion about such things. (Benyon, Turner, and Turner 2005, 315–16)

The rationale lets us know what the scenario is aiming to achieve. Both personae are described in detail (their names, jobs, age, the area where they live, and the characteristics of their apartment), and we are given clues about the date ("12.00 noon on August 15th") and the leisure time ("the remains of pizza and mixed salad mingles with a pile of newspapers on the kitchen table"). The scenario goes on to depict some possible interactions as a detailed story, with concrete examples of actions and the objects they are interacting with. The goal is to provide a rich description that facilitates the projection of the scenario onto various more concrete forms. Analysts can use their projections to explore technological issues, and users can use their projections to see if the story meets their requirements in enough similar circumstances.

In *The Sociological Imagination,* C. Wright Mills calls for a new perspective, the development of "middle-level abstractions" (Carroll 2000, 17). Carroll picks this up, arguing that scenarios can fill this role as they are less formal than traditional specification techniques.

This observation is remarkable in at least two respects. The first is the coincidence between Mills's idea of middle-level abstractions and the results of cognitive semantics, which considers basic-level categories as located at an intermediate, middle-level location in the tree of ordinate-subordinate categories. The second aspect of the observation is when Carroll points out that scenarios are neither formal nor technical in any fancy sense. Coming back to a previous idea, we need a wet discourse to capture the complexity of requirements but more formal tools in the form of dry discourse in later stages of development.

There is also a resonance here to Turner (1996) and Fauconnier and Turner (2002), when they emphasize aiming for a human scale as a key principle of blends. The technical level of SE description is usually not at a human scale (or at least not at a user's scale). Ordinary people cannot understand the dry discourse of formal systems development. They need stories at a level of abstraction at which they can make use and make sense of them. They need characters (personae) they can identify with and project their own actions onto. They need actions and objects that are described at a basic-category level so that they can project the story onto other examples. Scenarios need to be parables.

Although we do not have a complete specification for a scenario-based design, there are many heuristics for working with scenarios that can be useful. One method that exploits, explicitly, theories related to those presented here is that of Neil Maiden, P. Mistry, and Alistair Sutcliffe (1995), which draws on Eleanor Rosch's category theory. Many other proprietary methods are described in Alexander and Maiden (2004).

Diaper (2002, 379) argues that "it is possible to read almost all of Carroll's book making the assumption that very large numbers of scenarios will be required for the design of even a modestly sized system." The large number of scenarios suggested by Carroll (2000, 255) who says that "for any nontrivial system, there is an infinity of possible usage scenarios," corresponds to scenarios at different levels of detail, documenting the whole application at different stages (requirements, analysis, and design). As Carroll (255) explains,

"Scenario descriptions are fundamentally heuristics; indeed, they cannot be complete. . . . The incompleteness of scenario descriptions is an important property but not unique to scenarios."

We have already seen earlier in this chapter that the incompleteness is not the monopoly of scenarios, as it may also be applied to requirements in general. As Carroll (255) tells us, "The only complete specification of a system is the system itself."

David Benyon and Catriona Macaulay (2004) contend that there should be enough scenarios to scope the variety of domains that the system needs to cover, and suggest that ten to twelve should be sufficient in a system of some complexity. Domains are contexts of use, more abstract than the input spaces for blends and similar to their organizing frames. They can be concretized when required by blending them with specific circumstances. Domains are also included as a basic concept in Langacker's (1987, 147) cognitive grammar, where he sees them as "mental experiences, representational spaces, concepts or conceptual complexes." He, too, recognizes that domains have certain "dimensions" (which in terms of interactive systems design are things such as large or small domains, static or volatile, media rich or otherwise, and so on). According to Benyon and Macaulay (2004, 399), "The aim is to specify the scenarios at a level of abstraction that captures an appropriate level of generality that will be useful across the range of characteristics that is demonstrated within a domain."

Carroll (2000, 14) wisely points out that "one of the central properties of scenarios is that they are both concrete and rough, tangible and vague, vivid and sketchy." We would add that this is true of language and literature in general. Indeed, it is the inherently figurative nature of language that leads directly to the HCI-SE design problem of trying to satisfy both creative and technical concerns. Scenarios confront this problem by demanding literate users, analysts, designers, and implementers. Scenarios should include common confusions, mistakes, and breakdowns. They need to be written in a language that suits the "literary mind" (Turner 1996).

Finally, we need to consider the various purposes that scenarios can be put to and, returning to an earlier theme of this chapter, the viewpoint from which they are taken. For example, when considering the scope of a user interacting with the system we focus on an immediate scope of observing human actions, the learning experience, the performance time, and other social and behavioral factors. We are in fact looking at the usability specification.

When considering the same scope (interaction between the user and the system), but the immediate scope is the system itself, with the tasks performed with functions the system makes available, we are focusing on the functional specification. We might develop different scenarios for teaching or explaining than we would do for using them for systems design (chapter 4). We might shift the vantage point to observe the gradual moving of the immediate scope to more internal locations.

Writing scenarios is an activity of conceptual integration and as such we can apply the principles of blends. Central to these is the overarching goal of achieving a human scale, or being human centered as we might say in interactive systems design. At the most abstract, scenarios are blends between the activity space (including a consideration of the variety of people and contexts within which the activity takes place) and the technological space. For example, the previous scenario of the vacuum cleaner is a blend recruiting structure from two input spaces (see figure 7.15):

- The space of cleaning the house, an activity with needs, concerns, likes, and objectives; the goal could be described as "cleaning the house, rapidly and efficiently";
- The space of vacuum cleaners.

At different points in the design process, we can fix more or less of each space and explore the resulting ideas. This is essentially what we do as we aim to arrive at the corpus of conceptual and concrete scenarios. We can assume that the second space is already existent and explore the problems with current systems. We might use this to examine radical ideas such as a vacuum without dust bags at all or a robot vacuum subsequently using these input spaces to reflect on the activity space of housecleaning. We might use current technology as one of the input spaces and hence derive requirements through the principles of pattern completion. In the case of vacuum cleaners, many models do scratch the furniture and are difficult to keep clean. This might lead us to produce a list of incremental needs, concerns, likes, and objectives as a consequence of blending current vacuum cleaners and the activity of cleaning. This is the application of one of the governing principles, recursion, which implies producing many instances of the same blend at different moments of a life cycle.

Both activity and technological spaces are dynamic; the space of cleaning the house is an ongoing process modified not only by technological factors

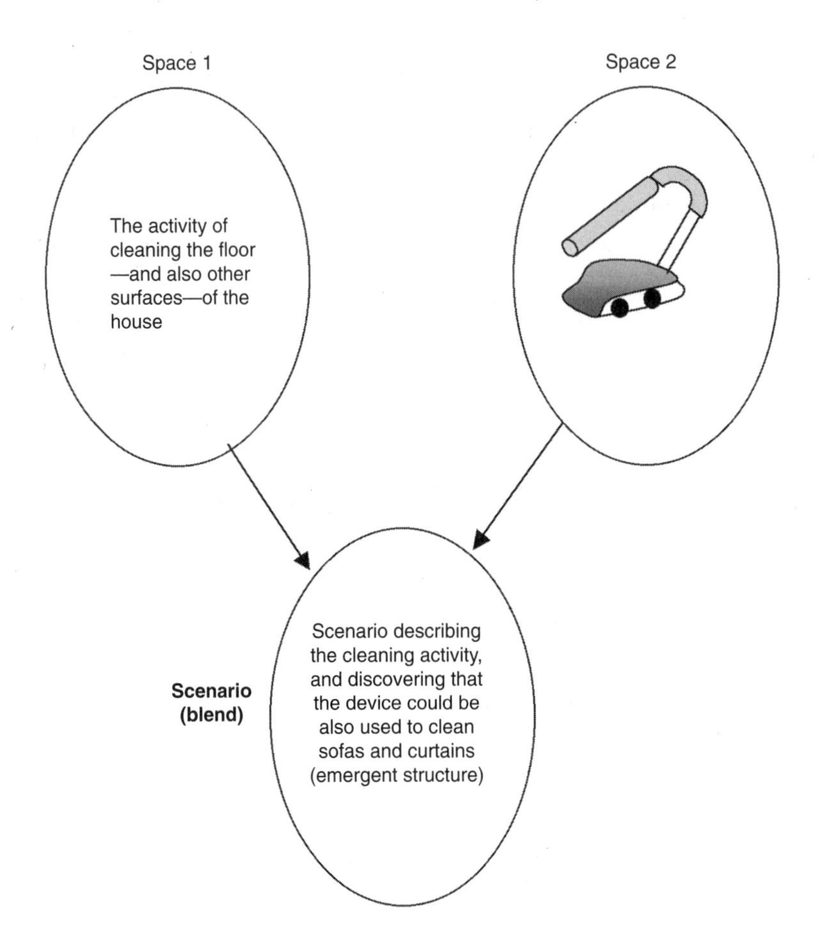

Figure 7.15
Scenario of cleaning the house with a vacuum cleaner

(such as those of the vacuum cleaner, yet also of the materials used to build the house and the furniture) but also by socioeconomic ones that might influence the time allocated to such an activity or the degree of care applied to it.

Use Cases

In the move from informal tools to more formal ones, use cases are at an intermediate point. They are semiformal artifacts, and as such the complementarity between formality and the possibility of representing human aspects (vividness, ambiguity, and complexity) is also at an intermediate stage. We witness the same complementarity principle that rules the physics of particles: it is not possible to determine with a high degree of precision simultaneously the position and speed of particles. We have to choose the variable we would like to measure with an indefinite degree of precision.

As we have seen when treating the characteristics of logic-propositional sentences, it is by restricting the number of mental spaces involved that we can get the simplicity needed to build a propositional sentence. Formal sentences of logical systems are possible because there is a considerable diminution of mental spaces involved, but most important yet, natural-language sentences are not objects of the same nature as logical propositions. This explains why we can capture complexity and the richness of vivid descriptions and experiences—when using natural-language sentences—as a consequence of creating a complex network of mental spaces and interconnections among them.

Recognizing the lack of power for such a purpose, Carroll (2000, 236) points out that

> scenarios are relevant and accessible to users not because they provide elegant hierarchical analysis of individual system functions, but because they provide rich, informal, and open-ended descriptions of real practice and experience. Use cases are very incomplete with respect to the experiences of the agents who play roles in the use case, the defining goals that cause the use cases to be enacted, and the circumstances that evoke those goals.

We agree with Carroll's position regarding the differences between both cognitive artifacts, but we are not proposing—as he seems to do—that use cases are an alternative to scenarios. If we have to choose, we also prefer scenarios to use cases, as they are more relevant, rich, and open-ended. But it is not a question of choosing between both artifacts, as use cases employed at an intermediate stage of development may be an excellent tool to continue further design steps using a more formal model such as UML diagrams. Use cases lack important features like explicating goals that cause the use case to be enacted, but we have already included all these human aspects of the system in the user stories and conceptual scenarios.

User stories, which describe the tasks at a general level, are the baseline or the individual contexts to use cases that must be developed at a later stage. The UML refers to use cases as the requirements model, so they are relevant as interactive descriptions between the actors. (We use the term *persona* when considering scenarios, while agents interacting with use cases are referred to by the term used by UML—*actors;* they are personae in a given role).

We concur with Carroll (2000, 237) when he continues his discussion about use cases, observing that "one should understand use cases as simplified views of task scenarios, simplifications that are suitable for particular roles in software design. They provide the critical link between scenarios as descriptions of use and scenarios as descriptions of software to support use."

Lauesen (2002, 92) gives some definitions of task and use case that can be helpful to differentiate both concepts:

A task is what user and product do together to achieve some goal (The product is usually a computer system)

A use case is mostly the product's part of the task
A human task is the user's part of the task

It seems—at first glance—strange to consider use cases as the product's part of the task, as the user is also involved in the interaction with the system. Maybe it's clearer when Lauesen (92) explains that "often, some kind of computer system was used before, and with the new product the computer system takes care of more of the task. In some cases the human part of the task disappears altogether, and we have a total automation of the task."

We can deduce that the user's part of the task includes all those actions the user does without using the system. This is a restrictive definition, as the user performs a task while interacting with the system, and consequently the use case would include part of a human task as well. In this sense, we could say that a use case is the product's part of a task and the user's part of the same task while interacting with the system.

If we need to make such a distinction it is because the concept of task used is broader than the specific set of actions performed with the system, and close to the concept of business process from which a task is always a component.

This consideration aside, we may accept the definition offered by Lauesen (126): "A use case is a sequence of related messages exchanged among the system and outside actors, together with actions performed by the system."

The definition is taken from a previous one—by Rumbaugh, Jacobson, and Booch (1999, 488), which states that "a use case is a coherent unit of functionality provided by a classifier (a system, subsystem, or class) as manifested by sequences of messages exchanged among the system and one or more outside users (represented as actors), together with actions performed by the system."

It is interesting to observe how Lauesen (2002, 127) concludes that "the definition only talks about the actions performed by the system (in our terminology the product), not the actions performed by the user." And being coherent with his point of view, Lauesen (92) describes the use case for checking in a booked guest as follows:

Trigger: Receptionist selects check in
Read booking number
Display guest and booking details
Read and store modifications
Wait for check-in command
Select free room(s)
Mark them as occupied
Add them to guest details
Display room number(s)
End use case

This point of view implies that all the interactions are observed from an internal perspective, where everything happens as if there were only a main actor enacting the use case. That is why the system reads the booking number, and later reads and stores modifications. We ignore everything about who is introducing such data, and the problems and concerns of such an external actor.

The description considers an observer (the architect or requirements engineer) from an internal perspective, and a scope that might vary from a closer location that is the system (foreground) until a far location (background) that is the interface, but always between the limits of the intended system. A

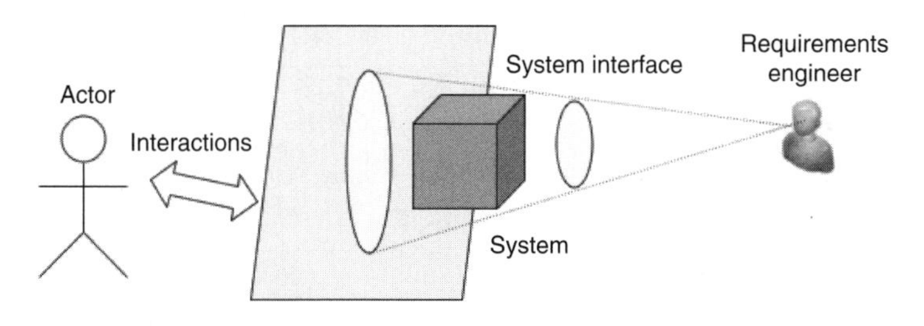

Figure 7.16
Description of the use case from an internal perspective

different form of depicting the use case is alternatively considering the actor and the system. Moreover, many examples of this type would describe the use case as follows:

Trigger: Receptionist selects check in

Receptionist	System
Introduces the booking number	
	Display guest and booking details
Introduces modifications	
Selects the check-in command	
	Select free room(s)
	Mark them as occupied
	Add them to guest details
	Display room number(s)
[Read room numbers and search keys]	

End use case

This alternate point of view implies that all the interactions are observed from an external perspective, where both the actor(s) and the system are visible simultaneously. This perspective is closer to what happens in the real scenario, and facilitates the finding of problems with interactions. When considering the use case from an external perspective, there are additional actions of the task that are immediately suggested by the description, such as looking for the room numbers and searching for the keys. In this case it is a part of the user's task, but it may occur that some important interactions might be ignored when only considering the internal description of the use

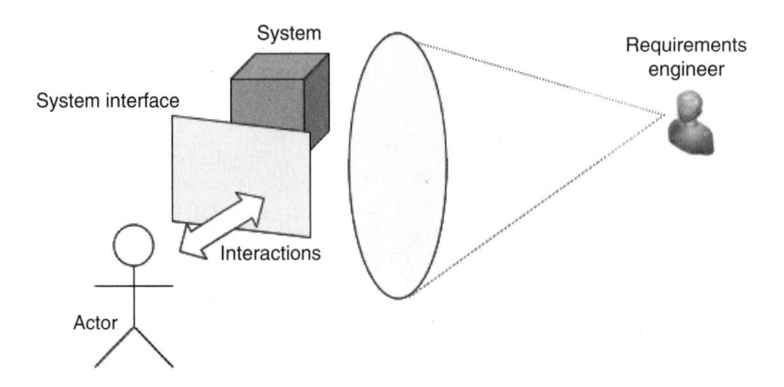

Figure 7.17
Description of the use case from an external perspective

case (as this perspective implies hiding the other key element of the interaction: the actor).

This is only an example of how changing the perspective in portraying a use case we can gain some advantages in the description. The description, in the style of scenarios, includes a flexibility that the internal one lacks. It is quite impressive how the changing of perspective allows us immediately to perceive things that the older view inhibited or hid.

Patterns

Patterns are a relatively new type of cognitive artifact aimed at offering some heuristic guidelines with an intermediate degree of formalization, halfway between scenarios and a concrete diagram such as a class diagram, or else for a given application. Patterns began in architecture where Christopher Alexander (1977) introduced them. Since then, they have moved into OO programming, design, and recently areas such as user interface design, Web site design, and so on. In engineering, of course, patterns have been in existence for an eternity: knitting patterns, patterns for the solutions of common engineering problems, and so forth. Mark Johnson points out that when understanding the concept of a schema more loosely than he does, it is possible to extend the list of image schemata he provides. Johnson (1987, 126) adds that "Christopher Alexander, for example, has developed an account of some 253 recurring 'patterns' that influence our experience. . . . Most of Alexander's patterns are not image schematic, in my sense, and would require a somewhat different kind of analysis than the ones given above."

While image schemata are the result of ongoing bodily experiences with the external real world, we might consider that patterns are the equivalent of image schemata when putting more abstract or cognitive experience in place of a bodily one. After a period of software development experience, we detect that some configurations of mental spaces appear over and over again. Another way of seeing patterns is considering them as conventional conceptual frames (chapter 2); in such cases, using a pattern would be the equivalent of framing a situation, seeing it as an instance of a general conceptual frame. We have described standard patterns of interaction (chapter 6) such as double click, drag and drop, and so on. Patterns will be the equivalent of frames for a group of people used to working together and knowing the details of a set of patterns, having previously practiced the patterns and collaborating among them with a suitable degree of communication. In such situations, patterns become more and more of a frame: somebody asks for a solution to a given problem and receives just the name of the pattern to be applied in such a context.

In order for a pattern to become the equivalent of a frame, there is a long history of training, discussions, and application of the pattern to concrete development situations. The name chosen for the pattern is also important. As we have seen in relation to scenarios, a name needs to activate immediately the network of mental spaces involved in order to mean something clear to the developer and for the developer to see how to frame the actual situation in terms of the pattern. So the vividness and experience of the name is related to its capacity to be highly figurative like the following ones from OO design: factory, bridge, decorator, facade, proxy, chain of responsibility, interpreter, mediator, observer, and strategy (Gamma et al. 1995). We know also that eventually the process of entrenchment makes the name more and more concrete, as it is associated to a set of concrete experiences of applying it to multiple software developments.

But there is another reason for choosing patterns as a tool for designing computer-based signs from metaphors and conceptual integration. In spite of the criticisms patterns might have generated, we prefer to use such a schema for representing the computer-based signs as our purpose is to use them in a more flexible way.

Some authors (Gartner et al. 1998, 10) include this cognitive process in a broader schema for cognitive models:

Domains Goals/principles/reasoning associated with recurring situations; serve as explanatory structure for expectations regarding a situation, as in "sorting activities."
Frameworks Domains with additional context information, as in "sorting mail" activities.
Cognitive Maps Frameworks that are oriented towards wayfinding; finding one's way through a problem, as in "sorting mail when address is incomplete."
Patterns Detailed, very context specific instantiations of frameworks, as in "sorting by zipcodes."

In this sense, we use the word pattern with an intermediate meaning, midway between patterns and cognitive maps. Even if we have adopted the classical formulation, it is evident that we are not dealing with classical classes and associations but with the vagueness of conceptual integration, derived from an initial metaphor. Even if we are going to use this concept as explained, it is worth using the classical structure for pattern definition—"name," "context," "problem," "forces," "solution," and so on—as this structure encourages designers to increase the precision of the conceptual integration development process.

While image schemata are structures that are constantly operating in our perception, bodily movement through space, and physical manipulation of objects, patterns are recurring structures we use in our professional life. That is, they are used in the context of more abstract contexts. They are conceptual configurations that frequently appear in the context of our everyday experience as software designers.

8 Designing with Blends

In the previous chapters, we have explored a set of conceptual tools that allow us to take an alternative perspective on cognition, HCI, and SE. From the notions of cognitive models, mental spaces, image schemata, basic-level categories, and imaginative projection, we have built up a view of cognition that distances itself from the disembodied world or the algorithmic manipulation of abstract symbols that characterizes traditional cognition. We live in a physical and social world, and this very existence has formed what we think and how we think. We feel what we think.

From this starting point, we have elaborated these concepts through many examples drawn from our domain of interest of software and people. Indeed, what motivated this inquiry was the mismatch between software and people, and we felt that a more embodied cognition might help us understand the problems people have with software and thus to design better systems. By moving away from the literal and into the figurative, we have understood how a number of key features of metaphors and blends can be useful. The process of designing with blends involves looking at the input, generic, and blended spaces, at different levels of abstraction, and at how blends result from compression of the vital relations. Designing with blends consists of understanding existing systems through analysis, and the imaginative design of new systems and devices.

Metaphor and Design

There have been many methods and much discussion about the role of metaphor in the design of human-computer systems, but not much has been motivated by the type of analysis that we have provided here. John Carroll and

John Thomas (1982) and Carroll and Robert Mack (1985) offer good design advice, and James L. Alty and colleagues (2000) supply a well-considered method for design with and for metaphor. Bonnie Nardi and Craig Zarmer (1993) argue that metaphors are good at suggesting a general orientation, but warn they are not good at accurately encoding precise semantics. As we have seen, this notion of a literal designation, or the encoding of meaning, is misleading. Don Norman (1998, 181) goes further: "Designers of the world: Forget the term 'metaphor.'"

By this we think that Norman is railing against some of the awful interface metaphors that are sometimes employed in user interface design. Norman (176) also says: "When I encounter a new situation, how do I know what to do? I look, listen, and copy. I try to understand what is happening. I see if I can find anything that looks familiar, and if I do, then I'll perform the actions that work in the familiar situation. . . . When I encounter a new piece of technology I do the same thing. I look at it and try to see if anything looks familiar."

For us this is the essence of metaphor—taking concepts from one domain and applying them to another, showing a *new* result and hence gaining understanding. Particularly in the early stages of design we find the fertility of concepts in informal cognitive processes, such as metaphors, blends, or stories.

There have been a few approaches at directly applying the concepts and constructs of metaphors and blends to user interface design and analysis. John Waterworth (1999) develops "schema space," an interactive system that seeks to exploit the power of image schemata. He uses centrality to show importance, paths to show links, and so on. Paul Maglio and Teenie Matlock (1999) use an analysis of the language people employ when browsing the Web, such as "I clicked on . . . and it brought me to . . . ," "I went to Google," and so on, to show the conceptual structure based on image schemata. They also use the idea of blends to explore issues of Web usage.

The mechanisms of conceptual integration are part of our deep cognitive processes, what Fauconnier and Turner (2002) call "backstage" cognition. It is not possible to describe blending as an algorithm or procedure that we could follow mechanically in order to arrive at a given goal. Nevertheless, even partial descriptions or guidelines about the interactions derived from an understanding of blending might be useful in the HCI discipline. In the development of a new software system we need to consider, on the one hand, a mainly creative process based on a new metaphor, which has to be explored and developed. We also need methods and techniques to help us understand the current situation and any current implementations.

When applying conceptual integration, or blends, to designing user interfaces, we propose two main processes. The first one is concerned with understanding which input spaces and frames are involved in any current implementation. The process of producing this first blend corresponds to what we usually do in the analysis stage of traditional software development. We study the domain by asking people, obtaining their stories, and examining their existing systems. From this we can identify input conceptual spaces and frame descriptions. The next part of the process is to select a basic set of main concepts, entities, or classes. We have also seen (in chapter 5) how, in traditional software development, new entities or classes appear as the analysis continues. Issues need to be solved to produce an improved situation.

The second process belongs to a lower level of abstraction in which we refine the concepts by bearing in mind the constraints of technologies. This might be considered the design stage of classical software development. Here we are dealing with objects that also often have a graphic representation (what we usually call icons) or other perceptible manifestation, so decisions have to be taken on the perceptual features to assign to these elements. Importantly, we must also specify the associated actions that people will perform to interact with them. The steps to be performed in the design phase are to consider each analysis element to assign its graphic features and each operation in order to assign actions we must perform. It is crucial to reiterate that the overall process is highly iterative, looking at blends and subblends, physical and conceptual features, doing design and analysis, and moving up and down levels of abstraction.

One of the few design theorists who also discusses metaphor is Donald Schön (1993). He emphasizes the critical role that metaphor has in "frame shifting" and "frame restructuring." By coming up with a novel, figurative way of seeing a design problem, new insights can be gained on how to solve the problem.

Analysis

Analysis is aimed at understanding the main concepts derived and issues involved in a domain. Gathering user stories as well as developing scenarios and personae will help to move from the concrete world of a real situation to the more abstract one of a domain of interest. The design can commence by analyzing user stories, detecting the input conceptual spaces, and finding a suitable frame description for each space. The aim here is to unpack the blend so that the designer can see where concepts have come from and which concepts are emergent in the blend. The designer will iterate around these issues, developing and exploring blends and subblends along with evaluating the integrity of different formulations.

In chapter 6, we emphasized the different levels of HCI: actions, tasks, and goals. We also stressed that designers need to reflect on designs at each of these levels, aiming to achieve a human scale in their designs—foregrounding the humanly scaled relations in a blend over the technological ones. Indeed, tasks can themselves be seen as blends. One input space is the space of technologies and the other is the space of activities and contexts (that is, the domain). Tasks should be designed at a human scale. This will also help them to disappear—in the same sense as a hammer *disappears* and integrates into an arm's extension—and give the illusion of nonmediation.

We also looked at the input spaces of the desktop interface (in chapter 3)—the real workplace desktop and the space of computer commands. As each of the input spaces has a different organizing frame, a detailed description of each one will be valuable. The description is the source for the detection of individual elements of one space that will be projected (or not) to the conceptual integration.

The frame of the real workplace desktop has elements like folders, documents, and trash cans (or wastepaper baskets). Other items could be added such as a calendar, a calculator, a telephone book, and so on. Interestingly, Microsoft Windows now has a recycling bin on the desktop—something not often found in offices. But in the selected list of elements in the original frame used for the Mac OS graphic interface, there were only folders, documents, and a trash can. In such a frame, we organize our documents into folders, so we have to open a folder to get a document; we write documents and then we archive them into folders, put them in a safe location, and so on. We can copy groups of documents, so while the original is in one folder, the copy is in another folder.

As we saw in chapter 6, Fauconnier and Turner (2002) analyze the desktop interface in terms of how the integration principle wins out over the topology principle in this blend. The topology is violated by having the trash can on the desktop (since it is not on the desktop in the real workplace), but the integration of the whole interface is maintained. Fauconnier and Turner also discuss how the copy and paste commands violate the topology of real workplace copying and pasting as there is no clipboard in the real workplace. Interestingly, our understanding of this part of the blend comes from the practice of journalists cutting and pasting articles in the days before word processing. Once again there is no secret clipboard, but there are multiple pieces of text that are reconfigured by pasting. Indeed, the copy-and-paste example is now fully reversed. One of authors (Benyon) once suggested to his children that they could do a cut and paste from a magazine into their scrapbooks. They looked at him, puzzled, before one of them said, "Oh, you mean like on the computer!"

Whatever the "real" derivation of the original input spaces to the desktop interface blend, the main concepts involved in the input spaces may now be considered. For example, if one of the input spaces is the office in general and not the desktop, it is clear that there are many more elements available. In chapter 6, we presented an example of office interface, broader than desktop and with more elements (see figure 6.3). There was a telephone and a door indicating the "exit" from the system. In the case of the desktop interface, we select a set of candidate elements to consider: the desktop surface, folder, document, or trash can (notwithstanding that this is not usually placed on the desktop).

It is also important to consider the behaviors of the elements. For instance, regarding real-world folders, there are operations like "open," "to put into another folder," and so forth. It is interesting to note that some operations such as opening a folder are derived from additional subblends. For example, before being able to double click the folder, we have produced a double-click blend as a new manipulation command (see chapter 6).

We may consider that such subblends have previously been built when the associated devices (say, the mouse) were created. Even considering that there is a simultaneous development of devices for the operations and interfaces, it would be convenient to define these operational blends first, and subsequently apply them to the interface features like folders and documents. This can be observed in the development of new media devices such as mobile phones and the iPod. The behaviors of the iPod's *click wheel,* the phone's *rocker switch,* or the personal data assistant's *navigation button* have to be learned alongside the concepts of the interaction.

From the frame of real-world objects, we project some additional operations. For example, to select an element is the equivalent of stating an intention to do something with it, such as looking at it. Before moving any object, I have to intentionally focus my attention on it or grasp it with my hand. So there is a selection of the object I will act on, and it is only after this selection has been made that I can move the object (see chapter 6).

The analysis must also concern itself with new concepts that are emergent in the blend. For instance, associated with the open operation applied to a folder and considering the constraint of a limited space available on the screen, we need a new space where we can show documents and other folders contained in the opened folder. The need for a new space leads us to create a new concept, a window perhaps, with new operations associated with it. This new emergent concept derives from a new subblend applied to two different input spaces: one is the desktop and the second is the space of buildings. In this second space of buildings, windows are elements through which it is possible to observe different scenes.

The concept of a window needs, in turn, the definition of new operations. For example, we need to define an operation to modify the size of the window. Some windows can be moved, some are fixed, some are *scrollable,* and some are not. Another new operation might be to browse the content of the window horizontally and vertically. Drilling down still further, we can see that these new operations derive from applying another subblend to two input spaces: the space of computer-based windows and the frame of human vision, where a person moves their head to achieve greater visibility or increase their field of view. This head movement has been projected into the window blend as an operation to browse the window horizontally and vertically.

So the process iterates and continues until the main conceptual integration, the desktop in this case, is stable. It must be taken into account that this stable condition for a blend is a relative one, and the whole process may imply months or even years of continuous reworking, as of the case of the desktop interface. Often, the meanings and behaviors of the elements in such a complex blend are formally defined as the elements of the desktop interface were in the Apple and Microsoft user interface guidelines. But it is also true that just as a blend becomes stable, so the demands of a situation require additional concepts and behaviors. The recent and rapid development of interfaces for devices such as phones and cameras illustrates this well.

Analysis is a detailed, sometimes painstaking process. As we saw in chapter 7, there are often multiple viewpoints to consider on a situation, and many vantage points that can be considered. A team of analysts will work individually and collectively to explore the domain, and discuss the different elements and the meanings that they bring with them. Having finally selected the elements of the blend and considered new emergent ones along with their operations, we can begin a first evaluation of the whole blend. A table such as the one in figure 8.1 can be used to present a general outline of the operations, actions, and transformations. It is also important to identify where constraints need to be applied because of the domain's logic or physical restrictions. For example, if folder A contains folder B, it is not possible to move folder A to folder B. A warning message must be used to indicate this, or the action needs to be prevented in some fashion.

We can also show the transformations that happen to elements when certain operations are performed. The trash can moving from an empty state to a full state, for example, changes its graphic representation. The sign is the same, but it is represented by a different icon.

In figure 8.1, we have shown some typical concepts from the desktop interface. Across the top we have a folder, a document, a window, the trash can in an empty state, and the trash can with something in it; and down the left-hand side we have a folder, a document, a trash can, a hard disk and a removable floppy disk. The cells indicate where and how different operations occur, and the transformations that happen. Of course this is only a tiny part of the behavior of the interface, used here to illustrate how the analysis can be helped. For example, when selecting a folder it changes from a light blue color to a dark blue one, and a document from white with some gray tones to dark gray; or when moving a folder/document to the trash can, if the trash can is empty it changes to the full state, otherwise it remains in the same full state.

In the case of a floppy disk, there is an eject operation when the disk is moved to the trash and the trash can does not change its state. This illustrates the famous anomaly with the original Macintosh interface, which has been discussed previously.

The analysis can continue by looking at the integrity of the blend and reasoning about it in terms of the principles for good blends (see chapter 6). In terms of the integrity principle, there is a violation because of the dual role of the trash can. The trash can usually contains anything that is dragged to it.

We have also seen how the framework of conceptual integration provides a number of useful principles to guide the analysis of an existing system or device. Examine an existing, or potential, design for its conformance to the principles of compression, topology, pattern completion, integration, web,

from/ to				 empty	 full
	select		open	move ⇒	move
		select	open	move ⇒	move
			open		moving folder/ document into
			open		
			open	eject	eject

Figure 8.1
Some operations assigned to interface computer-based signs

unpacking, relevance, recursion, and so on. This sort of critical analysis is vital during the design stage too. Analysis and design are highly iterative. Discussion will also roam over many levels of abstraction. Here we have been looking at detailed aspects of design, but such an analysis is just as important at a conceptual level. Recall from chapter 4 the different levels of HCI. Sometimes the analyst will be looking at organizational issues, sometimes at procedural issues, and sometimes at the design of icons or behaviors.

The overriding principle that Fauconnier and Turner (2002) advocate is to design to achieve a human scale, as mentioned earlier. This principle brings the analysis back to the central theme of designing for the physical, cultural, and social aspects of being human. Cognition is embodied. Cognition is felt through the ways that we, as humans, interact with the world around us. Ed Hutchins (1983), in a discussion of gauges, watches, and dials, makes a similar point when he argues that good design comes from making the salient conceptual features map onto the perceptual ones.

Another key message about analysis is to realize that it is about problem setting as much as it is about problem solving. Schön contends that how we frame the purposes to be achieved is critical to how successful the analysis and design might be. The metaphors we use frame our understanding of the problems. "Problem settings are mediated by the stories people tell," says Schön (1993, 138), so attend to these, and be creative and critical in the analysis of them. Frame restructuring—seeing things through the lens of a new metaphor—can be crucial to effective analysis and design.

Design

The second process belongs to the design level, in which we refine the analysis concepts and deal with the physical characteristics of the interaction. Conceptual design is concerned with bringing new ideas and actions to bear on a problem. Physical design results from taking the concepts and operations produced as one input space, and blending this space with the new one: computer-based signs.

The space of computer-based signs varies with the different platforms that we might be designing for. If we are designing for a specific organization, there may be guidelines determining certain aspects of the look and feel of a design. In different domains there are various constraints, and of course there are constraints imposed by the target technology. For example, a drag-and-drop style of interaction is generally not available on a mobile phone. Designing an interactive television application has to take into consideration that interaction is through a remote control device.

Design is about structuring interactions into logical sequences, and clarifying and presenting the allocation of functions and knowledge between people and devices. Designers need to be concerned with specifying how everything works as well as how content is structured and stored. They need to fix on colors, shapes, sizes, and information layout. They are concerned with style and aesthetics. This is particularly important for issues such as the attitudes and feelings of people, but also for the efficient retrieval of information and how people will understand the system.

In operational design, the designer concentrates on how to input data and commands, the events that trigger actions, what feedback is provided, and how people will know what they are able to do. Representational design is more concerned with the layout of screens, the overall mood and metaphor of the design, and the "story" the design is telling.

The idea of patterns—perceived regularities in an environment—has been adopted by designers of interactive systems and appear as interaction patterns. As we saw in chapter 7, interaction patterns can be identified at many different levels of abstraction. For example, on a normal personal computer, if you double click on something it opens it, and if you right click it displays a menu of operations you can perform. Macintosh computers have only a single mouse button so the right-click pattern is unknown to Mac users. Most playing devices such as VCRs, DVDs, cassette tapes, and MP3 players on a computer will have a play, stop, fast forward, and rewind interaction pattern.

Patterns build up into the complex interactions that we are familiar with and become entrenched. When you turn on your stove, you do not think of how to translate that intention into a physical action. But when someone new to the house tries to turn on the stove, they may have to consciously search for something, some sign, that looks like an "on" button and may have trouble working out which switch controls which burner.

The designer has to work through all the conceptual objects and operations that have been identified in the analysis phase, and consider the behaviors and representation of the computer-based signs that are to be created.

For example, the possible states of a folder are "closed," "opened," and "selected." Sometimes, the state of open folder may imply the use of a different image. In other cases—as in that of selected folder—we can use a different color to indicate it. Observe that the state of selected derives from a subblend using as the first input space—the analysis blend—and the second input space (or frame)—visual field or manipulative actions. A selected folder might correspond to a glance at the folder or to the folder in our hands (not yet opened)—that is, to an intentional act.

To each applicable operation, we need to associate actions we might perform using an external device like a mouse, joystick, or trackpad. This is also a subblend applied to the space of elements' operations and the actions performed using an external device. When executing this new subblend, we can produce new concepts not included in any of the input spaces. For instance, as we have constraints when using mice—we can press down the left or the right button, or sometimes there is only one button—we might need to associate to the operation—open a folder—a new action—using a double click. This is a new meaning not available in any of the input spaces, where we only had "to open a folder" or "to press the left button." The new operation appears in the blend, into which we project the concept of operation and the action of performing a double click.

Initial icon	Final icon	Operation	Consequences	Action	Place
		Empty	Delete all the objects contained in the trash	Click on the option "delete trash can"	Menu
		Select		Click on the sign	
/		Move	Included into	Drag and drop a document or folder on the trash can	Document, folder
/ Equal to final icon	(when dragging internal/external device)	Dismount/ Eject	the internal/ external device is dismounted/ ejected	Drag and drop a internal/external device on the ejecting device	Internal/ external device
/		Open	List all the items contained in the trash can. May be presented as icons or names.	Double click	Trash can

Figure 8.2
Table for representing the trash can blend

If we return to the trash can as an example, the designer can again list a table of the different operations and behaviors, and use the table to inspect the design for conformance with the principles of good conceptual integration (figure 8.2).

After performing this blend, we can make some considerations in relation to the context. As we have already assigned the manipulative operations click, drag, drop, and double click (which has been already assigned for opening the trash can as there is no order in the blend), let us suppose that we need a new operation. One possible solution would be to assign a triple click, but for each additional operation we would include an additional click and that does not appear to be a reasonable design solution. Therefore, other solutions need to be found such as displaying a menu of functions. The important issue here is that there is a difficulty in the blend and it has to be solved. The difficulty derives from the fact that there are only two or three elementary actions that can be used with the mouse, and we have an increasing number of operations to be assigned to them. Another aspect is the concept of a menu.

Of course, this is not just a problem in this design situation. Buttons, user actions such as clicking, menus of commands, and so on, are used on all manner of devices. As the functionality of the device inevitably increases, so the original design solution breaks down as more and more functions get loaded on to the few physical or perceptual features of the device.

The operation of putting something in the trash can is derived more or less immediately from the real-world image schema: we take an object and put it into the trash can. The equivalent with our signs would be to grasp and bring (to drag is the equivalent given the restriction of having only two dimensions) the object to the trash can. When we reach the trash can, we release (drop) the object. The same restriction of being in a two-dimensional space determines that we drop the object on another and not into another; a three-dimensional representation of objects would allow us to put, for example, a document into a folder. A solution provided with the later versions of Mac OS allows the user to move a document onto a folder, which then opens automatically and permits the dragging of the document into the folder or repeating recursively the operation in another folder contained in the first one. This is a further evolution of the desktop conceptual integration.

In this blend, the trash can will never fill up completely. This consequence is derived from the fact that the underlying operating system command implies moving the object from one location to another (or just marking it up), and if there was enough space to store the document (or folder) before the move, there will be enough space after the move as well. This feature is projected from the frame of computer commands and restricts the potential projection from the frame of real-world trash cans. It is something nobody could have anticipated since it emerged when making the blend. That is why there is no graphic representation for a possible *full* state of the can.

For the "open" operation, it is evident that the graphic representation of the half-filled trash can does not allow us to see anything inside it. After using the open operation, it would be necessary to enlarge the same graphic representation (a big trash can with enough capacity to list its contents) or choose an alternative graphic representation. As the window sign is also available for other purposes, it is the suitable candidate to be selected as a viewer for the trash can contents. So this is the solution that has been chosen along with a general solution to see the inside of other objects-containers (folders): a window as a view of the inside of a container.

This analysis would have continued thoroughly until the sign had been completely defined at a design level. This complete definition may need additional models in order for the sign to be fully specified. For example, additional state-transition diagrams would be useful as each state and transition has to be mapped with different graphic representations. In general, all the artifacts offered by the UML are available to create the set of diagrams necessary for a complete modeling of the sign. Once the complete set of operations is stable and has successfully passed the tests of the governing principles, it is time to continue modeling in the classical way. Using the UML, each operation could be captured as a use case (although as we have seen, we still believe that such a representation is inherently figurative).

We have also emphasized the need to design, at a human scale, for people's goals, and to design for a sense of presence so that people feel connected to the domain or inside the environment.

Designing a Home Information Center

In this section, we will use a case study to illustrate many of the of the analysis and design features that we have been discussing. The case concerns the development of a new concept for a device known as the HIC. It was a real project that involved one of the authors (Benyon) along with a small design team. A rich and extended description of the design can be found in the work of Benyon, Turner, and Turner (2005). That description provides much more detail on the overall process and is presented from a traditional perspective rather than the conceptual integration one that is provided here.

The concept for the HIC came from the observation that there are two typical situations in the home. The television, video, DVD, and music center are in the living room. This is a "lean-back" situation, where people are being entertained and they relax. In the home office, there is a personal computer. This is a "lean-forward" situation, where people are actively engaged with and focused on producing things. The relatively poor uptake of devices such as WebTV (which provided Internet access through the television) suggests that neither the lean-forward situation of a personal computer nor the lean-back situation of a television in a living room will be the right context or device for new services such as home banking, shopping, and so on. Instead, a new device, the HIC, is proposed. This should be a device where people can get at and provide information while they are occupied with other household activities.

The abstract concept of a HIC as a device to deal with "a move-around situation for infotainment" was initially translated into a number of high-level features and functions. Some of these were derived directly from the concept, whereas others were included in order to prototype the technology to evaluate its suitability.

In thinking about scenarios of use for the HIC, three general and highly abstract ones—informational, communicational, and entertainment—were envisaged. From these abstract ideas, eleven scenarios were developed that looked at more specific activities, contexts, and people, and explored the range of information content, input, output, media, and communication abilities of the HIC technology. These were: What shall we have for dinner? What shall we do tonight? News and e-books, entertain me, message board, traffic, new users, housekeeping, and/or payment. I cannot program my video because . . . Planning ahead.

Early ideas about communication centered on how the HIC might be used as a sort of "post-it" system (a first metaphor): one member of the family might leave a message for another. The HIC would also be used as a video phone, e-mail system, and so on. The informational scenarios concerned activities such as going sailing, skiing (hence finding out about the weather), or out to a restaurant or show. The entertainment scenario led to ideas that users might like to watch television on demand alongside a chat room, say. Other scenarios included integration with other devices, such as heating control and home security. The children doing homework was another, as were investigating, finding out, doing crosswords puzzles and quizzes, ordering videos, photographs, and so on.

The first thing we observe about the HIC concept is the name itself: infotainment—an integration of information and entertainment. The input mental spaces are working with a personal computer and the type of interactions derived from such activity. We need to type in commands, click or double click with a mouse, move a joystick, or via touching, read the information shown on the screen, and so forth. The activity of working with a personal computer implies the use of hands to communicate with the computer, as the usual interfaces are textual or graphic.

On the other hand, we have the input mental space of the traditional television, which allows for hearing and seeing information while we are occupied with other household doings. One important point here is that we would not need to constantly use our hands to interact with the device, except when we change the channel or increase the volume of the television set.

The requirements of the new device show that it will be used for helping with other home activities, such as cooking or maybe with some type of do-it-yourself projects. From this new mental input space, we can recruit additional features such as the fact that in other housekeeping, or entertainment, activities like cooking and do-it-yourself projects this usually requires us to constantly use our hands. In such circumstances, we need someone else to help us to search for or read a recipe in a book, or tell us how to prepare a particular recipe. So it would be essential that the new device be able to recognize spoken commands in order for us to continue with the current activity while asking for specific information.

Thus, we have at least three input mental spaces from which to recruit structure for the new device: it should offer the possibility of a classical personal computer interface (a keyboard, a mouse, or the equivalent, and a monitor), the image and sound quality we require from a television set, and the added spoken interface to leave our hands free when they are needed for other activities.

One of the scenarios, message board, began as follows:

> 07:45 Michael comes into the kitchen to prepare breakfast, activates the HIC, and asks for messages. The HIC identifies Michael, and informs him that there are three new messages waiting for him. Michael can see that two of the messages are work-related, and none of them are essential for him to read right now, so he instructs the HIC to forward those two to his account at work. The last message is from Caroline, a close friend of the family, who sends an invitation for dinner Thursday next week. Michael checks his calendar and sees that he is able to make it. He leaves a message for his wife, writing, "Dinner at Caroline is ok by me, are you available?—and will you tell her?" He then grabs a quick cup of coffee and dashes out of the door.

Recall how we suggested that scenarios are a good way of exploring potential designs. The design of the whole HIC involved analyzing, designing, refining, and evaluating many different conceptual and physical designs (see Benyon, Turner, and Turner 2005, in particular chapter 14). Here, we can illustrate issues of designing with blends by considering some of the many questions that are raised by this brief story. Just this one paragraph implies the HIC has the following functions:

1. Ask for messages.
2. Identify the user.
3. Inform the user that there are new messages.
4. Forward messages to another location or user.
5. Record verbal message.
6. Finish a verbal message.

Elsewhere in the full scenario, functions such as the following were identified:

1. Take a snapshot from the user.
2. Attach a snapshot to a message.
3. Set a priority to a message.
4. Send a message (automatically or when requested by the user).
5. Translate a verbal message.
6. Acknowledge that a message has been sent.

This list may be categorized as follows:

- Sending and receiving e-mail messages;
- Receiving (and sending) phone messages;
- Taking a snapshot (or a video);
- Recording and listening to verbal messages;
- Controlling a given device.

And for each category, we can include the corresponding functions from the list:

1. Sending and receiving e-mail messages:
- Ask for messages.
- Inform the user that there are new messages.
- Write a message.
- Set a priority to a message.
- Send a message (automatically or when requested by the user).
- Forward messages to another location or user.
- Acknowledge that a message has been sent.
- Attach a snapshot to a message.
- Forward a phone message by e-mail.

2. Receiving (and sending) phone messages:
- Answer a phone call.
- Record a phone message.
- Announce a phone message.
- Phone.

And so on. As we mentioned earlier, the process of design is highly iterative and detailed, so we can hope just to give a flavor of the process here. This is "middle-out" design (chapter 5). After having categorized the main interactions, we may proceed to an initial solution to the conceptual space of the message board, in which we will introduce a set of blends. We will present two main solutions, one based on an image-schematic framework and the other on a framework of categories.

Both of these frameworks aim to achieve a human scale—again, the overriding principle that Fauconnier and Turner emphasize. Image schemata are one of the basic building blocks of human cognition, according to Lakoff and Johnson, and so we feel they should be stressed in design solutions. This is also the approach taken by Waterworth and colleagues (2002), and it satisfies Hutchins's design guideline of placing the conceptual map onto the perceptual (Hutchins 2000, 68). An approach based on a framework of categories aims to exploit the human scale of people interacting with basic-level categories where interaction is most natural conceptually and perceptually.

A solution based on image schemata might be based on three of them: source-path-goal, container, and center-periphery. In this design, we may use a set of source-path-goal image schemata to represent different ways a message may come in and a set of similar image schemata to represent ways a message may go out. The second image schema, the container, is used as the base to build a blend that is connected to input and output source-path-goal image schemata. We use the third image schema, center-periphery, to place the blend at the center of the design in order to fix the attention of the user on this design element in which all messages are stored. This is illustrated, conceptually, in figure 8.3.

The interface concept is intended to be highly straightforward, but of course it does involve some duplication in that devices that are both input

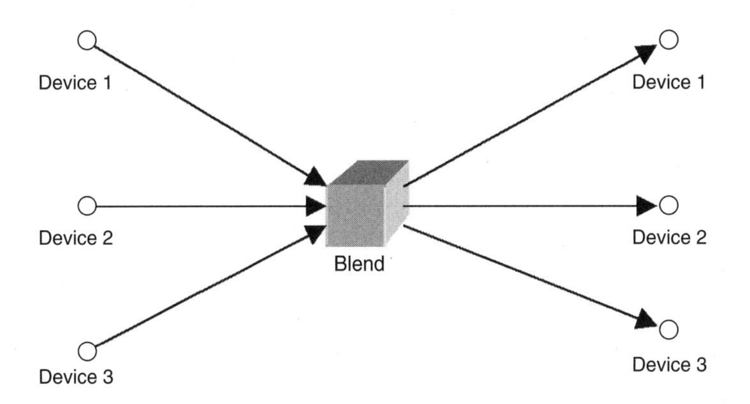

Figure 8.3

A first draft of the message board built with image schemata

and output will appear twice. The notion of messages moving from the input through the center, with the message contained and subsequently being sent, seems quite intuitive. It could be that we would include the people at this level of the interface. Particularly in the home setting where there are not too many people to be accommodated on a screen, including people would indicate where the message came from and where any message was to go. The forwarding of messages would then be also highly intuitive because it would be based on image schemata that are embodied and do not need additional information to be understood.

Of course, figure 8.3 is not intended to show how the interface would actually look, and in this part of the illustration we are not discussing the design of appropriate signs. Rather, we are concerned with the conceptual design. A design based on categories would look (conceptually) as depicted in figure 8.4. The design, here exploits a familiar distinction between objects and actions. One part of the interface identifies the actions and the other part the objects. Once again, we could include people objects at the interface or these can be included in the central blend of the message itself.

Another key design issue in this application was how to present the search results and let people move through them. In a number of scenarios, the user was presented with a potentially long list of search results. A generic and consistent design feature was needed to handle this. Another significant constraint on the interface for the HIC was that it should not look like a personal computer. Hence, we wanted to avoid scrolling at the interface. Reconciling these two design constraints—long lists of search results and no scrolling—

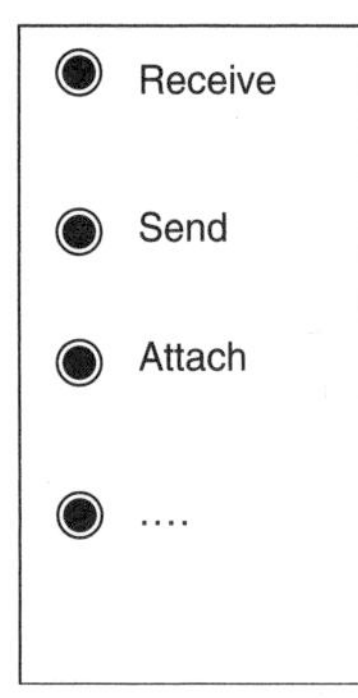

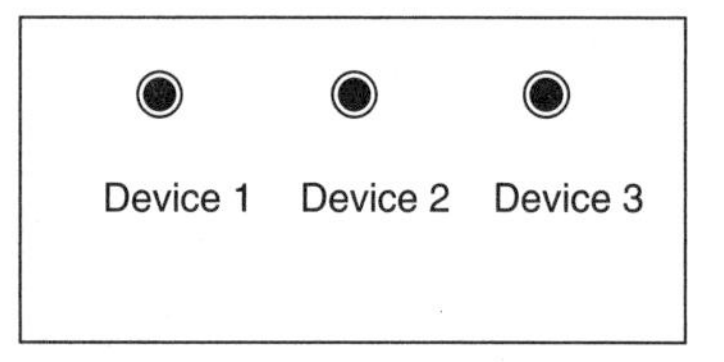

Figure 8.4
Message board design based on categories

Figure 8.5
A Rolodex

proved quite challenging. During the process of designing this part of the system, we explored a whole range of alternative visualization techniques that have been developed to deal with visualizations of large information spaces. We finally settled on the concept that any item returned from a search would be considered a "card," so we looked at the metaphor THE SEARCH RESULT IS A CARD. Cards do not have scrolling, so we were able to examine other ways of accommodating a search result that did not fit on a single card. Ideas of extensions cards, card part 1, card part 2, and so on, were explored. There was also the issue of how to present the whole information space that included all the search results. Here we considered various designs, such as a "gun barrel." The investigation led finally to the idea that THE INFORMATION SPACE IS A ROLODEX (figure 8.5).

We were now able to use these two basic metaphors to study how they would come together into a suitable blend of the interface. A card contains information, and the result of a search is information. Cards are stored on a Rolodex, typically in alphabetical order, so the search results can be stored on a Rolodex (though in the blend we might want to have other orderings, which might undermine the topology principle). With a real Rolodex, the person flicks through the cards with their finger or turns a knob on the side. Clearly, these physical aspects of the interaction will have to be replaced in the blend, which has to be displayed on a two-dimensional display device.

And so the discussions continued. An appeal was made to the governing principles of blends in an intuitive rather than rigid fashion. The focus was to maintain consistency with the overall metaphor and yet extend its meaning to accommodate the demands of this application. The blend from the space of the Rolodexes and the space of the search results developed its own, emergent structure. We felt that the design met the unpacking and relevance principles, and that it was appropriately humanly scaled. One area where we departed from the web principle was in introducing a history. We wanted to keep a record of people's previous searches so that they could easily retrieve them and to do this we developed an animation so that the Rolodex would shrink down to a separate part of the display—something real Rolodexes certainly do not do. We also needed to accommodate the results of large searches—when hundreds or thousands of results were retrieved. To do this we developed the concept of a "Rolodex tree," itself a blend from the Rolodex concept and a popular visualization, the "cone tree."

The final interface for the HIC is shown in figure 8.6. This depicts the miniature Rolodexes and the idea of the Rolodex tree. The interface contains three bars that hold important features of the HIC. Across the top is a category bar, showing the main information categories. On the left-hand side is the activity bar, and on the right-hand side is the object bar. This bar is also used for holding different content providers.

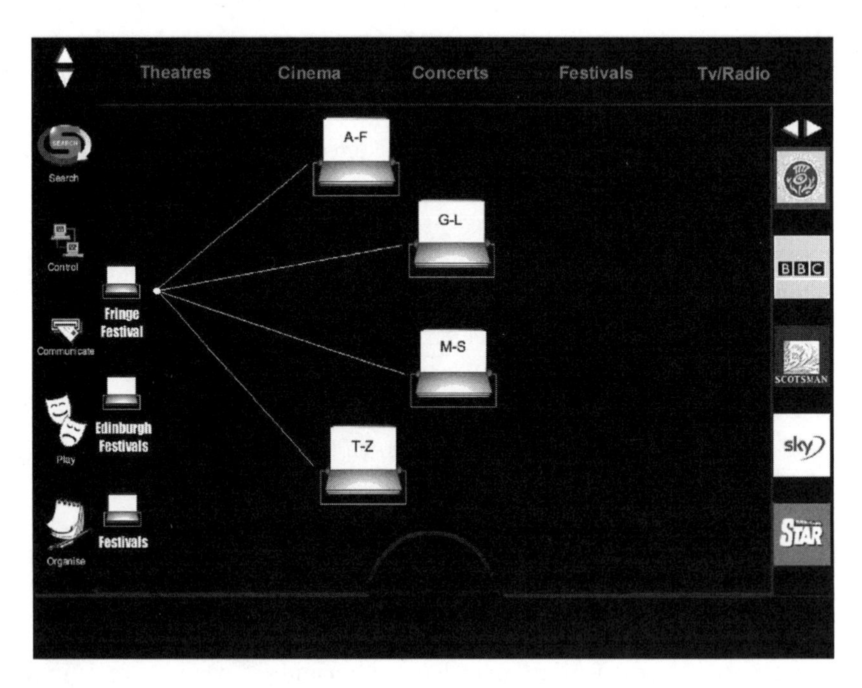

Figure 8.6
Final HIC interface

Of course, there were many more discussions and arguments within the design team during the development of the interface. The whole issue of how to move through the stack of cards in the Rolodex was one such debate. The pattern completion principle tells us to use existing patterns where possible. Up (or right) and down (or left) arrows are highly common signs to indicate next and previous: *up* is next and *down* is previous. But is "next" moving down or up through the alphabet? If it is the latter, than "up" is "down."

The interface was evaluated with people, and generally the concept was well liked and felt to be intuitive. One suggestion that arose from the evaluation was that the Rolodex should have alphabetical tabs on it (more like a real Rolodex) so that people could easily jump to particular parts of the information space.

Whatever the specific issues of the design that arise here—or pieces that you might like or dislike—the key feature of this description is to highlight how the concepts that we have explored can be brought together into a design process. The Rolodex certainly worked to promote the vital relations of the input spaces of Rolodexes and search results. Issues of ordering and access were preserved. The mess of search results that can arise from a large search is certainly not on a human scale. Borrowing for compression from the real-world Rolodex helps to manage that aspect of the HCI domain.

Conclusions

The main conclusion we may derive from this chapter is that the pragmatics of designing with blends are summed up in two phases: analysis and design. Designing by both image schemata and categories will help to ensure that the design is human centered, or humanly scaled. Using the governing principles of conceptual integration—in particular, integration and topology—helps to guide the choice of metaphors and blends used in the system.

During the analysis phase we produce the conceptual model of the interface, which is composed of a set of conceptual spaces. In order to structure a conceptual space, we use all the cognitive mechanisms, such as metaphors, image schemata, blends, projections, categories, and so on. These help to guide the development of an initial conceptual space, which needs to be refined at this early stage, allowing reasoning about the integrity and other aspects of the resulting interface.

We may use two ways of structuring the conceptual space: image schemata or basic-level categories. An important fact about image schemata is that they provide a level of representation intermediate between perception and language. This fact makes image schemata useful as designing tools, as they allow categorizing at an intermediate level, without the need to use linguistic expressions, thereby making the design *intuitive.*

The second framework we may use is based on categories (or concepts). In this framework, we use sets of categories to represent activities we will perform on entities and objects, which will support those activities. The main difference with designing by image schemata is that here we use a linguistic representation, even if concepts are represented as graphic signs.

An important fact is that conceptual integration is not a process that occurs in a given period of time. It may start with some elements of the integration, but persist for some months or even years, the way it actually occurred with the desktop conceptual integration.

9 Reflections

There are other books about the foundations of design and HCI and SE methods. These have been based on traditional psychology (Weinberg 1998), cognitive psychology (Norman 1998), ecological psychology (Gibson 1986), situated cognition (Suchman 1987; Clancey 1989; Lave and Wenger 1991); distributed cognition (Hutchins 1995), activity theory (Nardi 1995), philosophy (Dreyfus 1972; Winograd and Flores 1987), and more recently even embodied cognition (Dourish 2001; Agre 1997).

This book is based on the ideas of cognitive semantics, metaphor theory, and blending theory. These ideas have emerged in the last twenty years and remain in a constant state of expansion. Recently, a number of books applying cognitive semantics to different areas have been published: publicity and literature (Fauconnier and Turner 2002), social science (Turner 2001), mathematics (Lakoff and Núñez 2000), law (Winter 2003), and even music (Zbikowski 2002).

In *Designing with Blends*, we have sought to use some of the findings of cognitive semantics as a serious attempt to explain human creativity within the domain of people and their interactions with digital artifacts. The key concepts that have influenced our analysis include the importance of metaphor to cognitive processes and a theory of categorization that is not based on set-theoretical assumptions. This view of categorization and classification is particularly significant because much SE is predicated on finding and defining the "right" ontologies and classes of objects and relationships in a domain. It is difficult to reconcile notions such as the radial categories and the language games of human classes with the constructs provided by OO notations.

Another key issue that we have promoted is the bodily basis for cognition. Image schemata might be considered as the first cognitive constructs. They are so basic and general that they may be applied in any situation, even in prelinguistic contexts. We have seen that any graphic notation is based on image schemata and extended by means of metaphorical projections. It is also important to think in terms of image schemata when trying to create a new conceptual space for a user interface, as shown in the example of the HIC project (chapter 8). Basic-level categories are also central to this view: offering an explanation at a human scale for why we group things in particular ways and organize the hierarchies of categories that we do. Basic-level categories are basic in cultural, perceptual, and psychological ways.

A third major concept is that of mental spaces and how they are related through conceptual integration. The networks of models and frames that make up our thoughts and the process of blending are vital to the creation and interpretation of new ideas. Taken with the bodily basis of cognition, a view of cognition and action emerges in which there is a tight coupling of the two. This resonates with Dourish's (2001) embodied interaction and the ideas of McCullough (2004).

In a concluding chapter it would be nice to offer a new approach to HCI and a better methodology for SE that ensures great designs. But of course we cannot do that, nor would we want to do that. The worlds of HCI and SE as well as digital artifacts and people are evolving rapidly, and their interrelationships are complex. In place of method we provide debate and critical analysis. We will look at some emerging views of HCI, the roles of metaphor, models, and mental spaces in interaction design, creativity and conceptual integration, and some methodological contributions of this work.

Emerging Views on HCI

During and after the 2002 Association for Computer Machinery conference on human factors in computer systems, a Web site (ChiPlace) was maintained to link members of the global HCI community. The aim was both practical (to provide information about the conference and other events) and experimental in its use of community-building techniques. The forum was discontinued toward the end of 2003 owing to a shortage of volunteer time to manage the site. In 2003, there were two debates of particular interest: the question of HCI considered as a "navigation of information space," and another about HCI and interaction design (ID).

In his intervention to the first debate, one of the authors of this book (Benyon) proposed the following alternative: Is "HCI is a navigation of information space" a metaphor or a theory? Although this question did not elicit an explicit reply to the forum, following the ideas previously discussed in this book, we would say that there is no opposition between the terms metaphor and theory.

Theories are based on metaphors. Perhaps people may question this assertion, particularly with respect to the "hard" physical sciences. One might think that it could be true for social sciences, perhaps, where the type of phenomena considered may be interpreted through metaphors, but not in classical science. To answer this, we point to the work of Lakoff and Núñez (2000) to show how fundamental metaphor is even to such hard sciences as mathematics.

When Benyon says that "HCI is a navigation of information space," he is stating a general theory about HCI. As with all metaphors, the navigation metaphor determines the visibility of some aspects of HCI, while hiding others that could be important to the subject. One opponent of this view of HCI on ChiPlace answered that HCI is not just navigation but many other things as well: usability, visual presentation, or even data representation. Therefore, the entire subject of HCI would not be compressed into just navigation.

This issue is critical, as in all metaphors there are some *visible* and also some *hidden* aspects of the analyzed discipline. These hidden aspects are unthinkable in the theory based on a particular metaphor. We have already seen this question when discussing requirements and how they could be conceptualized: as *elicitation, capture, gathering, creation,* and so on. Each concept reveals key aspects (using another spatial metaphor, we would call them dimensions) of requirements that are valid simultaneously. The different views need to be considered alternatively or in sequence.

Another frequent issue associated with metaphors is the need to remember something obvious: that source and target domains are, in fact, different. In the ChiPlace debate, another opponent asserted that the concept of navigation in cyberspace has a completely different physics from navigation in the real world. The objects in cyberspace are not static, links can be created and broken, people can jump from one part of the space to another, and there is no bodily movement. While this is indeed the case, it is exactly the function of a metaphor: to bring together two different things, blending something new.

Associated with HCI as the navigation of information space, there are other concepts in architecture or interior design. When considering interior design, for example, we could analyze different places where the HCI phenomenon occurs—in particular, the workplace. One such workplace is the office, and the idea of using such an environment metaphorically may result in the desktop metaphor. Therefore, one possible useful application of the HCI IS NAVIGATION OF INFORMATION SPACE metaphor is the production of new, secondary metaphors to be applied to the design process. In this case, the source domain was a real space, but nothing prevents the use of virtual spaces or other source domains. The main metaphor may be considered constitutive of the discipline (HCI), while secondary metaphors are used to produce new designs.

Another interesting and current debate that surfaced briefly on ChiPlace concerns the opposition between HCI and the new discipline of Interaction Design (ID). At first glance, one could maintain that we are dealing with the same subject, but focusing on different aspects of it. In terms of scope and immediate scope (chapter 7), the scope is the general form and function of a software system. The immediate scope in the case of HCI is the way designers immerse themselves in the everyday activities and concerns of users, while in the case of ID designers are concerned primarily with values, preferences, and meanings—that is, aesthetics and semantics (Crampton Smith and Tabor 1996).

It appears as if we are dealing with a question of categorization, and hence we should decide whether both areas are included in a common category or are so widely separated as to define two different concepts. The problem with this type of categorization is the difficulty of finding a prototypical member. Both definitions might be candidates for a prototype, and we could then decide whether they define, for example, a graded or radial category. They are not physical things, which could be considered in relation to aspect, form, color, and so forth. Another aspect of the problem is that both definitions refer to an abstract and permanently changing discipline.

What Terry Winograd (1997, 156) considers as interaction design is also in line with the spatial metaphor, ID is the "design of spaces for human communication and interaction." So we have the metaphors HCI IS NAVIGATION OF INFORMATION SPACE and ID IS THE DESIGN OF SPACES FOR HUMAN COMMUNICATION AND INTERACTION. One conclusion here is that ID focuses on the design of spaces while HCI focuses on the use, the navigation, of such spaces. HCI is then concerned about such things as usability, visual presentation, or data representation, as noted earlier. Indeed, the subject of "information architecture" is an emerging area of study in HCI, primarily in Web site design. Information architecture concerns the structure and layout of information spaces. This debate illustrates how, when contrasting different definitions, new meanings may emerge. In the discussion about metaphor or theory it seemed that the concept of navigation left out such aspects as usability, but now that it is contrasted with ID, we realize that navigation implies the use of physical and cognitive artifacts. Navigation is not just about the movement through a space, it is about the architecture, visual appearance, and usability of that space.

On the other hand, the scope of Winograd's definition is wide open (as one of the discussants on ChiPlace pointed out). A space can mean anything from a bus stop to a shopping mall to cyberspace. In trying to illustrate the similarity between real-world navigation and navigation in information space, Benyon described how unstable some physical spaces can be. In the ChiPlace forum in 2003, Benyon used the example of a department store during the January sales: "Temporary signs had been put up to show people the way to departments and I had to search along the rails to find the right sizes because all the content was not organized as it should have been. . . . I finally found a new hat, the right size and took it to the cash register. They scanned my card and I signed my name."

Not only did finding the right hat take time because of the store's information architecture, even signing a name is part of the navigation. This might at first seem surprising (surely a simple piece of data entry cannot be considered navigation). Yet as soon as we project structure from the domain of real-world classic navigation into the cognitive model of the navigation of information spaces we see things differently. Writing in a logbook, for example, is an important part of real-world navigation.

In the debate regarding HCI and ID, Jonas Löwgren—in the ChiPlace 2003 forum—referred to the book called *Interaction Design* (Preece, Rogers, and Sharp 2002). Löwgren argued against the use of the term support in respect to ID:

In the preface, the authors define interaction design as "designing interactive products to support people in their everyday and working lives." But does it make sense to say that a computer game supports people? Even if it "supports" the player's assumed goals of experiencing excitement or challenge, how does it "support" the player's boyfriend's desire to see a bit more of his girlfriend? Is a teenager's experience of spending time in an online chat community primarily a "supportive" one? Does a piece of techno-critical digital art, such as the work by Anthony Dunne and Fiona Raby, "support" the viewer?

My point is not that "supporting" is necessarily bad, only that it implies a certain ideology: an HCI perspective of goal-driven users whose use should be made as effective and efficient as possible.

In this context, the term support is the cornerstone to develop some arguments in relation to an ideological use of discourse, and how such ideology can hide more general social considerations when analyzing the design of a game or a chat in just a narrow, traditional way. One possible conclusion to this discussion is the proposal to merge, or rather blend, the disciplines of HCI and ID into a new one: human-centered interaction design.

Personal Spaces

Dourish (2001, 118) points out that from an ecological perspective, cognition is not purely a neural phenomenon, but is located within (and throughout) a complex construct involving the organism, action, and the environment: "Ecological psychology studies 'knowledge in the world' rather than 'knowledge in the head.'" This was the conclusion James Gibson (1986) arrived at when studying visual perception, which is considered not as a link between optics and neural activity but as a coupling between the human being and its environment. Linking optics and a neural activity corresponds to an objectivist point of view, separating the body and the world. Whereas considering the coupling between the human and the environment takes into account the ongoing interactions between both aspects of the phenomenon—that is, it is the equivalent of embodied cognition.

This approach does not agree in dividing, for example, seeing and acting, as it views the two as deeply connected. The conclusions of ecological psychology regarding the impossibility of separating seeing and acting were experimentally confirmed. The experimental story was gathered by Francisco Varela, Evan Thompson, and Eleanor Rosch (1991), and tells how a group of newborn cats were separated into two groups. The first group was harnessed to a cart, which took the second group of cats. All the experiment was performed with a minimum intensity of light, so that the cats that pulled the carts continually interacted with obstacles put in the way, while the other cats could never access such types of interactions.

The result of the experiment is that the first group of cats continued seeing normally when the experiment was over, while the second group was unable to see and continued living as blind cats. That proves that there is not a passive relationship between light rays that go through the vision system and produce a final neurological activity. This neurological activity is also the result of actions that the whole body performs with its environment.

The idea of considering knowledge in the world in place of knowledge in the head goes in parallel with the theory of mental spaces. Back in 1985, Fauconnier (1994, xxxi) stated that mental spaces are "clearly theoretical constructs devised to model high-level cognitive organization." As with most scientific notions, mental spaces are connected to the real world through the theories of which they are a part. This has been called constructivist epistemology by Ronaldo García (2000). We have to think of scientific explanation as ascribing to the empirical relationships the necessary connections, which are verified in the theoretical structures of scientific theories.

The main argument that asserts that mental spaces are not purely "knowledge in the head" is that the objects of study are mainly language, text, pictures, or graphic user interfaces; they are social productions. Here also, we find a coupling between humans and their social or cultural environment. Using mental spaces, we can explain how language moves progressively from informal stages—implying several mental spaces and connections among them—to more formal stages with just one mental space. Sentences that unfold in just one mental space imply the speaker's origin or base along with the identity space-connector from and to the same space.

In general, we might say that the development of a piece of software progresses in a series of blends with the addition of new mental spaces. We start with a frame, basically the notation that we are using and continue adding mental spaces from the domain, then additional technological mental spaces, the security mental spaces, and so forth. Each new aspect we might consider in the design corresponds to a new mental space. But the notation and hence the frame is critical and defines the starting ontology. In SE, data-centered techniques such as entity-relationship models or dataflow diagrams provide a different ontology, or organizing frame, than OO techniques. The developer's view of the requirements (elicitation, capture, gathering, and so on) and the development process is critical to how the software is conceptualized and the mental spaces that are employed. It has taken many years to get HCI into mainstream SE. Even then, the predominant frame of HCI has been task based as opposed to goal based (see chapter 6).

Alistair Cockburn (2002, 146) explains the origins of methodologies:

> A methodology's principles are not arrived at through an emotional neutral algorithm but come from the author's personal background. To reverse the saying from *The Wizard of Oz,* "Pay great attention to the man behind the curtain."
>
> Each person has had experiences that inform his present views and serve as their anchor points. Methodology authors are not different . . .
>
> A person's anchor points are not generally open to negotiation. They are fixed in childhood, early project experiences, or personal philosophy.

In terms of cognitive semantics, an "emotional neutral algorithm" refers to the folk traditional approach, which considers that the mind and the body may be separated, while Cockburn's point of view highlights the embodied aspect of the methodology's principles. Another sentence points to "the man behind the curtain," a similar concept to that of backstage cognition applied by Fauconnier and Turner (2002). But the important aspect to highlight is when Cockburn writes that each person has had experiences that "inform his present views and serve as their anchor points." This is an expression that shows the origin of a metaphor, where past experiences are the source mental space, which is projected (that is, informs) onto one's present views—that is, a target mental space.

The other important assertion suggests that the past experiences are fixed in childhood from where they are projected to new mental spaces. The same idea is held by psychoanalytic theory (Lacan 1966), which considers that the unconscious is structured like a language, and particularly by metaphor and metonymy. Much of the work a psychoanalyst does is to establish relations (that is, projections) from a mental space (childhood, parents, actual work situation, and so on) to another (actual work situation, childhood, and so forth), the same way that metaphors do.

It is funny how Cockburn (2002, 147) describes some elements of a methodology, viewed as a preventive measure against repeating a bad experience the author has had: "Afraid that programmers make many little mistakes? Hold code reviews. Afraid that users don't know what they really want? Create prototypes. Afraid that designers will leave in the middle of the project? Have them write extensive design documentation as they go."

Kent Beck (1999) puts this point into a nutshell when he considers that "all methodology is based on fears." He also proposes to simplify the general design of a program to match a single metaphor. Examples might be: "This program really looks like an assembly line, with things getting added to a chassis along the line," or "This program really looks like a restaurant, with waiters and menus, cooks and cashiers."

Even knowing that words are not mirror images of an external reality, it is hard to get rid of expressions based on an objectivist philosophy or using the conduit metaphor to refer to communication in general. We quite likely have used such expressions throughout this book without being aware of doing that. For example, in Benyon and Imaz (1999, 163), we wrote that "the analytic, explanatory and communicative power of a conceptual model arises from the structure, operations and constraints which that model is able to capture," which may be considered as equivalent to the above ideas.

But to be consistent, we should have written "the analytic, explanatory, and communicative power of a conceptual model arises from the structure, operations, and constraints that the model is able to evoke." The former expression, including "capture" in place of "evoke," suggests that a model leads us to understand "just what the words say"—or what the model has introduced into itself. Nevertheless, the important fact is that we must be able to understand such expressions in a nonobjectivist way until a new, more suitable discourse is developed.

Fluency in Conceptual Integration

Conceptual integration is an ongoing work of the last ten years that continually includes new advances and refinements. An activity such as software design is aimed at providing imaginative and creative new solutions to problems created by humans, computers, and other digital artifacts, and their interactions. So new conceptual tools like conceptual integration, or blends, are quite relevant to HCI-SE. We have tried to show how ordinary concepts like entity and relationship, class (but also instantiation and object), user interfaces, and even scenarios may be defined as blends between different mental spaces. As blends are specified by constitutive and governing principles that have been defined by the authors of the concept (Fauconnier and Turner), we may use such principles as general guidelines not only in the process of designing new constructs and notations but also in designing new software systems.

If we think that our approach will be helpful to designers of new notations and methods, we should not forget to also believe that all software designers need to understand the constructs they are employing to elaborate their system models. Therefore, a better understanding of the underlying cognitive processes will be useful to anybody directly or indirectly involved in software development. These people include designers of notations and methods, software designers, and trainers who explain to software designers how to use the new notations.

It is clear, then, that our approach will not directly lead to the design of new models, notations, or diagrams, but we can explain how such constructs are built and how they work in terms of cognitive processes, considering that such explanations may be quite useful when designing new models. Consider an example from SE (see chapter 5). After understanding that we constantly employ a set of image schemata that are always the same (container, link, source-path-goal, and so forth), we are aware that we are representing an underlying image schema: that of container, link, and so on. This is quite independent of the symbols used in a diagram (rectangle, circle, or other). We are aware also that using a metaphorical projection from the image schema, we may create new constructs (states, processes, and so on), even if the basic symbol is the same (for example, a rectangle).

The constructs we use in SE are created on the basis of image schemata and metaphorical projections. It is a common way of imagining some constructs as containers, and so we associate with them geometric representations such as rectangles, circles, and so forth. We have seen that this is the same mechanism used with linguistic constructions, as when we say "we left this point out of the discussion," in which there is also a basic container image schema and a metaphorical projection: THE DISCUSSION IS A CONTAINER.

It is clear how new meanings emerge. It is apparent which metaphors we are employing, and most important, that we are constantly creating and using metaphors. Another consequence of this point is that we can enhance the design by studying alternative metaphors, as some of them let us see some aspects of a problem that other metaphors hide.

But beware: we might employ alternative metaphors and study the consequences on the current design we are working on. In relation to this aspect of producing new meanings and constructs, we have to bear in mind what Kay (1993) points out about his experience of teaching programming. He tells the story of teaching Smalltalk programming to a group of twenty adult nonprogrammers at Xerox PARC, who were asked to make a little database that could behave like a card file. After seeing that they could not even come close to programming it, Kay develops a solution and explains it to them. Finally, he discovers that they were not capable of doing it by themselves. Analyzing his solution, he finds that it is full of nonobvious ideas, some quite complex. As Kay (1993, 82) remarks, "The connection to literacy was painfully clear. It isn't enough to just learn to read and write. There is also a literature that renders ideas. Language is used to read and write about them, but at some point the organization of ideas starts to dominate mere language abilities. And it helps greatly to have some powerful ideas under one's belt to better acquire more powerful ideas."

Continuing the parallel, we would say that explaining how the cognitive processes develop is no guarantee of being able to apply them efficiently in order to produce successful metaphors, blends, or constructs. Knowing the mechanism of producing new meanings is a prerequisite, but it is not enough. Moreover, many people may produce magnificent conceptual integrations without knowing anything about such underlying cognitive processes. What is crucial is literacy, understood as a sound command of some area of knowledge.

Kay (1993, 83) argues for the importance of fluency, which he sees as the natural connectedness of representations, meanings, and a depth of knowledge: "The 'trick,' and I think that this is what liberal arts education is supposed to be about, is to get fluent and deep while building relationships with other fluent deep knowledge. . . . At the liberal arts level we would expect that connections between each of the fluencies would form truly powerful metaphors for considering ideas in the light of others."

Sometimes, the success of a blend may depend on social determinations or acceptance, like when we say, "This surgeon is a butcher." In such cases, it is difficult to find "an author" as the author is people in general; they are sayings without authors. If this book is intended to do anything, it is to increase the degree of literacy necessary to get some success in the difficult art of finding metaphors and blends as well as developing systems of digital artifacts for people.

Another question we have analyzed is that of formal versus informal methods. Cognitive semantics allows us to understand this important issue of HCI-SE: the intertwining between formal and informal tools. People are accustomed to prefer formal tools, because they are seen to have higher degrees of precision than informal ones. It is assumed that they possess a scientific rigor that informal methods lack. Why, then, would we prefer to use informal cognitive artifacts in the initial stages of design, like scenarios? Because they evoke more meaning than more formal tools allow: it is only possible to capture the vividness, richness, and complexity of human activities through informal tools. Later stages of development need to be specified with more formal methods, and consequently there is a loss of vividness and rich, open meaning.

Critical Perspectives

When considering cognitive semantics along with its possible repercussions on methods and methodologies, it is helpful to cite Dourish's (2001, 161–162) comment about design recommendations: "Given the variety of settings in which the embodied interaction approach is applied, it would be inappropriate to give rules or guidelines here."

One method to achieve the goal of designing improved notations and methodologies is by understanding what notations and methods are, how we build such constructs, and which cognitive processes are involved in the activity. Another important aspect of notations and methodologies is to know the range of validity and their limitations, as the discussion about formal and informal cognitive artifacts has shown.

At the same time, there is a need to enlarge the concept of methods and methodologies. In this sense, we wholly agree with Cockburn's (2002, 115) remarks about the concept of methodology:

> Your "methodology" is everything you regularly do to get your software out. It includes who you hire, what you hire them for, how they work together, what they produce, and how they share. It is the combined job descriptions, procedures, and conventions of everyone on your team. It is the product of your particular ecosystem and is therefore a unique construction of your organization. . . . Boil and condense the subject of methodology long enough and you get this one-sentence summary: "A methodology is the conventions that your group agrees to." "The conventions your group agrees to" is a social construction. It is also a construction that you can and should revisit from time to time.

In other words, a methodology is something that would help to improve the communication among a group of people, and thus the performance of the group as a team. That is, methodologies have almost everything to do with meaning and its production as a social construction. And a discipline such as cognitive semantics, whose concerns are the way language allows us to create meaning and how some cognitive processes constitute the base of creativity, is a perfect companion for such a goal.

The interaction designer Pelle Ehn expresses a similar idea (cited in Cockburn 2002, 241) when he argues that we need tools and models to help us reflect on our designs, and in the area of cognitive semantics, Turner (1991, 206) offers an equivalent thought: "When we understand an utterance, we in no sense are understanding 'just what the words say'; the words themselves say nothing independent of the richly detailed knowledge and powerful cognitive processes we bring to bear."

What Ehn calls "reminders for our reflection" are, in terms of cognitive semantics, the powerful cognitive processes triggered through a network of mental spaces. Models and diagrams, which Ehn speaks about, are the equivalent of words and sentences we employ in everyday language. They are tools to trigger cognitive processes by means of complex interactions through mental spaces. They are what Schön (1993, 137) calls a "generative metaphor," "carrying over frames or perspectives from one domain to another."

One of the strengths of a concept like blend is to explain the emergence of new concepts and constructs as an integration of previously available concepts and constructs. The concept of blend may be a helpful tool to analyze already-available blends (like the desktop metaphor), and diagnose some of its weaknesses and the reasons why they are weaknesses in terms of the governing principles. It may also be helpful to derive the meaning of constructs, as when considering a class as a blend compressing a whole business story into a set of operations (or a set of states to build a state diagram).

We concluded that conceptual integration would be more powerful in the early stages of development, when the use of informal methods is not only useful but also advisable. In chapter 7, we showed that scenarios are the type of informal tool advisable to capture much of the richness, vividness, and complexity of human interactions with the system. It does not mean that blends are not useful when analyzing or designing software systems—quite the opposite. A better understanding of what classes really are is evidently an advantage compared to traditional, objectivist approaches. Depending on how we consider classes, we can enhance our skills when designing OO systems, as this is an eminently creative activity. If we consider that objects are easy to design because they refer to objects in the real world (as the folk approach to design tells us), we will miss some important issues. The idea that classes represent a whole business story about entities, where we project in a compressed way all the avatars of the entities, implies immediately that we think of a way, or method, to elicit the whole story of entities.

Continuing with the idea of applying the concept of blend to the analysis phase of development, there is another interesting aspect of compression: creation by compression. Sometimes, we see that the addition of vital relations to a space can help it to achieve a human scale. It is intriguing to observe that when compressing outer-space relations into inner-space ones, we are constantly loosing the agent who performed the action over the entity (for example, the clerk who modified data in the order).

When building a class diagram aimed at performing a use case, for instance, we usually detect that we need to reintroduce the equivalent of the missing agent in the form of a control class. This is an example of creation by compression, as in order for us to achieve the human scale of tasks to be performed there must be somebody/something who performs them again. This is the emergence of new classes in the class diagram in order for tasks to be performed (and to achieve a human scale).

The inherent problem of HCI-SE—the difference between people and digital artifacts—will not go away while we have the designs of computational devices that we do. But with an educated and articulate team of designers and coders who are attuned to the ways in which meanings are made, designs might be better. We look forward to the software critic, or interaction critic, debating designs on a late-night television show much as the art critic does now. We expect our interaction designers and software engineers to be digitally literate.

Summary

The digital landscape is unfolding before us. It could turn out to be harsh and unforgiving, the province of technophiles surrounded by barriers to wider access. It could be open, welcoming, and inclusive. We can be sure that digital technologies will be pervasive and ubiquitous. We need to ensure that they commingle with people harmoniously. We can achieve this through sensitive, considerate human-centered design.

Cognitive semantics provides a perspective on this future landscape that allows designers to see things on a human scale, as embodied interaction. It also helps them to understand the historical development of HCI-SE. The transition from entity-relationship models to OO is a gradual move from simple blends to more complex ones, and as a change in the foundational metaphors THE SYSTEM IS AN INDUSTRIAL PLANT to THE SYSTEM IS A SOCIETY OF PEOPLE. HCI has also changed its foundational metaphors, moving from HCI IS A DIALOGUE to HCI IS DIRECT MANIPULATION. Direct manipulation is likely to remain an important constitutive metaphor as the interaction with digital artifacts becomes more physical. Other metaphors such as HCI IS NAVIGATION OF INFORMATION SPACE and HCI IS THE MANAGEMENT OF AGENTS will have their place. In SE, the agent paradigm may also develop in significance: THE SYSTEM IS A COLLECTION OF AGENTS.

Cognitive semantics also shows that the process of meaning production is quite different from what the usual theories propose: that there is a mapping between words or sentences and real-life objects or states. This is also the usual assumption of most methods in HCI-SE, which search in the erroneous hope of finding new paradigms of communication with the computer, such as natural language. Meaning emerges when—while interacting with a digital artifact or producing an utterance—we perform complex operations with mental spaces that take structure from real and continually evolving contexts: meaning is not directly assignable to sentences of natural language. For a computer to understand natural language, it would mean that the computer would have an embodied cognition and similar experiences to ourselves.

If the analysis provided here contributes to literacy in HCI-SE, then we will have succeeded. Understanding the conceptual foundations of the models, notations, and methods in HCI-SE, and understanding where those foundations have come from, provides a basis for that literacy. By deconstructing the metaphors and results of design—through examining the many examples that we have presented here—we hope to have exposed the foundations and skeletons that underlie this complex and fascinating endeavor that is the design of interactive systems.

References

Agre, P. 1997. *Computation and Human Experience.* Cambridge: Cambridge University Press.

Alexander, C., S. Ishikawa, and M. Silverstein. 1977. *A Pattern Language.* Oxford: Oxford University Press.

Alexander, I., and N. Maiden, eds. 2004. *Scenarios, Stories, Use Cases: Through the Systems Development Life-Cycle.* West Sussex, UK: John Wiley and Sons.

Alexander, I., and S. Robertson. 2004. Understanding Project Sociology by Modeling Stakeholders. *IEEE Software* 1:23–27.

Alty, J. L., R. Knott, B. Anderson, and M. Smyth. 2000. A Framework for Engineering Metaphor at the User Interface. *Interacting with Computers* 2:301–322.

Bannon, L. 1991. From Human Factors to Human Actors: The Role of Psychology and Human-Computer Interaction Studies in System Design. In *Design at Work: Cooperative Design of Computer Systems,* ed. J. Greenbaum and M. Kyng. Mahwah, NJ: Erlbaum.

Bartlett, F. 1932. *Remembering: A Study in Experimental and Social Psychology.* Cambridge: Cambridge University Press.

Barthes, R. 1957. *Mythologies.* Paris: Seuil.

Beck, K. 1999. User Story, <http://c2.com/ cgi/wiki?UserStory>.

Benyon, D. R. 2001. The New HCI? Navigation of Information Space. *Knowledge-Based Systems* 14, no. 8:425–430.

Benyon, D. R., and M. Imaz. 1999. Metaphors and Models: Conceptual Foundations of Representations in Interactive Systems Development. *Human-Computer Interaction* 14, nos. 1 and 2: 159–189.

Benyon, D. R., and C. Macaulay. 2002. Scenarios and the HCI-SE Design Problem. *Interacting with Computers* 14:397–405.

Benyon, D. R., and C. Macaulay. 2004. A Scenario-Based Design Approach to Interactive Systems Design. In *Scenarios, Stories, Use Cases,* ed. I. Alexander and N. Maiden. West Sussex, UK: John Wiley and Sons.

Benyon, D., P. Turner, and S. Turner. 2005. *Designing Interactive Systems: People, Activities, Contexts, Technologies.* Maidenhead, UK: Pearson Education.

Bødker, S. 1991. *Through the Interface: A Human Activity Approach to User Interface Design.* Mahwah, NJ: Erlbaum.

Booch, G., J. Rumbaugh, and I. Jacobson. 1999. *The Unified Modeling Language Users Guide.* Boston: Addison-Wesley.

Boyd, R. 1993. Metaphor and Theory Change. In *Metaphor and Thought,* ed. A. Ortony. Cambridge: Cambridge University Press.

Buchholz, H., A. Düsterhöft, and B. Thalheim. 1996. Capturing Information on Behavior with the RADD_NLI: A Linguistic and Knowledge Base Approach. In *Proceedings of the Second Workshop Application of Natural Language to Information Systems.* Amsterdam: IOS Press.

Buschmann, F., R. Meunier, H. Rohnert, P. Sommerlad, and M. Stal. 1996. *Pattern-Oriented Software Architecture, Volume 1: A System of Patterns.* West Sussex, UK: John Wiley and Sons.

Card, S., T. Moran, and A. Newell. 1983. *The Psychology of Human-Computer Interaction.* Mahwah, NJ: Erlbaum.

Carroll, J. 2000. *Making Use: Scenario-Based Design of Human-Computer Interactions.* Cambridge, MA: MIT Press.

Carroll, J., and R. Mack. 1985. Metaphor, Computing Systems, and Active Learning. *International Journal of Man-Machine Studies* 22, no. 1:39–57.

Carroll, J., and J. C. Thomas. 1982. Metaphor and the Cognitive Representation of Computer Systems. *IEEE Transactions on Man, Systems, and Cybernetics* 12, no. 2: 107–116.

Clancey, W. 1989. The Knowledge Level Reinterpreted: Modeling How Systems Interact. *Machine Learning* 4:285–291.

Coad, P., and E. Yourdon. 1992. *Object-Oriented Analysis.* Englewood Cliffs, NJ: Prentice Hall.

Cockburn, A. 2002. *Agile Software Development.* Boston: Addison-Wesley.

Colwell, R. 2003. Ground Bounce. *Computer* 3:11–13.

Constantine, L., and L. Lockwood. 2002. *Software for Use: A Practical Guide to the Models and Methods of Usage-Centered Design.* New York: ACM Press.

Cooper, A. 1999. *The Inmates Are Running the Asylum: Why High-Tech Products Drive Us Crazy and How to Restore the Sanity.* Indianapolis: SAMS/Macmillan.

Crampton Smith, G., and P. Tabor. 1996. The Role of the Artist-Designer. In *Bringing Design to Software,* ed. T. Winograd. Boston: Addison-Wesley.

Davis, A. M. 1993. *Software Requirements: Objects, Functions, and States.* Englewood Cliffs, NJ: Prentice Hall.

Degen, W., B. Heller, H. Herre, and B. Smith. 2001. GOL: Towards an Axiomatized Upper-Level Ontology. In *Proceedings of the Second International Conference on Formal Ontology and Information Systems,* ed. B. Smith and N. Guarino. New York: ACM Press.

Denning, P., D. Cormer, D. Gries, M. Mulder, A. Tucker, J. Turner, and P. Young. 1988. Computing as a Discipline: Preliminary Report of the ACM Task Force on the Core of Computer Science. In *ACM SIGCSE Bulletin, Proceedings of the Nineteenth SIGCSE Technical Symposium on Computer Science Education* 20, no. 1.

Diaper, D. 2002. Scenarios and Task Analysis. *Interacting with Computers* 14:379–395.

Diaper, D. 2004. Understanding Task Analysis for Human-Computer Interaction. In *The Handbook of Task Analysis for Human-Computer Interaction,* ed. D. Diaper and N. A. Stanton. Mahwah, NJ: Erlbaum.

Dijkstra, E. 1972. Notes on Structured Programming. In *Structured Programming,* ed. O.-J. Dahl, E. W. Dijkstra, and C. A. R. Hoare. New York: Academic Press.

Dori, D. 2002. Why Significant UML Change Is Unlikely. *Communications of the ACM* 45, no. 11:82–85.

Dourish, P. 2001. *Where the Action Is: The Foundations of Embodied Interaction.* Cambridge, MA: MIT Press.

Dowell, J., and J. Long. 1998. A Conception of the Cognitive Engineering Design Problem. *Ergonomics* 41, no. 2:126–139.

Dreyfus, H. 1972. *What Computers Can't Do: A Critique of Artificial Reason.* New York: Harper and Row.

Dreyfus, H., and S. Dreyfus. 1988. *Mind over Machine: The Power of Human Intuition and Expertise in the Era of the Computer.* New York: Free Press.

Egyed, A. 2002. Automated Abstraction of Class Diagrams. *ACM Transactions on Software Engineering and Methodology* 11, no. 4:449–491.

Ericksson, T. 1990. Working with Interface Metaphors. In *The Art of Human-Computer Interface Design,* ed. B. Laurel. Boston: Addison-Wesley.

Fauconnier, G. 1994a. *Mental Spaces: Aspects of Meaning Construction in Natural Language.* Cambridge: Cambridge University Press. (Orig. pub. 1985.)

Fauconnier, G. 1997. *Mappings in Thought and Language.* Cambridge: Cambridge University Press.

Fauconnier, G., and M. Turner. 1996. Blending As a Central Process of Grammar. In *Conceptual Structure, Discourse, and Language,* ed. A. Goldberg. Stanford, CA: CSLI.

Fauconnier, G., and M. Turner. 2002. *The Way We Think: Conceptual Blending and the Mind's Hidden Complexities.* New York: Basic Books.

Fillmore, C. J. 1977. Topics in Lexical Semantics. In *Current Issues in Linguistic Theory,* ed. R. Cole. Bloomington: Indiana University Press.

Fowler, M., and K. Scott. 2000. *UML Distilled: A Brief Guide to the Standard Object Modeling Language.* 2nd ed. Boston: Addison-Wesley.

Fritzinger, J. S., and M. Mueller. 1996. *Java Security.* White Papers, Sun Microsystems, Inc. <http://java.sun.com/security/whitepaper.ps>.

Gamma, E., R. Helm, R. Johnson, and J. Vlissides. 1995. *Design Patterns: Elements of Reusable Object-Oriented Software.* Boston: Addison-Wesley.

García, R. 2000. *El conocimiento en construcción. De las formulaciones de Jean Piaget a la teoría de sistemas complejos.* Barcelona: Gedisa Editorial.

Gardner, H. 1985. *The Mind's New Science: A History of the Cognitive Revolution.* New York: Basic Books.

Gartner, K., A. Rush, M. Crist, R. Konitzer, B. Teegarden, and B. McGibbon. 1998. *Cognitive Patterns: Problem-Solving Frameworks for Object Technology.* Cambridge: Cambridge University Press.

Gellerman, S. 1963. *Motivation and Productivity.* New York: Amacom.

Gentner, D., and D. Gentner. 1983. Flowing Waters or Teeming Crowds: Mental Models of Electricity. In *Mental Models,* ed. D. Gentner and A. L Stevens. Mahwah, NJ. Lawrence Erlbaum Associates.

Gentner, D., and J. Nielsen. 1996. The Anti-Mac Interface. *Communications of the ACM* 39, no. 8:70–82.

Gentner, D., and A. L. Stevens, eds. 1983. *Mental Models.* Mahwah, NJ: Erlbaum.

Gibbs, R. 1994. *The Poetics of Mind: Figurative Thought, Language, and Understanding.* Cambridge: Cambridge University Press.

Gibbs, R. 1998. The Fight over Metaphor in Thought and Language. In *Figurative Language and Thought,* ed. A. N. Katz, C. Cacciari, R. W. Gibbs Jr., and M. Turner. Oxford: Oxford University Press.

Gibson, J. 1986. *The Ecological Approach to Visual Perception.* Mahwah, NJ: Erlbaum. (Orig. pub. 1979).

Goldberg, A. 1995. *Constructions: A Construction Grammar Approach to Argument Structure.* Chicago: University of Chicago Press.

Greeno, J. G. 1983. Conceptual Entities. In *Mental Models,* ed. D. Gentner and A. L. Stevens. Mahwah, NJ: Erlbaum.

Haberlandt, K. 1994. *Cognitive Psychology.* Boston: Allyn and Bacon.

Heidegger, M., J. Macquarrie, and B. Robinson. 1978. *Being and Time.* Oxford: Blackwell.

Hollan, J., et al. 2000. Distributed Cognition: Toward a New Foundation for Human-Computer Interaction Research. *ACM Transactions on Computer-Human Interaction* 7, no. 2:174–196.

Hutchins, E. 1983. Understanding Micronesian Navigation. In *Mental Models,* ed. D. Gentner and A. L. Stevens. Mahwah, NJ: Lawrence Erlbaum Associates.

Hutchins, E. 1995. *Cognition in the Wild.* Cambridge, MA: MIT Press.

Hutchins, E. 2000. The Cognitive Consequences of Patterns of Information Flow. *Intellectica* 1, no. 30:53–74.

IEEE Std 1471–2000. 2000. *IEEE Recommended Practice for Architectural Description of Software-Intensive Systems—Description.* <http://standards.ieee.org/reading/ieee/std/se/1471-2000.pdf>.

Imaz, M. and D. Benyon. 1996. Cognition in the Workplace: Integrating Experientalism into Activity Theory. In *Proceedings of the Eighth European Conference on Cognitive Ergonomics,* ed. T. Green, J. Cañas, and C. Warren. Le Chesnay, France: EACE.

Imaz, M., and D. Benyon. 1999. How Stories Capture Interactions. In *Human-Computer Interaction INTERACT '99: Proceedings of the Seventh IFIP Conference on Human-Computer Interaction,* ed. A. Sasse and C. Johnson. Amsterdam: IOS Press.

Jarke, M., and K. Pohl. 1994. Requirements Engineering in 2001: (Virtually) Managing a Changing Reality. *IEEE Software Engineering Journal* 9, no. 6:254–263.

Jirotka, M., and J. Goguen. 1994. *Requirements Engineering: Social and Technical Issues.* Burlington, MA: Academic Press.

Johnson, G. 1994. Of Metaphor and the Difficulty of Computer Discourse. *Communications of the ACM* 37, no. 12:97–102.

Johnson, M. 1987. *The Body in the Mind: The Bodily Basis of Reason and Imagination.* Chicago: University of Chicago Press.

Juristo, N., A. M. Moreno, and M. López. 2000. Linguistic Instruments for Object-Oriented Analysis, *IEEE Software* 17, no. 3:80–89.

Kay, A. 1993. The Early History of Smalltalk. In *Proceedings of the Second ACM SIGPLAN Conference on the History of Programming Languages HOPL–II.* New York: ACM.

Lacan, J. 1966. *Écrits*. Paris: Seuil.

Lakoff, G. 1987. *Women, Fire, and Dangerous Things: What Categories Reveal about the Mind.* Chicago: University of Chicago Press.

Lakoff, G. 1988. Cognitive Semantics. In *Meaning and Mental Representations,* ed. U. Eco, M. Santambrogio, and P. Violi. Bloomington: Indiana University Press.

Lakoff, G. 1993. Contemporary Theory of Metaphor. In *Metaphor and Thought,* ed. A. Ortony. 2nd ed. Cambridge: Cambridge University Press. (Orig. pub. 1979).

Lakoff, G. 1996. *Moral Politics: What Conservatives Know That Liberals Don't.* Chicago: University of Chicago Press.

Lakoff, G., and M. Johnson. 1980. *Metaphors We Live By.* Chicago: University of Chicago Press.

Lakoff, G., and M. Johnson. 1999. *Philosophy in the Flesh: The Embodied Mind and Its Challenge to Western Thought.* New York: HarperCollins.

Lakoff, G., and R. Núñez. 2000. *Where Mathematics Comes From: How the Embodied Mind Brings Mathematics into Being.* New York: Basic Books.

Landay, J., and B. Myers. 2001. Sketching Interfaces: Toward More Human Interface Design. *Computer* 34, no. 3:56–64.

Langacker, R. 1987. *Foundations of Cognitive Grammar.* Vol. 1. Palo Alto, CA: Stanford University Press.

Lauesen, S. E. 2002. *Software Requirements: Styles and Techniques.* Boston: Addison-Wesley.

Lave, J., and E. Wenger. 1991. *Situated Learning: Legitimate Peripheral Participation.* Cambridge: Cambridge University Press.

Leont'ev, A. N. 1978. *Activity, Consciousness, and Personality.* Englewood Cliffs, NJ: Prentice Hall.

Licklider, J. C. R. 1960. Man-Computer Symbiosis. In *IRE Transactions on Human Factors in Electronics.* HFE–1, (March): 4–11. <http://medg.lcs.mit.edu/people/psz/Licklider.html>.

MacLean, A., V. Bellotti, R. Young, and T. Moran. 1991. Reaching through Analogy: A Design Rationale Perspective on Roles of Analogy. In *Reaching through Technology: Proceedings of CHI '91.* Boston: Addison-Wesley.

Madsen, K. H. 1994. A Guide to Metaphorical Design. *Communications of the ACM* 37, no. 12:57–62.

Maes, P. 1994. Agents That Reduce Workload. *Communications of the ACM* 37, no. 7: 30–41.

Maglio, P. P., and T. Matlock. 1999. The Conceptual Structure of Information Space. In *Social Navigation of Information Space,* ed. A. J. Munro, K. Höök, and D. Benyon, 132–154. London: Springer-Verlag.

Maiden, N. A. M., P. Mistry, and A. G. Sutcliffe. 1995. How People Categorise Requirements for Reuse: A Natural Approach. In *Proceedings of the Second IEEE International Symposium on Requirements Engineering,* Washington, DC: IEEE Computer Society.

Mandelblit, N. 2000. The Grammatical Marking of Conceptual Integration: From Syntax to Morphology. *Cognitive Semantics* 11, nos. 3–4:197–251.

Margolis, E., and S. Laurence. eds. 1999. *Concepts: Core Readings.* Cambridge, MA: MIT Press.

Martin, J., and C. McClure. 1988. *Structured Techniques: The Basis for CASE.* Englewood Cliffs, NJ: Prentice Hall.

McCullough, M. 2004. *Digital Ground: Architecture, Pervasive Computing, and Environmental Knowing.* Cambridge, MA: MIT Press.

Merleau-Ponty, M. 1962. *Phenomenology of Perception.* London: Routledge and Kegan Paul.

Miller, G. 1956. The Magical Number Seven, Plus or Minus Two: Some Limits on Our Capacity for Processing Information. *Psychological Review* 63:81–97.

Minsky, M. 1975. A Framework for Representing Knowledge. In *The Psychology of Computer Vision,* ed. P. H. Winston. New York: McGraw-Hill.

Naduri, S., and S. Rugaser. 1994. Requirements Validation via Automated Natural Language Parsing. In *Proceedings of the Twenty-eighth Hawaii International Conference of Systems Science: Collaboration Technology, Organizational Systems, and Technology.* Los Alamitos, CA: IEEE Computer Society Press.

Nardi, B., ed. 1995. *Context and Consciousness: Activity Theory and Human-Computer Interaction.* Cambridge, MA: MIT Press.

Nardi, B. and C. Zarmer. 1993. Beyond Models and Metaphors: Visual Formalisms. *User Interface Design: Journal of Visual Languages and Computing* 4:5–33.

Neisser, U. 1967. *Cognitive Psychology.* Englewood Cliffs, NJ: Prentice Hall.

Newell, A., A. J. Perlis, and H. Simon. 1967. What Is Computer Science? *Science* 157: 1373–1374.

Newell, A., and Simon, H. A. 1963. GPS: A Program That Simulates Human Thought. In *Computers and Thought,* ed. E. A. Feigenbaum and J. Feldman. New York: McGraw-Hill.

Norman, D. A. 1981. The Trouble with UNIX: The User Interface Is Horrid. *Datamation* 27, no. 12:139–150.

Norman, D. A. 1983. Some Observations on Mental Models. In *Mental Models,* ed. D. Gentner and A. L. Stevens. Mahwah, NJ: Erlbaum.

Norman, D. A. 1998. *The Invisible Computer: Why Good Products Can Fail, the PC Is So Complex, and Information Appliances the Answer.* Cambridge, MA: MIT Press.

Odlyzko, A. 1999. The Visible Problems of the Invisible Computer: A Skeptical Look at Information Appliances. *First Monday* no. 9 (September). <http://firstmonday.org/issues/issue4_9/odlyzko/index.html>.

Preece, J., Y. Rogers, and H. Sharp. 2002. *Interaction Design: Beyond Human-Computer Interaction.* West Sussex, UK: John Wiley and Sons.

Propp, V. 1958. *Morphology of the Folktale.* The Hague: Mouton. (Orig. pub. 1928.)

Putnam, H. 1975. *Mind, Language, and Reality. Philosophical Papers, Vol. 2.* Cambridge: Cambridge University Press.

Putnam, H. 1981. *Reason, Truth, and History.* Cambridge: Cambridge University Press.

Reddy, M. 1993. The Conduit Metaphor: A Case of Frame Conflict in Our Language about Language. In *Metaphor and Thought,* ed. A. Ortony. 2nd ed. Cambridge: Cambridge University Press. (Orig. pub. 1979.)

Rohrer, T. 1995. *Feelings Stuck in a GUI Web: Metaphors, Image-Schemata, and Designing the Human-Computer Interface.* Center for the Cognitive Science of Metaphor, Philosophy Department, University of Oregon. <http://metaphor.uoregon.edu/metaphor.htm>.

Rohrer, T. 2005. Embodiment and Experientialism. In *The Handbook of Cognitive Linguistics,* ed. D. Geeraerts and H. Cuyckens. Oxford: Oxford University Press.

Rumbaugh, J., I. Jacobson, and G. Booch. 1999. *The Unified Modeling Language Reference Manual.* Boston: Addison-Wesley.

Rumelhart, D., and J. McClelland. 1986. *Parallel Distributed Processing: Explorations in the Microstructure of Cognition. Volume 1: Foundations.* Cambridge, MA: MIT Press.

Sachs, P. 1995. Transforming Work: Collaboration, Learning, and Design. *Communications of the ACM* 38, no. 9:36–44.

Schank, R., and R. Abelson. 1977. *Scripts, Plans, Goals, and Understanding: An Inquiry into Human Knowledge Structures.* Mahwah, NJ: Erlbaum.

Schön, D. 1993. Generative Metaphor: A Perspective on Problem Setting in Social Policy. In *Metaphor and Thought,* ed. A. Ortony. 2nd ed. Cambridge: Cambridge University Press. (Orig. pub. 1979.)

Seibt, J. 2001. Formal Process Ontology. In *Proceedings of the Second International Conference on Formal Ontology and Information Systems,* ed. B. Smith and N. Guarino New York: ACM Press.

Sfard, A. 1997. Commentary: On Metaphorical Roots of Conceptual Growth. In *Mathematical Reasoning: Analogies, Metaphors, and Images,* ed. L. English, Mahwah, NJ: Erlbaum.

Shackel, B. 1959. Ergonomics for a Computer. *Design* 120:36–39.

Shneiderman, B., ed. 1980. *Software Psychology: Human Factors in Computer and Information Systems.* Cambridge, MA: Winthrop Publishers.

Shneiderman, B. 1983. Direct Manipulation: A Step beyond Programming Languages. *Computer* 16, no. 8:57–69.

Shneiderman, B., and P. Maes. 1997. Direct Manipulation versus Interface Agents. *Interactions* 4, no. 6:42–61.

Siddiqi, J., and M. C.Shekaran. 1996. Requirements Engineering: The Emerging Wisdom. *IEEE Software* 13, no. 2:15–19.

Suchman, L. 1987. *Plans and Situated Actions.* Cambridge: Cambridge University Press.

Sutcliffe, A. 2002. *Multimedia and Virtual Reality: Designing Multisensory User Interfaces.* Mahwah, NJ: Lawrence Erlbaum Associates.

Sutherland, I. E. 1963. Sketchpad: A Man-Machine Graphical Communication System. Baltimore, MD: Spartan Books.

Turing, A. 1936. On Computable Numbers with an Application to the Entscheidungsproblem. In *Proceedings of the London Math Society* 2, no. 42:173–198.

Turner, M. 1991. *Reading Minds.* Princeton, NJ: Princeton University Press.

Turner, M. 1996. *The Literary Mind.* Oxford: Oxford University Press.

Turner, M. 1998. Figure. In *Figurative Language and Thought,* ed. A. N. Katz, C. Cacciari, R. W. Gibbs, and M. Turner. Oxford: Oxford University Press.

Turner, M. 2001. *Cognitive Dimensions of Social Science: The Way We Think about Politics, Law, Economics, and Society.* Oxford: Oxford University Press.

U2 Partners. 2003. *UML: Infrastructure Version 2.0.* January 6. <http://www.u2-partners.org>.

Varela, F., E. Thompson, and E. Rosch. 1991. *The Embodied Mind.* Cambridge, MA: MIT Press.

Waterworth, J. A. 1999. Spaces, Places, Landscapes, and Views: Experiential Design of Shared Information Spaces. In *Social Navigation of Information Space,* ed. A. J. Munro, K. Höök, and D. R. Benyond. London: Springer-Verlag.

Waterworth, J. A., A. Lund, and D. Modjeska. 2002. Experiential Design of Shared Information Spaces. In *Designing Information Spaces: The Social Navigation Approach,* ed. K. Höök, D. R. Benyon, and A. J. Munro. London: Springer-Verlag.

Wegner, P. 1997. Why Interaction Is More Powerful Than Algorithms. *Communications of the ACM* 40, no. 5:80–91.

Wegner, P., and D. Goldin. 2003. Computation beyond Turing Machines: Seeking Appropriate Methods to Model Computer and Human Thought. *Communications of the ACM* 46, no. 4:100–102.

Weinberg, G. M. 1998. *The Psychology of Computer Programming.* New York: Dorset House Publishing Company. (Orig. pub. 1971.)

Weiser, M. 1991. The Computer for the Twenty-First Century. *Scientific American* (September): 94–100.

Weiser, M. 1993. Some Computer Science Problems in Ubiquitous Computing. *Communications of the ACM* 36, no. 7:75–84.

Williams, M., J. Hollan, and A. Stevens. 1983. Human Reasoning about a Simple Physical System. In *Mental Models,* ed. D. Gentner and A. L. Stevens. Mahwah, NJ: Erlbaum.

Winograd, T. 1997. The Design of Interaction. In *Beyond Calculation: The Next Fifty Years of Computing,* ed. P. Denning, and B. Metcalfe. London: Springer-Verlag.

Winograd, T., and F. Flores. 1987. *Understanding Computers and Cognition: A New Foundation for Design.* Boston: Addison-Wesley.

Winter, S. 2003. *A Clearing in the Forest: Law, Life, and Mind.* Chicago: University of Chicago Press.

Wirth, N. 1971. Program Development by Stepwise Refinement. *Communications of the ACM* 14, no. 4:221–227.

Wittgenstein, L. 1953. Philosophical Investigations. Ed. G. E. M. Anscombe and R. Rhees. Trans. G. E. M. Anscombe. Oxford: Blackwell.

Young, R. 1983. Surrogates and Mappings: Two Kinds of Conceptual Models for Interactive Devices. In *Mental Models,* ed. D. Gentner and A. L. Stevens. Mahwah, NJ: Erlbaum.

Yourdon, E. 1989. *Modern Structured Analysis.* Englewood Cliffs, NJ: Prentice Hall.

Zbikowski, L. 2002. *Conceptualizing Music: Cognitive Structure, Theory, and Analysis.* Oxford: Oxford University Press.

Index